PENNY FOOLISH

PENNY FOOLISH

A Book of

Tirades
&
Panegyrics

by

OSBERT SITWELL

Essay Index Reprint Series

BOOKS FOR LIBRARIES PRESS, INC.
FREEPORT, NEW YORK

First Published 1935
Reprinted 1967

LIBRARY OF CONGRESS CATALOG NUMBER:
67-28767

PRINTED IN THE UNITED STATES OF AMERICA

PREFACE

THE MAJORITY OF the contents have made their appearance in the pages of the *Sunday Referee*; other pieces have been published by the *Daily Telegraph*, the *Morning Post*, the *Daily Mail*, the *Daily Express*, the *Evening News*, the *Spectator*, the *Week-End Review*, *Harper's Magazine*, the *New York Herald-Tribune* and *Harper's Bazaar*. The author wishes to take this opportunity of offering to the editors of these journals the customary acknowledgments.

CONTENTS

vi

CONTENTS

CONTENTS

THE
BEST
YEARS
OF
LIFE

THE
BEST
YEARS
OF
LIFE

W E CAN WATCH, again, how the years built themselves
up; how they began, out of darkness, with small visual impressions that even to-day are borne back unexpectedly on
a tide of summer scent; the smell of hay, for example, or
of some particular flower; the smell of box hedges or of seaweed drying on the rocks in the wind, or, it may be, of
some pungent food.

But these sensations, agreeable though they were, are not
coherent enough to justify us in describing infancy as "the best
years of life". . . . Afterward there came, for me at any rate,
a year or two of unpleasant grappling with the primary problems of Latin and arithmetic; an epoch invested also with a
certain magic derived from the study of atlases and books of
history: for then insinuated themselves into the consciousness
all those queer names—names which seemed to stand for so

much, but in reality conveyed so little; Ethelred the Unready, Canute, William Rufus, Richard Cœur-de-Lion, and many other such high-sounding syllables. . . . Yet all these things we accumulated, in reality constituted—so one was given to understand—only a preparation for "the best years of life".

At last dawned the awful morning which, convention led one to believe, formed the threshold of them. School to me had always been an intimidating prospect, and I shall never forget the sensation of gratitude that I experienced toward the only person who, in advance, told me the truth about it. He was an acquaintance of my parents, considered rather a worthless, feckless and extravagant being, but, guided by some instinct of genuine kindness, he interviewed me before I went to school, gave me a sovereign, and said, at the same time, "My boy, most people will probably tell you that the next few years will be the best years of your life; but don't you believe a word of it. They will be perfectly horrible and a dreadful waste of time. You must never expect to know a moment's happiness until you grow up."

This information was, at any rate, encouraging and of use, for had I really, when at school, believed that it *was* the best that existence could offer, the blackness of despair which engulfed me would have been even darker. Several years of life at a private school followed: and then I moved to Eton, with its beauty, ineptitude and snobbishness; and from there proceeded to an Army tutor's. These last months were, rather unexpectedly for one of my temperament, enjoyable.

After that came a year of agony during which I was

attached to a cavalry regiment; a life fit only for horses and dogs—which were, indeed, considered by the officers (and very rightly) as being by far the most important members of their community. I escaped, eventually, to join my own regiment, and in it spent a year or two of great happiness. But the war broke out, and quickly put an end to that.

I am prepared to think that the long, the—as they seemed —endless years which were wasted in a horrible, deplorable and, as all now see, pointless struggle, *might* perhaps have been the best of my life; but since I was a soldier, and not a politician or an Army contractor, they were certainly the worst and most harrowing. Not only all that and more, but they were, in addition, the most boring. The war ended; but even so great a relief could not rid me at once of the great burden of unhappiness it had engendered.

Nevertheless the year after the war—I was twenty-six— proved one of the most agreeable of my life, for then one was able once more to travel freely abroad, to recover all the joys of European civilization; which had been in abeyance during the whole war period. I visited Venice and Rome and the cities of Spain. Even the Riviera, with its vacuous, rose-pink, middle-class tidiness seemed a paradise. Moreover, during the years that followed, I was, for the first time, able to work at a job congenial to me—writing. And this added a certain quiet pleasure—broken only by the fits of temper engendered by criticism—to my life.

Yet, invincibly sanguine, one cannot help but hope that the best years of life yet lie hidden in the future? . . . An old friend of mine once confided to me that he had never known happiness until he reached seventy. I can quite understand his point of view; no need to be afraid, at that age, of *giving too much trouble*. A man of three score years and ten can advise and interfere when he wishes, without the least dread of retaliation: he is too old to be worried, but not too old to worry other people. If, by that time, a successful author, he will have become automatically a "Grand Old Man". Everyone will laugh at anything serious the "G.O.M." says (since there is his reputation for wit to be considered), and will be serious when he says anything funny (because deference must be paid to sagacity as much as to wit). Moreover, a "Grand Old Man" can speak without being answered back. He can talk when he wants to, and be quiet when he wants to: and his silence will be considered no less pregnant than his utterances. . . . Would not these be the best years of life?

ON
PRIVATE
SCHOOLS

Those who come of Anglo-Saxon breed are people of strange and savage customs, especially where the young of their race are concerned. The more wealthy, the more fortunate, bring up their children until they reach the age of nine or ten in circumstances, if not of luxury, at least of happy plenty. Every little ailment is attended to immediately, and they go short of nothing they want. Their diet is carefully studied, they are taught the rudiments of many obsolete crafts, such as riding and old-fashioned politeness; while they learn, too, the names of cinema stars, wild flowers, butterflies and of the various brands of milk chocolate. . . . And then, suddenly, just as they have reached an age when their intelligence and sensitiveness, which have after this fashion been encouraged, can respond to the stimuli of their surroundings, they are whisked off to places of dreary internment, where the most extraordinary tribal values and standards prevail: and though these, as it were, labour camps are varied according to their years, they remain in one or another of them (unless they have the good fortune to be expelled with ignominy) until such time as their characters have been formed in the same hard, dense and unpleasant mould as that of those who teach them.

The arguments bandied about in favour of English schools as a form of upbringing always seem to me very faulty. The chief one in current use is to name some man, notoriously a half-wit, and say, "Look at *him*, now! He was never at school." But then, since schools in this country are the established rule, the fact that he never entered such a place of learning merely indicates that he was always mentally wanting. . . . Otherwise he would have been sent to one, willy-nilly; for, if they belong to the comfortable classes, the parents of any child who is not sent to school remain, among other parents, until death, under the intolerable, atrocious stigma of being "unusual".

And yet what strange, Spartan modes are these, to apply to boys of whom their parents hope that they will, when they grow up, one day rule their country, governing it, fighting for it, thinking for it! I believe that the children of working-class homes, though (as we hear so frequently stated) "denied the opportunities which money affords", are better, more kindly and more sensibly brought up than the children of those possessed of money to spare. . . . Notwithstanding, directly a poor man has made a sufficient fortune to enable him to do so, he sends his children to "a good school": so strongly anchored in our blood is the instinct for this sort of education.

8

What, then, does "a good school" signify; what qualities indicate it as such? . . . Difficult to define, these special marks of differentiation are, perhaps, easier to describe from personal experience. At the moment, however, I will deal only with those places in which are confined the very young, leaving the "public schools", as they are called, for a later scrutiny.

Thus myself, for example, was placed at a particular private school, which in those days had become fashionable, because —as frequently before I went there, I heard my elders remark to one another with an air of contentment—the headmaster was "the best dribbler in England". Innocent in those faraway times of the meaning of Association Football terms, this phrase used greatly, and often, to puzzle me. What could be the purpose, the significance of this so desirable and yet, as it seemed, mystic accomplishment; one, moreover, which so ill accorded, as far as my experience went, with their code of nursery behaviour? Nor, when I came to think of it, had I ever noticed that my parents chose as their friends those endowed with any special aptitude for dribbling.

But what a life ensued for me when at last safely placed under the tutelage, spiritual as well as mundane, of this grand, though well-meaning, dribbler! What vistas I see again of fog and rain and wet grey flannel (I can still smell it), of plungings through ink in the morning, and through mud in the afternoon, of pens and benches and indiarubber, of food which, though intended to be healthy and plentiful, was in reality of an ancient-British, Stonehenge variety, and, finally, of occasional nostalgic lectures, mostly about the Holy Land, accompanied by lantern slides and delivered by

9

various aged clergymen, each with a different kind of impedi-
ment in his speech; that is to say, that one would indulge
in an ordinary stutter, another betray an inability to pronounce the letter "s", substituting for it the letter "f"
(so that he conferred, as I see now, upon our everyday speech
the feeling of those old books in which the long "s"
occurs), another would whistle at unconjecturable intervals,
thereby imparting an extra, if unusual, interest to his dis-
courses, another would have no roof to his mouth, while
again another would, from time to time, lose his voice
altogether and mouth at the assembled school after the
manner of a rebellious goldfish.

Then, too, I recall those hideous, appalling school con-
certs, where, in an atmosphere of unscented soap and scented
brilliantine, blossomed that clean, sportsmanlike sense of
fun which, together with a rare aptitude for Alpine accidents,
is the badge of schoolmasters all the world over. . . . A
series of hymns to the wheezy following of a harmonium
also presents itself in my memory: until, at long last, the
term ended in a frenzy of ritual. Thus a certain day was
appointed, forty-eight hours before the school broke up—
called "pay-day"—on which every boy could pay off old
scores without fear of rebuke, "bashing" and being "bashed"
to one's heart's content. These were hours of black eyes, miss-
ing teeth, bloody noses and whirling fists. . . . During the last
week, too, of holding their usual class during the afternoon,
the masters would, as a further treat, read aloud a few chapters from some incomparably boring novel by Sir Walter
Scott: and there would be more chapel and prayers than ever,
and a certain amount of speechmaking, to be followed by an

"end-of-the-term supper", greatly appreciated by the young. Now, at last, the school cook could manifest in a thousand ways her hellish ingenuity; tipsy-cakes, crazy concoctions of cream, turned inside out by a thunderstorm, almonds, synthetic jam—containing wooden splinters intended to summon up in the uninitiated the idea of raspberries or strawberries—and custard, vied with quaking jellies that radiated the most terrifying green and red fires, volcanic and sulphurous, and little cakes, composed equally, it seemed, of cocoanut-matting and cold cream.

These may seem frivolous objections to a school: but what did we learn? To support the Navy League, and to shirk the necessity of lessons by means of shining at games. . . . We learnt, too, that in our free country stupidity was no disgrace. (This lesson, as we shall see later, was subsequently emphasized by a public-school education.) Indeed, I know of nothing more saddening than to visit a young relative at such a school: for the child that one knew as a delightful, original being, full of affection, has been converted into a horrid, stupid, hard-hearted little boy, his head full of shibboleths and cricket averages. That which now most concerns him is whether his trousers are turned up at the ends, like those of other boys, and whether, after all, Jenkins will play for the school?

ON
PUBLIC
SCHOOLS

PUBLIC SCHOOLS ARE to private schools as lunatic asylums to mental homes; larger and less comfortable. The public school, it is true, allows more individual liberty than the private school, and it must be admitted that up till the time of the war no special effort was made in these institutions toward education. This, where an intelligent boy was concerned, constituted an advantage. It did not waste his time, it did not oblige him to fill his head with useless tags of Latin and arithmetic, but instead afforded him the necessary leisure in which to read and to think.

Since the beginning of the nineteenth century the public school has injured incalculably the English governing classes. It has weakened them, and sapped their strength. The remark, attributed to Wellington, that Waterloo was won upon the playing-fields of Eton, in the end became more responsible

12

for the loss of the Boer War and the length of the Great War than any other hypothetical epigram of any other great man. It will be noticed, to the contrary, that when a particular streak of political acumen is visible through the generations of any family, the members of that family were never sent to a public school.

The popularity of the English public school arose with the industrial revolution and the necessity, which the middle classes then began to feel, of becoming gentlemen. In result, the public schools developed merely into so many large-scale factories of that boring and emasculate commodity, the English Gentleman. To be an E.G. it was necessary to possess a fixed income and a certain *savoir faire*, to hunt and to have very little education; and it was toward this goal that the public school aimed. But alas, the middle classes were not successful in their ambition; because, by sending their sons in overwhelming numbers to the public schools, they fashioned them—though it must be admitted, without meaning to—in their own mould. Games, which I propose to discuss at some length in two further essays, were now substituted for blood sports. And, much as blood sports are to be condemned, at least a certain primitive force and purpose inspires them.

Dr Arnold, as Lytton Strachey pointed out in *Eminent Victorians*, was one of those most responsible for the nineteenth-century development of the English public school. It was in his day that the boys, no longer allowed to roam about, observing birds and flowers and butterflies, were first obliged, instead, to concentrate their ambition and energy upon the pursuit of a football, cricket ball or some other spherical object. Even now, compulsory games are still in force, so that at this moment, all over England, poor little boys are being compelled to spend their time in this un-utterably boring manner. . . . Let me offer them one word of help and advice. . . . If they must play in a compulsorily organized game, then let it be football; which can only last for a short time, during which it is possible, with a little trouble and with the aid of the specially armoured boots that etiquette decrees for such an occasion, to inflict considerable damage on those who deserve it. A cricket match, on the other hand, can endure for three days and fill the soul with an almost intolerable sense of *ennui*.

Here I should like to recall an incident. Some years ago the Provost of Eton, Dr James, sent a circular round to all old Etonians, inviting them to subscribe sums of money in order to buy more land for playing-fields. This letter was addressed to myself among others, and in reply I offered to send a cheque if the Provost would ensure that these playing-fields should not be used for the odious habit of compulsory games, which had ruined the minds of so many of the most intelligent of my contemporaries? . . . Alas, on this point he would offer no guarantee.

I seldom visit Eton now, so bored was I during my time there. Indeed, the most agreeable hours I spent in that place were during the recurrent few days of each winter term in which the town was flooded. This imparted a certain remote-ness and watery, Dutch interest of detail to the landscape and pleasantly varied the normal course of the day's work. Moreover, there was then, given good luck, a chance of catching a severe cold through getting wet, and the comfortable prospect, in consequence, of being able to spend a day or two quietly in bed, reading, without being forced to see either masters or comrades. Anything, indeed, like a thunderstorm, that lifted life a little out of its ordinary rut, made it more bearable, and even a school concert, full of boys singing:

"At Flores in the Azores
Sir Richard Grenville lay,"

was less intolerable than the more normal hours of *ennui*.

And then the masters! Public schools are so obsolete that they yet rest upon an old monastic basis; the majority of them, even to this very day, still favour clergyman as headmasters—an absolute anachronism. It is difficult, of course, to be a schoolmaster—we all admit that: but a clergyman is the last man in the world to be allowed to deal with growing boys; for, whenever a clergyman becomes a schoolmaster, he always tends to become either severe and cranky or playful and self-advertising.

As I have said, I seldom visit Eton now. Too many pitiful ghosts haunt its lanes and quadrangles, and the mere sight of a master slouching in his cap and gown down one of its narrow alleys fills me with misery. But the other day I spent an hour or two there, and wandered round the cloisters, observing the alterations that had taken place. The chief change seemed to be the enormous number of memorials erected to my contemporaries: for I belong to that unhappy generation which came of age during the years in which the "Great" War broke out, and most of my friends and enemies at Eton are now either maimed or have long been dead.

15

It had always seemed to me that schoolmasters particularly love memorials: stained glass windows and Gothic lettering, carved ivy borders and brass eagles; and in this direction the war has, no doubt, added an interest to their lives. Just think of the wall tablets and the windows that have been unveiled! Think of all the singing in the school chapels, of the choir practices, and of the many charming little ceremonies which have celebrated the fulfilment of that education which I saw in progress round me. . . . Throughout my school years I felt that, if this education were intended to turn out a type, and if that type were going to rule the country, some great disaster must be on its way for us. So strong was this impression that, while still at Eton, I asked my father, who had also been "educated" there, whether the boys had been as stupid in his time as they were in mine? He assured me that they had been, and this comforted me. But I think he was wrong.

Well, the disaster came; and the public schools are still devoted to the same ideals, and thus will be ready for the next disaster which they are helping to bring about. The community which they turn out is now, therefore, to be regarded, not so much as one of English gentlemen, as of English dead. They constitute, in fact, no longer factories of gentlemen but, instead, so many corpse factories.

Their methods are antiquated to such a degree that it is almost impossible to remedy them. From the class-conscious point of view of those who dread government by the workers, the most desirable thing in the world would be democratization of the public schools. If miners and millhands could only be educated at Eton, there would never be any strikes, or if there were, these would be unsuccessful; would mean no more than an Eton and Harrow match. Always teach people of whom you are afraid "to play the game"; in other words to be hoodwinked throughout life, and to be contented with conditions with which they have no right to allow themselves to be contented.

ON
ANONYMOUS
LETTERS

IT IS CURIOUS, I think, that no public man has yet collected anonymous letters; and that no expert has studied them in the past; for, almost as I write, I notice that a book called *Anonymous Letters* has just been issued by Methuen, in which the expert, Dr Saudek, describes in minute detail, and with very interesting examples from real life, the clues afforded by handwriting in blackmail and forgery cases. On the Continent, of course, the handwriting expert is a much more significant figure than in this country, and before many great foreign businesses will even consider the engaging of a new clerk, he must submit his handwritings to this expert. In the case, moreover, of some anonymous letters —the ones which, when a crime is committed, from time to time overwhelm the police with hints, whether true or false—experts on handwriting can offer much valuable assist-

18

ance as to the traits of character manifested in this way. Many of these letters are very frightening from the brutality they display; from the sinister suggestions they throw out.

Intimidating, again, are those peculiar messages which, every now and then, the victims of split personality post to themselves—often without the more normal occupant of their shell being aware of it. Numerous cases of this kind have occurred both here and in America; but in fiction the most brilliant example is to be found in a short story by Mr Aldous Huxley, which appeared in almost his first book of short stories, *Limbo*. Just as curious psychic happenings in a house as a rule turn out to be the work of a young servant girl, so most usually the victim of a split personality proves to be of this age and profession. The cases vary, but some there have been in which the girl has written letters about her own moral character to her mistress, and in others has attacked that of the mistress herself.

Then there are countless anonymous letters of a more humble kind; unsigned, and of splenetic protest, to public men. They run, I fancy, always on much the same lines as do the manias of lunatics, are marked, similarly, by the symptoms of an egoism so intense as to be diseased, and by a certain lack of imagination and humour.

But I must first define what I mean by an anonymous letter. All writers, for instance, have received helpful criticism and advice from people who do not wish to trouble them for an answer, and who therefore, with true Christian charity, refrain from signing their names; but these letters, full of good sense, whether hostile or comforting, do not in any way come under this grouping. I do not want merely to indicate their lack of signature. No; the qualities which characterise the real anonymous letter—except, of course, in the case of obscene-letter-writing (which is indeed a form of mania)—are a certain vague pomposity and a great contempt of all but traditional ideas. The greatest scorn of these writers is reserved for those who tend a little to think for themselves. Thus any article written on games, public schools or army life, always draws the anonymous-letter writers and shows them at their most perfect. New ideas knock against and hurt them: and their letters thus constitute a lower parallel to those number-less ones which angry old gentlemen indite to the papers, to protest against the manner in which they have been bumped against in buses.

Here, perhaps, I may quote a typical letter, which I received as the result of the foregoing essay on public schools. There is manifest in it a certain dropsical unwieldiness of phrase, and a flat staleness, combined with a genuine gift for anticlimax. Only a well-known signature could lend to it any dignity. The talent for anticlimax is particularly well shown in its final paragraph, which refers to the old Etonian tie (let me hasten to add that I have *never* worn one).

To Osbert Sitwell, Esq.

SIR,

Self-inflated cads are to England, what upstarts are to the Englishman of integrity; pernicious and contemptible. (Choice of the word "cad" is emphasized, because to the Englishman of integrity, it means something that is pernicious and contemptible.)

As you doubtless had it in your head that before the War no especial effort was being made to educate boys in Public Schools, may I suggest that you begin your education as soon as possible, beginning with the elementary Unwritten Laws of Decency? But no! Further reference to your scurrilous article, reveals that you regard this lack of education as an advantage to the average boy, or, as you would have it, the average intelligent boy. Apparently intelligent boys "read and think", while the more stupid of their fellows are content to do "an incredible amount of harm to the English governing classes". In point of fact, if an Etonian really employed the time at his disposal in the normal, and intendedly hard-working way, reading and thinking would be but poor euphemism for a slacker.

Eton, the finest school or college in this world, is a shrine of great tradition, and has, through the Grace of God, produced the most noble types of English gentlemen. However, taking yourself as an example, it will be plain that there are exceptions. Mr Sitwell, I hope you do not often wear your O.E. tie; it is plain that the privilege is lost on you. And, if you go about saying the things about Eton that you write, it can only be hoped that your own kind are the only people that harken to you.

Being able to admit, through the Press, that you were bored while at Eton, is an absolute record of bad taste and effrontery. I only wish that you had been washed away in the floods that seemingly provided your only amusement.[1]

The anonymous-letter writer of this kind is always *grand seigneur* in tone. He does not rely for the making of his effect on freshness of point of view, or on thinking for himself. No, he is a great gentleman imbued with all the Boer War ideas of chivalry, and one who, it will be seen, comes from "a famous English public school". After the fashion of Mr H. G. Wells's *The Bulpington of Blup*, "a very gallant gentleman", he might have stepped straight out of the pages of Mr Noel ("Society's Hero") Coward's *Cavalcade*, with its servants' hall glamour.

[1] Italics are mine.—O. S.

GAMES (1)

As a Menace to the Country

Y FEAR AND detestation of games is founded in the first place, I think, in love of my country; chiefly, then, on patriotic grounds I abhor them. . . . When England was making her way from a small island to the principal power, first of Europe, and then of the world, no organized games existed in this fair land. Almost the first mention of them in our history is the unchallenged fact that Drake nearly missed destroying the Armada through untimely indulgence in a game of bowls.

At school—and, when discussing games, one must, alas, inevitably hark back to those places of incarceration and torment—the authorities arm themselves with the excuse that the playing of them prepares a boy for leadership in the life which is to follow. . . . But, that being so, where, I ask myself, are now my—or your—great contemporaries in the worlds

22

of cricket and football? . . . The answer is, of course, "Still playing them!": (though that an adult should, of his own accord, engage in such orgies of futile infantilism is hardly credible!) . . . As to qualities of leadership: was a particular devotion to golf or cricket ever recorded—to take a few great English names at random—of Raleigh, Marlborough, Henry V, Peterborough, the Black Prince, Pitt, Fox or Nelson; any more than of such negligible highbrows as Shakespeare, Milton, Pope, Keats or Blake? . . . To look further afield, neither Alexander the Great, nor Caesar nor Napoleon, seem to have had much time for this sort of thing; yet each one of them, you might have thought, displayed a certain capacity for inspiring his men.

Of course we are compelled to admit that our governors in the Houses of Parliament have, for the past three decades or so, played golf: but then consider to what a pass they continually lead us! Does anyone nowadays think favourably of politicians as such; has not their very name become a by-word for platitude, banal blatant blather and incompetence? . . . Indeed, it may be claimed that golf nearly lost us the last war: all the statesmen who allowed us to blunder into it were golf-addicts. And most certainly it will lose us the next one, unless we have the good fortune to become embroiled with another golfing nation.

And a chance of this now fortunately exists: for, albeit one of the foremost methods of propaganda by which our opponents kept up their flagging spirits during the "Great" War, and prevented their people from giving in, was the statement that, if the English won, they intended everywhere to introduce compulsory games, nevertheless, since we were nominally victorious, the nominally vanquished, looking round after the battle for the cause of their failure and our success, decided "It must be due to games! They say so themselves", and proceeded to inflict on their own countries this barbarous English habit.

Sometimes I wonder. . . . Abroad we are still held to be the most subtle diplomatists in the whole world; we have now taught other nations "to play the game". Is this a piece of deliberate, diabolic guile: for the practice of games, by inculcating a blind, "My country-right-or-wrong" team-spirit, teaches a nation to be warlike without being certain to win and, when actually engaged in the struggle, to fight as though playing a game; with the Almighty looking on as an omnipotent umpire, ever there, ready to declare a "foul", should one occur? . . . Have we, then, of a purpose set their feet on the wrong track? And, as I hear of our continual defeats [1] at the hands of France, Germany, America, Italy and Greece, a thrill of patriotic emotion runs through me and, murmuring "There Is Yet Hope", I wonder if, after all, this particular objection of mine to games—as a menace to the country— may not be mistaken? Perhaps we shall be more evenly pitted, one against another, in the future. . . . We have taught young foreigners, too, how to waste *their* time and undermine *their* health.

Moreover, our fellow-nations are very readily learning this lesson of ours. I think that Germany, for one, now plays the game; that is to say that Hitlerism (I do not mean Fascism,

[1] This was written two years ago. Since we refused to pay any more instalments of the American Debt, there has occurred a marked, if regrettable, recrudescence of victory.

which I admire) is a true development of the English public-school spirit. Certainly the descriptions of the concentration camps, called into being by the present régime, read, in our newspapers, very much like a word-picture of life at Eton, when I was there—save that the inmates are older and, no doubt, more intelligent.

Nevertheless, when all these arguments have been stated, it remains indisputable that England was built up with the brain rather than the foot (although it is this member which every schoolboy from the age of eight to eighteen is now taught to regard as all-important) and that, in the world as it was, the national mania for games did, I apprehend, help consider-ably to lengthen the duration of the war. The "team-spirit", of which in those ugly and ever-deplorable days we heard so much, undoubtedly prolonged it and, as well, aided the final exhaustion: for the end of the shambles resembled the result of a tug-of-war wherein one side suddenly lets go. The Allies sprawled on the ground: and there, indeed, they continue.

Further, while the game-playing spirit endures, so long can there be no peace in Europe: because it inspires us always to support the weaker side; which policy, however noble in intention or as a gesture, is dreadfully, horribly unwise. Directly a nation begins to be prosperous and powerful, we, for our part, begin immediately, almost automatically, to dislike and disparage it. But, in future, would it not—should the League of Nations fail—be better, instead, to try to form an alliance with the strongest—rather than the weakest—group of powers? . . . Alas, we shall never even attempt such a thing: for it will be time to "have a go at the other fellow", time to enter for the challenge-cup again!

GAMES (2)

As a Pernicious Influence on the Individual

F AR, THEN, FROM preparing a boy for leadership in adult life, all that the school obsession for games really accomplishes is to afford a pleasant existence to him who likes playing them. To others, however, compulsory-games come as a disaster, as well as a bore. (I hyphenate the words, since for them—as for modern warfare—a new designation should be invented, both having long outgrown their names.) When once they become compulsory, they cease to be games, and, with that, all their virtue—for what it was worth—dies. Indeed, upon the individual, they exercise as pernicious an effect as upon a country. For example: how brutally ugly they are to look at, with the single possible exception of lawn-tennis, a harmless, silly, rather pretty dissipation! Consider cricket: it does not even possess the dramatic, exciting side to it—and certainly not the splendour of pageantry—that go far toward excusing the bull-fight in Spain. It is thus infinitely more degrading to the spectator.

And here, perhaps, we may touch on another problem; the influence of games on those who watch them. At school, of course, small boys are often compulsory spectators of games, as well as compulsory players. They cannot help it. It may be, even, that they find it less boring, if much colder, than to join in the sport themselves. . . . As for the adult—if you can call him such—spectator of games, though it necessarily damages his esthetic sense, I do not in other respects take a very serious view of his failing. It must be very dull for him, poor man; but, at any rate, it must be *healthier* for him than if he were to *play* himself. Moreover, through this process of substitution, he may in time get rid of the craving. Further, the sight of a crowd on the way to a football ground should, in certain directions, help to reassure us. Some there are who have pronounced England decadent, have alleged that enjoyment is now the order of the day here: but let us remember, for their refutation, the thousands who will sit in the rain for hours in order to watch a football match. Surely *that* is a sign, a symptom, of the toughness and vitality of the race? . . . Let us recollect, too, that, though foreigners might misconstrue the complaint that some of its addicts have registered of recent years (that cricket was but dull fun), reasoning that this indicated an enfeebling of the national fibre, yet the only suggestion—put forward by the same people who complained— for the brightening and speeding up of the game, was a proposal to lengthen the natural span of a Test Match from three to four or five days!

But to return to our sheep (and what sheep they are!) the

influence of games upon those who play them is quite a different matter. After all, cricket, golf and football, whether to watch or to play, remain merely so many devices for wasting what is, so far as we know, the only span allotted to mankind in a world full of wonders: for, though it may be argued that they often occupy but a very small portion of twenty-four hours, they are yet so tiring that the rest of the day must likewise be spent in stupor. Thus, for instance, whenever you hear someone remark, "After a day's hard work, I go to the theatre to be amused, not to be made to think!", that person thereby announces himself, you may be sure, a game-fiend. Such fatigue results from over-exercise, from using the wrong muscles in the wrong way, at the wrong age, but never from brain work. A healthy man can derive more pleasure from the use of his brain than from the use of his feet.

What, then, you ask, gentle reader, is the cause of the "game-habit", hardly less injurious in the end than that of opium or hashish; how do men, reasonable in other respects, acquire it? . . . Usually its origin is to be traced back to schools: but, in after-life, it springs, as a rule, more immediately from over-indulgence in food. People choose to think that over-eating can be remedied by over-exercise. It is a vicious circle. Over-exercise makes them over-hungry. Once you take to it, violent exercise becomes a necessity throughout your life. You cannot go without it. The game-addict, unless specifically equipped for his career by Nature, must, in order to "keep fit", play—or should we write "take"?—more and more games. (Here, in parenthesis, note the coincidence that the word *take* is, through some process, perhaps, of unconscious identification, used of both exercise and drugs.) As with soporifics, the need for games increases with the years that pass. But, since the constitution of a man can only withstand this sort of life so long as he is young, directly he grows too old, too exhausted by exercise to indulge in it any longer, he dies. (It is, of course, common knowledge that athletes are apt to die young, their systems outworn, their hearts and nerves run down, their power of resistance at an end.) . . . Yet actually two brisk walks of from twenty minutes to half an hour each, or a swim of fifteen minutes a day are quite sufficient to keep a man healthy in body. But there also exists the mind. "EAT LESS AND THINK MORE" should be the slogan of all who have leisure.

Some game-fiends, exceptionally strong to begin with, do contrive, by one method or another, occasionally to prolong their existence into middle age: and nothing is more sad, more despicable, to the really healthy man, than to see these poor, tortured creatures running all over the place in sweaters, racing over muddy ground, and toiling over golf-courses, in a constant, ineffectual effort to regain the health which all these exertions, all this morbid attempt to escape from the reality of life, have destroyed. If you ask them what they are doing, they pant out, peevishly enough, that they are "trying to keep fit". . . . But what for? What, indeed, can be the purpose of trying "to keep fit", when all their time is absorbed in doing so? Against what hour of trial are these wretched victims of delusion preparing; for deathbed or Day of Judgment?

Yet games have their uses. There is, after all, a good side to them. The game of golf, for example, can be played alone

—a great advantage. Further, a cricket course, a golf ground, a football pitch, each acts as a temporary internment camp for all those who practise, or are interested in, the particular vice to which it is devoted. Thus the man free of these habits and healthy in mind and body, can look at his watch on a summer day and say to himself: "It's safe now: all the worst cricketers" ("worst" being used in the sense of most addicted) "are at Lord's or at the Oval; all the worst golfers are isolated on their 'blasted heaths'. I can now walk abroad without fear of being bored by a single one of them." . . . Lastly, as I have stated, such games soon intern their habituals even more securely— this time in their coffins. For Nature very sensibly concludes that if a man will, of his own choice, thus waste his time and energy, this world cannot hold much interest for him. And so, cutting down his life's span by a decade or two, she, with combined wisdom and kindness, removes him from it. *R.I.P.!*

ON
BROADENING
THE MIND

"TRAVEL", YOU HEAR people say, "broadens the mind"
—as if that were a recommendation!—and, in consequence,
it is often suggested to many young men of the more
leisured classes as a fitting close to their education. Another
instance of our illogicality: for the aim of education, I take
it, is to enable the child to grow up into a man well equipped
to grapple successfully with life, and so be happy in it. Yet
surely one would presume on looking round, that, to attain
this end, the absolute essential was to have not only a narrow,
but a resolutely shut, mind? And why, for example, seek to
broaden a mind, when several hundreds, or even thousands,
of pounds have already been spent upon a continuous and
very expert course of narrowing it—by means of the private
school and public school systems?

Travelling does, indeed, open our eyes, the eyes of even

the most unobservant, a little to the future; which, if happiness is your aim, is inexpedient. It is not, for example, encouraging, nor does it tend to promote the *bourgeois* belief in human progress on which contentment largely depends, to journey through China and find the Chinese people, with their strange instinct for the future, everywhere repairing the walls, long disused, of their towns and villages, and putting up new ones where necessary, in preparation for another thousand years or so of chaos. . . . And, again, to observe the different rites of different religions, which yet all present so close a parallel to those of your own church, might arouse disturbing thoughts. You should never, if you value happiness, allow yourself to question your beliefs. Indeed, if you lack them, you should go out and find them, for, just as the Chinese are rebuilding and patching their walls for their bodily security, so many people to-day return to narrow and outworn creeds for the protection and comfort of their minds. . . . Close your mind and shut your eyes, and you may be happy, and not only happy but great; for most really great men, that is to say, men of action as opposed to men of thought, have been narrow-minded and lacked vision. What man not blinded by a single purpose would have dared, like Clive, to conquer India (and will *broad*-mindedness enable us to keep it?) . . . Alexander the Great, as a boy, is said to have tamed his horse Bucephalus by riding it toward the sun, so that it became dazzled, blinded to all else, and in like manner he allowed the thought of conquest in later years to narrow his own great mind, so that he could perceive nothing but its blaze.

In politics, then, never entertain a doubt, nor in religion:

if you are an esthetic conservative, condemn out of hand all modern poetry and painting, but without reading or seeing it; or if a radical, despise all ancient things, forbidding yourself to recognize the worth of Raphael or Titian, El Greco or Gainsborough. The pleasure you will obtain from scouting them is quite equal to any you might derive from a more broad-minded appreciation of their beauties. Assign to your personal or inherited belongings a special artistic or historical interest, and to your home, even if it be one out of a row of two hundred similar houses, a particular air of handsomeness and comfort; think your carpets softer, and your children better at sport, than your neighbours'. And, above all, acclaim, without knowing any other, your own land as the most beautiful and most just, the least selfish and most intelligent, full of the best-dressed men and women, the most profound cricketers, the most subtle golfers and the best tadpole-fishers of any country in the world. . . . That way lies peace and contentment.

In all truth, a man whose mind is said by his fellows to lack breadth is from the first in a strong position where life is concerned, well adapted for its struggles, and certain of happiness, even if congenitally unfitted for conversation. And nothing can be done about it; the narrow mind narrows further with the years, inevitably; in the same way that the broad mind broadens. . . . Thus, to strike a personal note, my whole life has been spent in an endeavour to narrow rather than broaden my outlook, and to debase rather than improve my mind: but it has proved a hopeless struggle. I was afforded every advantage in that direction; I was sent to good schools and taught cricket and Latin: and yet it never made me into either a good cricketer or an adequate classical scholar; in only one direction did I show promise, by preferring my own native language to that of other countries, a preference founded, no doubt, on laziness, but a necessary ingredient of the narrow mind. . . . Finally, in, as I suppose, despair, those responsible for my welfare decided that a cavalry regiment would prove the best finishing-school for me, and accordingly I was for eight months attached to one of those now obsolete institutions: but did this, even, make for my happiness by destroying my intellectual and esthetic interests? Alas, not in the least! I could still see not one, but a thousand, sides to every question, and, in consequence, still found myself inclined to waver mournfully in my opinions.

As for that cavalry regiment, it was, indeed, an extraordinary and even useful, experience, enabling me at an early age, and without travelling to distant and unhealthy parts of Africa, to make myself acquainted with the customs and comprehend the mentality of the members of any primitive tribe. No life shared with savages of the Congo or with the web-footed natives of New Guinea could have been more strange; none could have seemed so far removed from the life proceeding round it. In all other aspects, indeed, it constituted the antithesis of travelling, for everything was a restriction. The objects, a stranger would have pronounced, to which these barbaric clans were dedicated must be horse and dog (even the crocodile, formerly venerated by the Egyptians, was a more sensible and seemly object of respect). Of all animals the horse influences the average Englishman to the greatest extent; the magical creature seems able to conquer his whole interest, his whole life, and to prevent him from thinking about anything else. A special language, even, of hoofs and hocks and fetlocks and a thousand other such terms, has to be used in his worship; a language as complicated, to express a process of thought as subtle, as any needed for the comprehension of the more involved problems in higher mathematics. Moreover, the devotee must dress in special clothes, and bestow every hour upon his god: that way, too, lies happiness.

Such experiences, even if they do not successfully straiten the mind, do, in a sense, help a little to prepare their victims for life. However much of horror and *ennui* the world may hold; whatever, for example, your experiences of first-class modern warfare, they will probably, nevertheless, come as a relief after days spent at school. Many a youth, leaving school to join the Army during the war, found life in the trenches less of a strain upon the nerves than had been every-day school existence; indeed, infinitely preferable to it in every way. In that sense Waterloo was perhaps really won upon the playing-fields of Eton. . . . So let us narrow our minds and take heart for the future.

IN PRAISE OF INDOLENCE

THERE WAS A time when laziness, now proclaimed as a virtue, was condemned as a vice. "Satan", they used to tell us, "finds some mischief still for idle hands to do." . . . But many people now realize, only too well, that, in order for this proverb to contain truth, the word *"idle"* should be rendered *"restless"* or *"busy"*: because over-intense activity is often a form of nervous disease, a kind of mental St. Vitus's Dance. The idle man is usually a good-natured one; at worst, harmless; whereas the men who do the harm, the Napoleons and Lenins and Hitlers and rabid newspaper-peers, are obliged by their natures to be for ever frantically striving. . . . Poor creatures, they cannot rest until they are worn out. Pleasure has little meaning for them, and they are the victims of continual indigestion; mental not less than physical. Avoid, I should counsel you for your own good, the man who has no use for sleep and says so: it is the sign of one who wishes to be a superman, and who will, if you give him time, undoubtedly tell you that he glories in battle and he considers that Effort is the Aim of All Life. Beware, too, of the sort of old people who subsequently, in their obituary notices, are said to have "remained active until the end".

Effort is of no avail in itself; nor should it be necessarily awarded admiration. It requires, often, as much effort to lose a battle as to win it; because the stupid commander, aware of his inferiority, has to be even busier than the clever one, and tends to fussiness in detail. Cleverness no more consists in an infinite capacity for taking pains than does genius; they both consist, rather, in an infinite capacity for inducing others to take the pains for them; and the right ones, at that! The generals and statesmen, on both sides, who were responsible for such endless disaster and loss of life during the last war were, on the whole, a painstaking and un-imaginative body, always busy, and indeed inclined to parade the fact. The Devil himself is evidently a busy lost soul, end-lessly coming and going about his work. . . . The lazy man has seldom forged or murdered. All the grand embezzlers and treasure-rooters of the last decades, Jabez Balfour, Bottomley, Ivar Kreuger, Hatry, were all intensely *busy* men. (Their activity, indeed, was a constant advertisement for them.) Further, both religious communities and germs only begin to persecute when they are active.

Effort for Effort's Sake, then, as a doctrine is outworn; he who follows it might as well devote his life to dumb-bell exercises for all the good he does. And, in fact, almost the only effort which it is worth making continually—and that more for the sake of self-respect than because of any positive utility—is the effort to combat human stupidity. It can be done, though, quietly; very quietly. . . . A word in time—like "Why?"—saves nine; so that, when people begin offering you such sentiments as "You see, *I* believe in . . ."—whatever it may be, Christian Science, a Big Army, or the Survival of the Fittest, always interject "Why?": for a belief which has so urgently and swiftly to be introduced into conversation is sure to be mystical rather than reasoned, the result of faith rather than of thinking. And faith should serve as the basis of a religion, but never of an opinion.

Consider the Epochs of Effort. The Victorian Era was the most consciously devoted to this curious ideal; the chief effort being, in reality, to sell something. The singular fact emerges that Charles Darwin, albeit a great man of whom most of the Victorians intensely disapproved, nevertheless through the medium of his theory of "The Survival of the Fittest", did much, however unconsciously, to give them support. He imparted to their often iniquitous proclivities an ethical foundation; because, for each rival merchant knocked into the workhouse, for each business assassinated, for every native murdered or enslaved in order that his land might be appropriated, the persons responsible for these results could, when occasionally their consciences stung them, always comfort themselves with the reflection: "It can't be helped. . . . Survival of the Fittest, and all that. . . ." The theory was applied to everything in the universe; the very laws of the universe itself were interpreted in terms of Effort and Will. And it is only of recent years that more probable but very opposite explanations have won acceptance from science; such, for example, as the one which tells us that the earth, in the course which it pursues round the sun, and the moon, in the course which it pursues round the earth, are not following any dictates of Effort, but are, instead, merely following the Line of *Least* Resistance! . . . And who knows but that many of those who prate of Effort and of Doing are not, in fact, following the same course? It is more difficult for many of them to think than to act; while to think straight would be more difficult still. The clamour, for instance, that has been raised recently in this country, by an identical set of people, for economy on one hand and ten thousand more airplanes on the other, is a very good example of the difficulty which so many experience in thinking straight. . . . It is easier to demand, than to think out the results of the policies you are demanding.

I should not, therefore, perhaps so much advocate laziness, as strive to uphold the cause of mental activity against physical, and of honest mental activity against dishonest. . . . Yet there is much to be said on behalf of sloth. Nearly every great invention has been the result of natural indolence in the inventor, and in its turn has helped on the cause. Some child, working in a factory in Victorian times, found it tedious to turn a wheel: by the clever adjustment of a piece of string to another wheel he found it would continue to work of its own accord. This was a "labour-saving" invention: in other words, it pandered to laziness and was the result of it. But, also, it saved the proprietor expense, and so we were spared all the talk, to which we should otherwise have been treated, of the beauty of labour and of the joy of work. This has always been the course of true invention.

As for the benefits of physical activity, the idea of "regular physical exercise" is another fruit of the conception that to keep busy is necessarily an admirable thing in itself. And exercise, excessive physical exercise, kills more people a year in England to-day than do many diseases of which men stand in dread. It is, perhaps, itself a disease of the spirit. . . . Alas, if only those addicted to it would sit down for half an hour with the same solemnity they apply to golf, and devote this time instead to thinking, results might be achieved that would astonish the world! As it is, they prefer to dissipate their energy in perspiration.

Where myself is concerned, even, I have never yet been able to attain to the pitch of sloth which is my object. Seven years spent in the Army made me, against my better judgment, to some extent an exercise-addict; so that, my system craving it, I must always obtain an hour or two of sharp walking a day. I have tried to reduce it, but have failed. . . . On the other hand, the waste of time thus incurred reduces my capacity for work, and so, in a sense, constitutes laziness of a kind.

FRIENDS
AND
ENEMIES

FRIENDS

HOW GAILY PEOPLE enter upon friendships, as though nothing in the world were so easy and so free of all risk! In consequence they never fail to be surprised by the disillusioning rows and rumours of rows which ensue. . . . Because true friendship being an art, as well as a question of feeling, is one which cannot always be mastered in a few years, even by those fortunate individuals most gifted in that direction: a fact, in a sense, generally recognized, since one excuse habitually advanced by lazy, cuckoo-like parents anxious to dispose of their offspring is, "The boy must go to school soon, or he won't *learn* to make friends". . . . Actually he seldom does. . . . And if the unfortunate little wretch was you, and if you were bullied into incurring such friendships, how much and how often have you not regretted them in later life! For very strong are the tentacles of that octopus, the professional, old-public-schoolboy friend, ever eager to "see a lot of you" during his frequent, if short, visits to London. You never had much in common except a compulsory propinquity, and now, luckily, even that is lacking. . . . The man who, at forty, is still surrounded by such weazen or chubby-faced old-boys, with their excruciating, palsied chatter of "Do you remember Jones Minor?", is one who knows so little of friendship that he deserves to be still at school. . . . Women, I think, are more sensible in the matter, having less scruple in dissolving unnecessary old ties, and more scruple about allowing themselves to be wickedly bored.

Nevertheless, friendship, if it is to be profitably practised and understood, requires a long and difficult apprenticeship. . . . In several directions a blunder is only too easy. There are those, for instance, over eager for friendship, who force boring, unwanted confidences upon you, and tell you "all about" themselves: while others will tell you nothing. The speeding up of life, it is true, has made friendship a finer if more difficult art. It is possible now to have different worlds of friends in different countries, not one of them aware of the existence of the other; though it then becomes necessary to keep, after the fashion of a conjurer, these various groups for ever in motion, spinning them with both hands. Not a moment of rest does it allow: but in this way it is possible to enjoy more friendship to-day than ever before.

Yet, on the contrary, even apart from the language problem, difference of nationality can act as a barrier. The Englishman finds American men often too much inclined to presume on a possible interest in themselves, to tell their lives (which seems longer to tell than to live): and the American finds an equal difficulty with the restrained and uneducated Englishman, who appears to him to be at once foolishly complacent and foolishly shy. . . . Then friendship with a German entails listening to long-familiar and extremely lengthy passages, often vilely rendered, of Shakespeare, or else an impassioned disavowal of war-guilt: for every German is a born propagandist. . . . Indeed, it is much easier to found a true friendship with a member of some distant country, remote from us and our ways of thinking, than with our own blood-relations.

For this reason, perhaps, English people used, before the war, to possess so many Russian and Polish friends. Having no community with us of religion, politics or thought, they were oblivious of the little mannerisms and tricks which in us may irritate our fellow-countrymen: while, even when themselves cultured, they could be amused by the ignorance of an unlettered Englishman, taking him to be typical and therefore interesting. . . . And the Englishman, for his part, will overlook all erratic behaviour in such a foreigner: for he likes to hear broken English, is entertained by it and yet feels a sentiment of pity for him who speaks it, comparable to that which he experiences at the sight of a dog or a child crippled from birth; and pity breeds a sort of understanding. . . . As for friendships with members of the Balkan races, for many of our nation these are still easier to contract: because, these people so recently freed from Turkish domination, not being so sure of their civilization as their western neighbours, cling all the more tenaciously to every convention, of thought as well as of usage: and, in consequence, to make any observation that is not trite and hackneyed amounts to bad form, may endanger the drawing-room if not the state, constitutes the same sort of bad form as would to play a piece of good modern music on an uncracked piano at a village concert.

But let us look now at our English friends, and our ways of making them. . . . Often, bored by the dulness of those who attached themselves to us in early life, we begin, when intellectually of age, to demand of friendship the qualities of liveliness of fancy, of intelligence and wit; false objectives, which, though they help the hours to pass quickly and with zest, will in the end become responsible for devastated feelings; because those possessed of wit naturally like to use it, and can use it best on those whom they best know. . . . If, notwithstanding, we care to maintain such friendships, it is wiser to ignore these titbits of things said about us by our lively companions (and so diligently collected and brought round to us by those other, strong, faithful-even-in-adversity friends, who, it must be remembered, can only prove *their* faithfulness in *our* adversity, and therefore long for the chance, and delight to serve us with our heads on platters) and merely content ourselves with reflecting how often we have been led into similar sharp-saying ourselves and how thoroughly we have enjoyed it.

Moreover, it remains entirely our own fault. We all know, each one of us, that the stupid make the most faithful friends. If you must have faithfulness, be content to rely on dogs (or upon those human beings who most resemble them): for the friendship of a dog, or of an old general, implies devotion without criticism. The very dumbness of their friendship makes it so admirable, so dependable. Where possible, then, cultivate deaf-mutes, to whom spoken treachery is forbidden by their affliction, and whose friendship, as with a dog, must ever be that of the eyes rather than of the ears and the tongue.

But, undoubtedly, a code of friendship should be initiated: so that it could be scored, like a game. Each type of friend should be listed and carry so many marks. . . . How much rather, for example, would I be disturbed by a drunken friend at night than by a sober telephone-fiend friend in the morning! (Oh, those morning and evening telephonic tin-tinnabulations, that eager, insistent ringing which breaks up a day's work, that voice which says so ungrammatically, "It's only me. . . . I thought I'd ring up!" . . .) Then there is the timid friend who cannot and will not say what he means; and the sort of friend who seeks to demonstrate his friendship by tiring you out when you are ill, and subsequently attending your funeral service: the huffy friend, too, who delights to recall "old times"; those delicious old times, so happy for him, when, too young to choose your own friends, you were surrounded by inherited impedimenta—distant cousins or the children of your parents' friends—and forced to indulge in the most odious and uncongenial pursuits, such as shooting harmless rabbits. And there is, further, the dentist friend (to which type I am conscious that myself belongs) who always appears when you have toothache, plaguing you with the name and virtues of his dentist, the skill of his drilling, the efficacy of his probes. . . . And oh, in good climates, in Italy or the south of France, there are the picnic friends, who will not be satisfied until they have kidnapped you for the whole day, taken you to a place you have never wished to visit, and then obliged you, under abominable circumstances of discomfort, to swallow quantities of cold, indigestible food the while the hottest of hot suns scorches your uncovered head. . . .

Notwithstanding, how far am I from despising friendship, in which, indeed, is contained almost the whole sweetness and savour of life. What curious devotions one is privileged to witness! The family friend, for instance. Before the war there were few households which did not include some such lonely, isolated figure, bachelor or unattached old lady, who had adopted a whole family and, with utter disinterestedness, would use the influence acquired to smooth every difficulty out. And what, too, of the devotion so often shown by domestic servants; the quality of which is all the more rare and to be valued because, though such a thing is obviously beyond all possibility of being bought or sold, it appears, in the eyes of the stupid, paid for in hard cash?

FRIENDS
AND
ENEMIES

RECENTLY A GREAT friend of mine, to show his affection for me, rose specially from bed, with a temperature of 103 and a bad attack of influenza on him, in order to meet me at the station on my return to London; with the result that I was in bed for a fortnight. No enemy could have done more. Often, after the same fashion, it is not easy to locate friends and enemies or, further, to distinguish one from the other, on so many occasions do the two appear to exchange places in a night. You may go away for three months and, when you return, find all your enemies friendly, all your friends hostile. Even the proof of friendship, which the loyal friend displays from time to time, giving the coin a ring to demonstrate by its sound that it *is* true, does not lack disadvantages.

Friendship is defined in the dictionary as "mutual attach-

D

ment"; but "mutual interest" would approach more closely to a correct definition, and one which would apply as nearly to enemies as to friends. By interest, I mean more than curiosity—I want to indicate a compelling feeling of interest which cannot be repressed, and yet which does not wholly arise from curiosity or the scientific spirit.

If, therefore, devotion, the former basis of friendship, is not accepted as sufficient, then interest must replace it. But, alas, those in whom it is possible to feel interest are only too prone to the use of ear and tongue. Never, probably, was such a time as the present for treachery and backbiting. Drawing-room, studio and restaurant echo with malicious titters and vindictive laughter. But treachery, that most deadly fault, and one to me quite unforgivable, appears at any rate to be a vice of those swift in the race, and not of the slow and halting. Alcibiades was treacherous, but one cannot say that he was stupid. A peasant, in spite of a natural bent for it, finds it harder to be treacherous than a politician. Moreover, we must remember that the possibility of being treacherous is only given to a friend. "A treacherous enemy", however often we hear the phrase or read it, is a silly contradiction in terms, and merely constitutes a libel on a plausible and clever enemy, possessed of a tactical sense. And further, while, as I pointed out in the preceding essay, it is of course possible to-day to enjoy more friendship than ever before, this statement takes on as its corollary the fact that, at the same time, one is forced to endure more treachery.

Sooner or later, accordingly, it is better to adopt the doctrine of Swedenborg; that it does not matter whether we love or hate those whom we see constantly. Nevertheless some design, the full extent of which we fortunately cannot perceive, exists in life, and thus there are people we shall have to see and go on seeing: for fate only provides us with these few as the intimate human material of a lifetime. This specially selected company moves constantly round us, marching in and out of the army of supers and acquaintances to join, part from and rejoin us; swinging in and out of our lives, just as the little figures swing in and out of a toy Swiss hut, to foretell good or bad weather. Once recognized as a principle of life, this leads to true forgiveness, to a general amnesty.

Precisely this matter of mutual interest, too, divides friends from acquaintances. How impossible it is to feel an interest in the latter, and how awkward and difficult are those pretences to interest that politeness forces one to frame —that fine rain of false questions which a casual and un-wished-for bump in the street entails! "Where have you been this winter? How is your mother? Have you skated at all? What are you doing now?" and all the rest of that pain-ful, familiar chatter. So obvious has the lack of any bond become, that the questioner never waits to hear the answer. Indeed, it is well to avoid acquaintances at all costs: for they are merely the figures that block up the exits and entrances to the stage. Better is it to encounter an enemy than an acquaintance—more feeling can be derived from it.

The modern changes in manners has affected both friend-ship and enmity. Sherlock Holmes went through life calling Watson, Watson: if he had lived now, thirty years later, he would have called him Peter, or Evelyn, or whatever his name was, within three hours, because to the young of our time, a surname is a frosty hedge that cuts one off from the true personality of its owner—makes him seem merely a member of an ancient tribe rather than an individual of to-day. The Christian name, on the other hand, is the most personal belonging of its proprietor, the most intensely individual thing that he possesses. Yet our fathers could pass through half a century or more of surname-calling without finding their friendship frostbitten. But then, in those times even husbands called their wives and wives their husbands "Mrs F." and "Mr F."; while, further, in that otherwise most informal country, America, husbands and wives still address, and refer to, one another in the same manner; whereas to-day, in Europe, every enemy presents his Christian name to us, as well as every friend. Whom you call by his surname cannot constitute a real enemy, being too distant to injure or be injured.

Two final words of advice to the neophyte: never forgive your enemies—it only makes them more bitter; and never introduce one intimate friend to another—an act always fatal in its consequences and extremely painful, as you see yourself gradually forced out and barred from the newly forming circle.

THE
WHITE
MAN'S
BURDEN

CERTAIN PEOPLE EXIST whom the experienced can at once recognize under the classification of the White Man's Burden; and, indeed, the cleverer among them acknowledge such identity of their own accord. These happy beings, by no means confined to any one class, are those on whose behalf others willingly work themselves to the bone; who can, without danger to themselves, become implicated and entangled in a thousand troubles, and yet, whatever the cost in labour or money, will always be rescued, though this salvage work will entail an absolute lack of exertion on their own part. They ever float on the surface, in bright, never-ending sunlight, wearing perpetual and quite natural smiles. They go anywhere they want to go, do anything they want to do, and yet no evil consequence will ever befall them. Providence reserves the pains which, according to every moral rule, their behaviour should incur, for other people. They are debited, reader, to your account and mine.

The White Man's Burden, as I have written, is not confined to any one class; we have all seen the labourer whose bicycle is wheeled along for him by his comrades, the shopkeeper whose business is carried on by domestic slaves; but certainly he is most to be sought, most at ease, most active, in an artistic environment. Eager to attend parties, he can sit up all night without feeling in the least debilitated next morning. He never works, for his work is a pleasure to him, and the harvest of his agreeable labour he disposes of with a born facility. Publishers scramble to accept his books, directors of galleries rush after his pictures. He can paint or write music as easily as he eats and drinks—not that this in itself indicates that he necessarily paints or writes well; in instance of which the reader will remember the story of the discerning lady who, expatiating upon the work of a novelist remarked finally, "Dear Mr Dash . . . he writes as easily as he breathes . . . but then some people don't *like* being breathed upon".

But it must not be thought that the W.M.B. is in any way a parasite; far from it. He labours, but with more ease and with more pleasure than the average man. No: that which distinguishes him from his fellows is the fact that everybody —even those who do not like him—are always willing to labour, indeed slave, for him without comment. Further, the W.M.B., by nature clever and intuitional, seems as a rule to be conscious of his birthright, and is therefore inclined to be difficult and a bully. When, however, for a moment he forgets his genius, he becomes the gayest, most amusing of companions.

Many of us have a streak of the W.M.B. in our composition. I myself was always conscious at school, and, of later years, in a military hospital, that my comrades would look after me without much effort on my part. Yet I could never attain to the full stature of a W.M.B. I have to be pleasant, and to work a little, to gain my effects; and, alas, I am always forced to rescue myself from the troubles into which I fall.

Of course, those who do not understand the nature of these rare beings remain to a certain degree unappreciative of them; and this accounts, I apprehend, for the unflattering portraits which we find of them in literature. The finest example of a White Man's Burden to be depicted in a novel is, I think, Mr Skimpole, of *Bleak House*, with his peaches and champagne, his charm and his wit (his wit seems to me undeniable), but Dickens has misunderstood him and, by an underlining of his faults and an underrating of his very real distinction, has in this case spoilt the balance of character. Mr Skimpole, it is plain, realized to the full his destiny; and this was apparent to Dickens. He knew that he would ever drift on the tide of life, enjoying himself, supported, as a great ballerina is supported, by a crowd of satellites, by a mob of struggling, eager, drowning friends and relatives. *Somebody* would always come to his rescue. Meanwhile, as we see, he pursued his delightful, his effortless way, a child of pleasure.

"This is our friend's consulting room (or would be, if he ever prescribed), his sanctum, his studio," said my guardian to us.

"Yes," said Mr. Skimpole, turning his bright face about, "this is the bird's cage. This is where the bird lives and sings. They pluck his feathers now and then, and clip his wings; but he sings, he sings!"

He handed us the grapes, repeating in his radiant way, "He sings! Not an ambitious note, but still he sings."

"These are very fine," said my guardian. "A present?"

"No," he answered. "No! Some amiable gardener sells them. His man wanted to know, when he brought them last evening, whether he should wait for the money. 'Really, my friend,' I said, 'I think not—if your time is of value to you.' I suppose it was, for he went away."

Not even the French or Russian revolutions, had they occurred in his time, would have been able to spoil his manner of life or dispossess him of his birthright. The Communists would have laboured on his behalf as willingly as his rich friends.

Another chief characteristic of a W.M.B. is his inevitability: impossible to avoid him. For example, on one occasion I was on a visit to Paris, where I had not stayed for many months. At any rate, I felt as I journeyed there, I have escaped seeing Smithers (as we will call him); for I was angry with him for the trouble to which he had put me, and I knew that he had been left behind in London. That evening, however, I visited a *boîte*, and there he was, in the doorway, waiting to receive me. I explained to my companions that I could not face it. . . . We left, deciding to visit another *boîte* instead. But there he stood again, waiting for us, expectant and unsurprised, though we had gone there directly in a fast car and he could not have been aware of whither we were going.

Many other curious points require elucidation. Thus,

though the W.M.B. often accomplishes much good work—
and if not good work, at any rate, much work—he seems to
the outward eye to have all eternity at his disposal. Never in
a hurry, always able to drop in and see his friends or, in his
turn, to receive them, his books appear, as though they were
mushrooms, in a night.

And not only does Providence itself take care of the
W.M.B.; there exists invariably, attached to him by some
invisible thread, a special kind of human being. Just as the
crocodile is inevitably accompanied by the crocodile-bird, so
the W.M.B. bears always with him, at his beck and call, a
type of individual whom we may christen the "retriever".
Retrievers, of course, exist also on their own, and are sometimes to be found elsewhere than in the wake of the W.M.B.
Divided into several groups, they nevertheless fall roughly
into two main classes: firstly, those who collect all your
former acquaintances—people who have bored you twenty
years ago, and of whom with great difficulty you have rid
yourself—and then, without warning you, fling them at you
in a lump, asking you to tea to meet them or, at any rate,
organizing an encounter of some kind, without explaining
who is going to be there; secondly, those retrievers who bur-
row you out in order once again to expose you not merely to
your own bores, but to your own liabilities—such as the
W.M.B.

For instance, you will say to your W.M.B. that you are
away, offering several excuses. At once the retriever will
come round, will worry you until you forget your excuse, will
force you into saying yes, you will come to tea, suspecting
no link between them. You will go, and there you will again

meet your fate. . . . The best retrievers of the collecting sort are those who live in country houses. In these vast depositories they can secrete any number of former acquaintances of yours, people whom you have forgotten long ago and with difficulty, and then, without a warning word, bring them over and unload them on you in your own home.

RULES
FOR
BEING
RUDE

BEING RUDE, I suppose, is an art like any other, governed by strict rules and subject to a code. It requires, for its full development, either native genius or, at any rate, an inherent talent. . . . A lady to whom George Moore had read a story, once remarked: "What enormous talent you have, G. M.", and received the reply, "No, I started with a very little talent, but I have cultivated it every day". . . . In the same way, there are those among us who, born with however small a talent for being rude, have cultivated it to a truly remarkable extent.

Let it be clear from the beginning that by a *natural talent* for being rude, I do not intend to signify natural rudeness. A man naturally rude is indeed temperamentally, but very effectually, barred from ever gaining any results from his insolence. He is merely rude—"a rude sort of chap"—

whereas to exercise the art of being rude, to extract from it
the utmost flavour, you must be, by nature, kind and
generous, and have, in addition, acquired beautifully polished
manners, so that your rudeness tells to the full. Thus it will
be seen that the pleasures of rudeness are essentially those of
an old and civilized society; which explains why the eighteenth
century was the grand epoch, the golden age, of rudeness as
of so much else. It is of no use to be rude in the backwoods:
there, among so many too liberally gifted by Nature in the
same direction, you would be merely another backwoodsman.
Further, avoid at all costs being rude without intention; do
not ever allow yourself to become a rudeness-gusher, with a
perpetual supply of that commodity, on which the world
can depend.

Consider the technique of your art, by no means an easy
one. It is difficult, even, to find a subject upon whom to
practise. First of all, let us establish that those—if any—to
whom it is permissible to be rude, must be of your own age,
sex and standing: never be rude to those older or younger or
poorer than yourself. You must, in addition, carefully select
your setting, your background. Just as if you were a great
pianist, or a great violinist, you must have an audience to inspire
you to the full use of your powers: yet you must never be rude
in your own house (a great pity, for it would enable you to
grapple with your foes with much more facility); nor must
you be rude to them in their own homes (a still more
grievous injunction, because meditate for yourself upon how
enjoyable would be a daring Jameson Raid or verbal hold-up
of your enemies in their own beastly homes); nor, again, must
you be rude to them in the houses of common friends, of

neutral powers, as it were. . . . I have even heard an old gentleman once lamentatively protest: "I'm surprised, that's all: rude to me in *my own motor-car!*" . . . Thus it becomes plain that the path of true rudeness never did run smooth, is beset with difficulties and trammelled with the reddest of red tape.

What pitch, then, what scenery, should you choose for your brief battle (it must be brief, too, very brief, to be effective)? How can you entice your quarry, all unsuspecting, into the street, and there assassinate him with a word: for being an enemy he would, unless bent on the same errand, scarcely wish to find himself in your company? You must, I apprehend, make a careful study of his ways, in order to meet him as though by accident, all unwary, walking along the pavement or entering a place of amusement. A railway carriage, again, offers a splendid *décor* and no opportunity for your quarry to escape.

On the other hand, if you are thoroughly acquainted with the canons of your art, with the commandments that govern its exercise and the old-fashioned limitation which tradition has placed upon it, your knowledge affords you several pleasures and advantages which ignorance would forfeit. Thus you can meet a person—as he thinks, by chance—in the street, and be very rude to him without his having any cause for complaint (it is all the more startling for your victim), or you can be extremely cordial and polite in the house of a common friend one night, insult him the following evening in a restaurant, and then go out of your way to be amiable once more the day after. . . . This adds perplexity to insult. . . . And, though you follow the old rules that framed the

impromptu nimble wit of Lord Chesterfield and the stentorian and calculated insults of Dr Johnson, yet modernize
your technique, making it adaptable and elastic, with plenty
of give and as much take. . . . But do not dash at it: remember
you must play your opponent for weeks, as though he were a
trout in some limpid stream. Disarm him with interest and
amiability and the charm of your companionship, lull him
into a fictitious security; then choose your opportunity, and
do not spare his feelings. . . . Better still is it, if you can,
to induce *him* to afford you the exercise of your art: persuade
him, though he remains unaware of the process, to write to
you asking for some favour, and then crush him.

As for the manner of being rude, never allow yourself at
the moment to show any emotion, least of all anger. Dislike
should breed contempt, but never rage: for such anger, after
the fashion of love, has a flame to it, and offers heat, so that
your opponent can avail himself of it and forge himself
armour, and even, it may be, a sword. Conscious that he has
made you angry, his replies now come to him all the more
easily. . . . No. True rudeness should be cold, and at the
same time, perfect in form, exquisitely delivered, so that,
going away discomfited, your enemy will ponder, "Can I
have heard aright? Did he really say it, really *mean* it?" will
tell people of the occurrence, in order to have their opinion
on it; will even, in his folly, deliberately ask their advice. . . .
Many days he will turn it over in his mind, and in this way
the wound you have given him will fester, scar him for life.

Moreover, should your opponent, too, be gifted, never
grudge him the effect he desires. If he is rude, adequately
rude, in return, show your pleasure and appreciation: but do

not retort more than once. . . . Never allow rudeness to degenerate into a wordy duel, into a vulgar quarrel. . . . No, if you can, pick a moment when he is surrounded by friends —his friends—and then, into the momentary silence which the strength of your personality should be sufficient to enforce, interject a poisoned sentence. . . . Above all, eschew humour, that antidote to wit.

PAST
AND
PRESENT

HINTS
ON
LIFE

(1) MANNERS

THE MINING VILLAGE which lies beyond the gates of the house wherein I sit writing does not offer many attractions to the reader. There are the usual papers, *Herald*, *Mail* and *Express*, and specialist journals, too, devoted to the sports connected with whippet and pigeon. These the younger men may be seen reading, during their hours of leisure, the while they squat on their hunkers in the pale northern sunlight. For the rest, a motor-library now calls three times a week with a selection of novels: food for the mind, in much the same way that the continual supply of travelling ice-cream, borne in the gaudily painted vehicles that have inherited the decorative tradition of the old hokey-pokey stall, is food for the body.

Alas, the travelling library has to a marked extent damaged the business in books, formerly carried on by the combined stationer's and post-office. This shop no longer buys many new books: and most of the more modern ones have, in the course of years, been sold out. The result is that on its shelves still linger the most queer survivals, so that when you put up your hand to reach them, it is as though you had entered another plane of life. On this dusty shelf still filters the radiant sunshine of times past: the middle-aged Queen Victoria yet remains in the seclusion of a very black and lonely widowhood at Balmoral, and King Edward, then the debonair, baccarat-playing Prince of Wales, resides at Marlborough House. All goes well for the capitalist system—soon Rhodes will be fingering diamonds and gold-dust in South Africa, and the last great period of imperialist expansion will be inaugurated.

Examining these shelves, then, I found one day a book with the somewhat equivocal, almost epicene, title of *How to be a Lady and Gentleman* (but never, indeed, were the valuable hints, which it undoubtedly contains, more needed). Alas, the date of issue is not given, but numerous references occur in it to "the Gracious Lady who now presides over us", and by internal evidence it cannot have appeared much later than 1870. (I note in passing that the same firm which published it—Cameron, Ferguson & Co. of Glasgow—gave to the world two musical handbooks entitled respectively *The Concertina without a Master* and the *Complete Tutor for the Concertina*.) Even its index of contents is a delight, for there are model letters, as well as instruction on every polite subject.

The author, we note, is very much opposed to "Modern Dancing", by which term, I presume, she (for I deduce that the author is a woman) signified the waltz and polka.

Dancing has too generally degenerated into vulgar jiggling [she writes]; couples scuffle and spin about, as if they were determined to exhaust their physical energies by bouncing down all who would participate in the enjoyment with them. The rudeness of their reckless evolutions is equally out of taste with their absurd wrigglings, when, in the midst of their boisterous plunges, they appear suddenly seized by St Vitus, and their muscles take on a tremulous but fitful motion. . . .

Quite a new light is this on the Victorian Age. And what a familiar ring the denunciation possesses for younger people! But were all her hints really necessary, I wonder? The following caution, for instance: "Avoid all ungraceful habits such as using a knife in eating"?

The guests at a Victorian dinner-party certainly seem to have behaved rather queerly. "Let no one ask for soup or fish twice, because by so doing part of the company are often kept waiting for the second course; and while thus disengaged they generally occupy themselves by looking at the awkward, and perhaps somewhat greedy, consumers of the second portion". (No such "Oliver Twist" fears intimidate, I hope, the braver, if smaller, eaters of our era?) But other Victorians seem to have gone still further; for the author remarks, apropos of finger-glasses, which "come on with the dessert", that

many persons wet a corner of the napkin, and wipe their mouths, but it is best only to dip the fingers. An odious custom of gargling the mouth is adopted by some few, who think that a foreign habit cannot be unseemly. Let nothing induce you to imitate them.

Nearly all the model letters are good, infused with the stateliness and swinging rhythm of Victorian English. To read the list of them, alone, is a pleasure.

To a Friend, on the Evil Consequences of a Love of Dress.

From a Niece to her Aunt, offering her Consolation on the death of her Uncle.

From a Mother to her newly married Daughter, on Domestic Economy.

From a Young Lady, accepting an Offer of Marriage.

From a Young Lady, declining an Offer of Marriage.

On the Advantages of Simplicity and cultivating a Contented Spirit.

A New Year's Letter from a Son to his Father.

A New Year's Letter from a Daughter to her Mother.

On the Folly of keeping up Appearances beyond our Means.

On the Folly of Ostentation.

To a Young Mother, on the Proper Education of her Children.

On the Moral Influence of Gardening.

On our Social Duties to the Poor.

To a Brother, on the Evils of Indolence.

From a Mother to her Daughter, warning her against marrying a Spendthrift.

Let me now quote one or two letters in full:

*Letter from a Niece to her Aunt offering her Consolation
on the Death of her Uncle.*

My Dearest Aunt,—Too well, alas! do I know how sad it is to realise the loss of one so dear, so long and fondly loved; and I feel how cold and powerless are words to express sympathy my heart would offer. But Hope is mingled with our sorrow, for we know "our loss is his gain", and it is a sweet thought that he has but preceded you a few short years to his Father's home, where he waits to welcome you with more than human love; and though each hour his gentle tenderness, his voice and smile, are missed, yet, who would wish him back? Rather let us rejoice that his Christian pilgrimage is ended; that the solemn moment of separation is over, and those dear eyes for ever closed upon this world of weariness and change, and opened to the fullness of God's glory,

70

to the depth and height, the length and breadth, of His goodness. We know that God afflicts not willingly, and though each earthly tie be severed, and the voices which made the music of our life are hushed for ever, still can we rest passive in His hands, knowing that "He doeth *all* things well". Our few remaining years will soon pass away, and then, when the day is ended, how trifling will seem this world's sorrows: and its dreams of love and glory how unsatisfying! It is upon Christ *alone* that our hopes and desires can sweetly sleep and calmly rest. May, then, each trial be a cord of love, drawing us closer to Him!

How much do I long to be with you once again, and hear from your kind lips all the particulars of my dear uncle's illness; it will do us good to recall the happy days we all passed together; to read the books he read; to see his chair, and tend the flowers he loved:

> "Though each a tinge may wear
> Of something gone".

I trust soon to feel your soft kiss of welcome on my face, and hear your fond "God bless you", which expresses so much, and recalls so many joyous meetings, and sweet though sad adieus. For a short time, my own kind aunt, farewell; and believe me, with every prayer for your present and eternal welfare that a loving heart can offer,

Ever most affectionately yours,

EMMA.

And

From a Mother to her Daughter, warning her against Marrying a Spendthrift

My Dearest Leonore,—In opposition to all your beloved father or I can say to you, you still persevere in your intention of marrying Arthur Fitzgerald; thus wilfully uniting yourself to certain misery. Though not brought up in the midst of luxury, yet, my child, you well know that nothing needful for your comfort has ever been wanting; and you know, too, the horror with which *debt* has always been regarded by myself and your father, and how we have always taught you to regard it as near akin to a crime to owe any

71

person a farthing while you had the means of paying it in your power; and in spite of all our earnest endeavours to teach you aright, and our many entreaties to you to beware of letting your affections become entangled with any one not worthy of you, what is it you now propose to do? To unite yourself to one whose whole aim in life seems to be to spend money, and to waste his substance. I grant you that Arthur is handsome, gentlemanly, and fascinating —talented also; but these attractions, alluring as they now appear, will not suffice for happiness in married life. All spendthrifts are necessarily selfish, and after the novelty was over, Arthur's old ideas and habits would come upon him again, and you would find yourself the helpless victim of a selfish man. To indulge *himself*, he would not scruple to deprive *you* of every necessary, without even considering that he was doing so; and by degrees you would find yourself reduced to absolute want; and believe me, my own dear child, there is no surer destroyer of love than poverty with its train of attendant evils. You have heard, no doubt, of the lovers who, being thrown into a dungeon together, and left to die of starvation, at first comforted each other, then turned away, and each groaned in solitude; then they began to loathe each other, and finally died invoking the bitterest curses upon each other! all their love being, in adversity, turned to mortal hate. Such, my Leonore, in a less degree, will be your lot, if you marry Arthur Fitzgerald. Your love will cool, your eyes will be opened, and you will see the glaring defects of his character; and then, my dear child, how miserable, how truly miserable you must be! A husband's faults are sacred: in your own bosom you must carry the consciousness of what he really is, while the world envies you as wife of the handsome Arthur Fitzgerald. Oh! then, my daughter, how sincere but fruitless will be your regret at having spurned a loving mother's advice! Reflect then, while there is time, and, by giving up Arthur Fitzgerald, make happy

Your affectionate mother,

LILLIAN MAY.

Poor, handsome, gentlemanly Arthur!

Perhaps the most acutely revealing anecdote in the whole book is told in a chapter entitled "Recognitions". It consists of a Warning against Familiarity and is calculated to bring a blush to any save a Victorian cheek.

An individual who filled a gentlemanly position in the world, and derived an excellent income from a place in some public office, dined one day at the Beefsteak Club, where he sat next to a man of the highest rank—a noble duke—who conversed most affably with him on the general topics of the day. A short time after, the same individual chancing to meet His Grace in the street, encouraged by his previous condescension, accosted him most familiarly, by saying—"Ah, my Lord, how d'ye do?" The Duke, who was not a little surprised, answered by saying—"May I know, sir, to whom I have the honour of speaking," drawing himself up at the same time. "Oh! why, don't you know? we dined together at the Beefsteak Club, the other evening! I'm Mr Salcombe, of the Treasury." "Then," said the duke, turning away, "Mr Salcombe, of the Treasury, I wish you a good morning."

Be careful, therefore, with regard to claiming acquaintance.

(2) SUCCESS

YESTERDAY, once more looking through the treasure trove in the local stationer's, I came across another book—booklet rather (for it is curious that so important a subject can be dealt with in the small space of seventy-eight diminutive pages)—entitled *How to Succeed in the World*. This work was published in 1883 by a firm with the strangely assorted, though poetical, names of "Tubbs, Brook, and Chrystal". It hails from Manchester, and the author of it was—I hope still is—a certain Dudley Armytage, Esq. "Esquire", unusual on the title page, I suppose denotes, in itself an outward and visible sign, an inward and spiritual success?

A perusal of the book raises the question of whether success to-day means the same thing as it signified fifty years ago. Frankly, after reading Dudley Armytage, Esq., I doubt it. In some ways the book is not as original in its information as I could wish, or as was my other find. The author relies too much on the worldly advice of such platitudinarians as Emerson, Washington and Franklin. On the other hand, a certain pleasure is to be derived from observing how the strangest names are waved at us from its pages, as banners of success; can it be, we wonder, that the names of our great millionaires, our famous press-barons and industrialists, will prove as ephemeral, so that within a period of fifty years they will be but unwonted syllables on the lips of an uncaring generation? Who, for instance, was Mr Stanley Budgett, with his strangely business-like nomenclature? But perhaps every-one save myself is aware of his identity?

Would I had read this book in earlier years! On the first page is the sentence:

It would be well for the youth to pause at the entrance to the world of active life, and before its cares and worries have clouded his perceptions or embittered his mind, to ask himself the object with which he plunges into its labours or anxieties.

Too late! Too late! Some of the hints, again, seem better balanced as sentences than helpful as precepts. What are we to make of:

The individual demands companionship, even as work asks for rest, and as weariness seeks for recreation:

and do we concur in the following sentiments?

In some cases it will be found that success has been obtained by unworthy means, by sharp practice, and by actions which, if not absolutely illegal or dishonest, are at least an uncomfortable approximation to them. But, in the majority of cases, it will be found that the men who have succeeded in business, if not claiming to be in advance of the majority of their own age, have at least been fairly on a level with it.

Dudley Armytage, Esquire, retains, I notice, a curious belief in the diary as a means to success, remarking that the record of trifles enables their importance to be seen. Again he holds that the safest plan is to reply to all letters at once: but, in these days, unaided and without a secretary, this is not so easy.

Finally, let me quote another sentence, while recommending that our millionaires take it, too, to heart:

It is a fallacy to suppose that culture is any detriment to commercial or business success. It was remarked of the great American millionaire, Mr A. T. Stewart, that he was a diligent reader of Horace, and the same delightful classic was the pocket companion of one of the best known and wealthiest of the many engineers whom Manchester has produced.

VICTORIANISM:
AN
ENGLISH
DISEASE

W<small>E ARE NOT</small> cleverer in our generation, but we are quicker, much quicker, than our fathers; more subtle, more in touch with real life, more understanding, more able to act swiftly on swift decisions, less intimidated by catchwords. We do not accept our judgments ready made. We can comprehend that all sorts of rights go to the making of a wrong; that two wrongs *do*, sometimes, make a right. We can see that many gradations of colour go to the composition of the proverbial "black and white", and that simple things are often not so easy as they appear. We are, in fact, the only people who can take charge of this age and guide it.

But never, alas, has it been so difficult to oust the old and the elderly minded. The age is still dominated by the greybeard and his spiritual children. Wherever you look in England—in politics, in the Church, in art, in the theatre or in literature—the old bar the way and muddle the path in front of us. This, of course, is a natural sequel to war—or, at a. / rate, to a war where the young and strong fight and perish, while the old govern and survive.

Yet Italy, Germany, Russia—all were in the war. Within ten years they have become new countries, revitalized, full of new men with new ideas. All these lands prosper. Only England clings to a Victorian past, and suffers in consequence.

No doubt the Victorian Age *was* a great one, the best qualities of which will ever exact the respect, as the worst must arouse the disgust, of later epochs. But "Victorianism" —by which I mean the survival of Victorian ideals, methods and ways of looking at things, into an age totally unsuited to them—is a thing mean, boring and detestable, a thing thin-blooded and lifeless. And just as ivy clings to, and in time ruins, any old building which it finds in its parasitic embrace, so Victorianism is smothering our country, draining England of her vigour. And we—even if "we" are not yet the whole nation—are sick and tired of it. England has had in the past many great eras and must have others in the future. The Victorian was, after all, only an episode in our history.

If Victorianism will not die, it will have to be blown up with dynamite, for it is dangerous to the nation. Austria perished as a world-power because her people could never be brought to understand that the Empress Maria Theresa was dead . . . and behaved, right down into the opening years of the twentieth century, as though they were existing in the middle of the eighteenth. They never modified their ways of thought until the most brutal reality forced them tò do so. Russia, again, could never forget Peter the Great; and the toll of suffering exacted for this loyal and amiable fault is beyond compute. England must forget the Victorian Age.

But the old men, the old familiar faces, the old-minded, are in the way. Their whiskers adorn every academy; they possess the country. Their ideas are Victorian, but bad Victorian, dead and mouldering. There is no force in them, and no prestige any longer attaches to them. They do not understand post-war life or circumstances.

In politics they discuss measures that in other countries are long-buried or long-enacted. They argue and wrangle over things which are matters for expert decision, rather than for long-winded, half-hearted and amateur discussion. But the talk goes on, the talk that represents dead ways of thought, and under its cover the decay steadily increases. Things happen which nobody wants to happen, and for which no one is responsible. Every Englishman desires beautiful, clean cities and a beautiful, clean countryside. Every day the cities lose more and more of their amenities, and the countryside becomes more and more defaced.

In England the arts are not always considered in connection with national life. But a vigorous nation thinks vigorously. Let us take the drama. In France, Germany, Italy—and in Russia—the theatre has blossomed anew since the war. There the laurels have gone to the men who have produced new ideas, and have worked at them in a new way. Here they have been awarded to those young men who deck out old ideas in the old, familiar way, imparting to them merely a new veneer of cheap smartness and an empty rattle of witless epigrams, rapid and vapid as the sound of a ping-pong ball hit backward and forward over its miniature net.

With painting, it is a little better, for the critics of the daily Press are alive to their responsibilities, and receptive of new ideas. . . . And yet, though we possess painters of great ability and talent, young artists the equal of any we have had in the past, you can look for their work in vain on the walls of the Royal Academy, that resort of old women with an afternoon to spare in London, that hideous museum of antique fashions.

In literature, we still abide in a mild, debilitated Victorian age. Only a few lonely, and by now rather cross, old prophets stand apart. These, at their death, will be honoured: for death reconciles the stupid to the clever (the only thing that ever does); but the power is held by the Victorianists. The chief successes of the younger men are earned by those who continue their methods, and so merit their blessings. In poetry, the merits and demerits of free verse are still discussed, though the last words on this subject were said long ago—by Milton and Dryden respectively.

The national life is thus engulfed in the past. But sooner or later, Victorianism, and its old men, must go. If they cannot be moved from their Parliaments and Academies, then, in time, these will lose the respect of the nation. Other institutions will be set up in their stead, inevitably, and will win the respect they have lost: and this is what is meant by "Revolution".

We must remember that Queen Victoria is as dead as Queen Anne. To say this of one monarch should not seem more disrespectful than to say it of another. Queen Victoria was at the head of a great nation in a great age. In this, only, need we emulate her. . . . The Victorianists are as dead as Queen Victoria.

79

THE
EDWARDIANS;
THE
RICH MAN'S
FEAST

A LITTLE WHILE AGO we used constantly to read in the papers such paragraphs as this: "It is now the fashion to decry everything Victorian, and to speak of the great Vic-. torians themselves with contempt". . . . Before now, I have been myself accused of this heinous misdemeanour.

Yet I doubt very much whether these accusations were ever justified. Certainly to decry the Victorian Age was never the *fashion*; for—apart from Victorian morality, which has undoubtedly been discarded and which only, in fact, began to ravage the country after the Crimean War, when the failure of our arms and the first revelation to the world of the ineptitude of our generals led to a most virulent and bigoted revivalism—this epoch has always remained for the majority of English people the Golden Age. It was an age which they find it easy to understand; an age of plain-speaking and comfortable living, of easy interference with the affairs of foreign nations, of fogs, and of a convinced and sanguine patriotism. Its poets could be comprehended—only too easily—while its musicians chiefly wrote anthems, or tunes which, at any rate, resembled hymns already popular and familiar. The world was ordained, under English guidance—or rather, synonymously, under the guidance of the English Comfortable Classes—to advance from triumph to triumph; through steam to petrol, and from the electric telegram, as it was at first called, to telephone and phonograph. It was a wonderful, happy, if rather self-complacent age, in which there could be no suspicion of unexpected future developments; no seeds of decay existed. Even the ruthless satire of those humorous twins, Gilbert and Sullivan, could reveal no hidden sore. . . . As for the great men of the later Victorian period, as for those whom this generation is now arraigned for reviling, no words, it is true, were bad enough for them at the time: Darwin, impious atheist; Swinburne and Rossetti, mad *poseurs*; Whistler, horrid little American bounder; but the really good and great, the territorial magnates and millionaires, the top-hatted poets and the respectable painters, such as Leighton, were universally revered and personally adored.

These, then, were some of the features which helped to compose an age to which numberless people still remain faithful; so many, indeed, that one is driven to the conclusion that Victorianism must be a national rather than an epochal trait; a quality innate, if sometimes latent, in the British people. To-day, with the pillars of the Victorian world— such as the Gold Standard—lying shattered and smashed all round it, Britain rather touchingly yet clings like a child to

Queen Victoria's voluminous and billowing skirts; refuses to emerge at all from behind them. . . . Who can doubt that the future will witness fresh outbursts of Victorianism from this country; any more than that, when Julius Caesar first landed among our naked, if exotically dyed, ancestors, even then some form of Victorianism, whether more primitive or no than in its subsequent full flowering, brooded dully over the country? Certainly Victorianism, as he shows us in the *Dunciad*, ruled in the early days of Alexander Pope.

Thus, if occasionally people have of latter years mocked the Great Age, this was but a pretence; only so that, by speaking and thinking of it, they could live in it over again. . . . But at last, I believe, the centre of interest has a little shifted: for the Edwardians can by now be seen in full perspective, and their rotund and splendid figures seem, more than those of their more severe predecessors, to engage the attention of the young.

And what, indeed, are we to make of those gay ten years, that strange culmination to the long Victorian Era, or of the beings who presided over this essentially Rich Man's Feast? How are we to judge them, or that fat, placid, kindly yet exciting period, when the only voices that broke the harmony were the rough Scottish tones of Keir Hardie, denouncing the wealthy, the gallant accents of Lord Roberts, alone prophesying war, and the enraged and, it then seemed, slightly hysterical tones of the suffragettes, as they chained themselves to the railings of Downing Street or slashed old masters in the National Gallery? What a delicious, halcyon period it was!

The attraction of these years derives in part from the fact

that the King was a character, always able to make himself
popular, and one who preferred to surround himself deliberately with certain people, rather than simply to accept or
inherit those whom he found there; that he liked, in fact,
to be amused. Thus for the first time since the death of
his great-uncle, King George IV—and, as for that, for only
the second time since the death of Charles II—it became
fashionable to be, at any rate a little, intelligent, and the
possession of wit, and even of some eccentricity, was considered preferable to mere dulness, however worthy. Much
outward splendour was joined to these happy circumstances,
for the King understood the value of pageantry, and the shell
and form of life, the big parties and entertainments, continued in the same mould as in previous reigns. The traditional English life still prevailed: so that, in effect, the
members of the ruling classes remained true to traditions, in
which—if they were intelligent (and then, they sometimes
were)—they could no longer believe.

Thus, though it deemed itself imbued with a new liberty,
it was a tremendously conventional age; for, no longer be-
lieving in anything, the penalties for any breach of the code
yet remained the same. The Victorian religious edifice had
collapsed under its own weight, but the Edwardians continued to worship in it as though it still stood. Divorce
remained unforgivable; though no stigma attached to the
conduct that had caused it, unless divorce followed. Outward
life was everything, and material prosperity was marvellously
maintained and increased, until it seemed as if the sub-
stantial, vulgar dreams of the Victorians were, after all, to
be realized.

Alas! that decade in which all men grew richer and all women prettier passed very rapidly. . . . And what did it leave behind it? Must we judge it by its works, of which the World War was the chief; by its Sargent portraits of hard-faced women in soft, filmy hats; by its lack of poetry and contempt for it; by the *Merry Widow*, that unique expression—as had been Gilbert and Sullivan of the late Victorians and Offenbach of the Second Empire—of the humour, romance and ideals of its period; by the bold, towering, cosmopolitan figures of Boldini, advancing, with ropes of pearls, out of their canvases; by the gold boxes and kick-shaws of Fabergé and the sudden popularity of papers such as the *Sketch* and *Tatler*; or can we rely upon our own memories of it, as a period of intense sweetness and activity, when even the newspapers seemed more concerned for the invention of new sweet-peas and the revival of cookery than in the fomenting of wars, when everyone appeared gay, and when people, even those who were not kind by nature, were mostly good-humoured; when, in fact, hatred had not as yet inherited the world?

ON
PROGRESS

THE MATERIAL HEAVEN of the Edwardian reign, and of the first few years of King George's, seems very remote from the present time. In those happy days every faith, even the faith of the Socialists, was justified, for it looked as though, if wealth were redistributed, there would soon be enough money to go round . . . As for the upper and middle classes, they lived in circumstances of profusion, and there was provided for them a constant flow of pageantry and amusement, which in no way was allowed to be spoilt by the frantic bustle which grew to be the mode in the later post-war years. The great feudal families still maintained to a certain degree their influence, though even then it was weakening; but to possess many connections in the world of politics and fashion was an advantage, rather than a disadvantage, to more serious work. In the evenings the houses of the great squares of London opened their doors; light poured out from the balconies, and with it came the music of the waltz; for jazz only began, with such tunes as "Everybody's Doing It" and "Alexander's Rag-Time Band", in 1910 or 1911. The world anticipated no future but a continued steady progress, although one of the questions most frequently put to a dancing partner was "Can you reverse?"

There can, I think, be no doubt that civilization itself is proving triumphantly that it *can* reverse. A year ago, for example, Germany exploded back into the times of Odin and Thor—that horrible German world where the heroes drank blood out of skulls and wore skins instead of clothes (and never did a race exist more unsuited by nature for the display of its bodies!). Many people in Germany, it is said, have actually advocated a return to the cult of Thor and Odin; but such an apostasy could make no difference, for whatever god or gods the Germans worship will always remain the identical barbarous gods under a different name. In any case, the old, kindly German of Bach and of Mozart is dead, and the Wagner lovers have reaped their reward in the revival of a boisterous and fictitious past. Every morning, as you take up a paper, the first question you ask yourself is: What have the Germans done to-day?

But while the appearance of the world in the pre-war years of which we are writing was that of a great comity of nations advancing, more or less at a level rate, year by year, the impression to-day is of a hundred or so insane states, all —not advancing—but diverging in different directions; backward, forward or sideways; but these alleys are no cul-de-sacs, for at the end of nearly every one of them stands plainly destruction. The rate of their progress toward this goal is variable, but the pace has so much increased recently as to have become visible: it is as if microbes had grown so large that they had become perceptible, or as though one were watching a comet with its golden tail falling from the sky. But the eyes of the observers are blank with apathy, and human beings appear to reserve their terror for mice rather than men. Any idea concerned with the modern world of literature or art terrifies the average man, and also angers him; but, singularly enough, ideas in general do not frighten him —or, at any rate, do not frighten those who do not understand them. . . . A mouse, though, is something smaller and more tangible. And yet, it seems strange that so many people should be more frightened by those soft and furtive rodents than by the enormous menace of events; a menace that surrounds them on every side.

Everybody, for instance, appears to be delighted to see a battleship launched. The prow is wreathed in flowers, champagne bottles are showered on it, flags decorate every building in the vicinity, and old men make interminable speeches. The armament firms and the corporations provide lunches. The very people who stand on chairs in order to avoid a mouse when it runs into the room are precisely those who cheer most wildly when they see a battleship glide smoothly into the water; only launched that it may one day destroy their fellow-men. It is true, of course, that, comparatively, battleships can achieve but little harm; for they are obsolete —as obsolete as the sailing-ship—but this hardly affects the principle.

And the more frightened the human race becomes of the

things it makes, the more it calls for the things of which it should be frightened; the more terrified we grow of the possible destruction that can be wrought by airplanes, the more stridently we demand more airplanes to destroy our neighbours. You can see many women who would run at the mere sight of a mouse, regarding with complacency some tank or cannon, erected in a public place as a memorial. Hardly ever, in any country in Europe, will you find an inscription under such a monument of a kind to discourage war. It is, therefore, a source of some pride to me that I am responsible for one of them. The Parish Council of my native village invited me some years ago to lend a small portion of land upon which to erect a cannon, presented to them by the War Office. I replied that this instrument of war was a very ugly thing, that my views on war approximated to those held by the Quakers, and that I could see no point, therefore, in lending them any land for such a purpose. They replied that my views were coincident with their own, and was I still adamant? To which I answered that I would lend the piece of land if I were allowed to write the inscription under the cannon, and penned the following paragraph, which to this day stands under the gun.

THIS GUN HAS BEEN ERECTED HERE TO REMIND THE PEOPLE OF ECKINGTON OF THE WICKED FOLLY AND WASTE OF WAR RESPONSIBLE FOR THE DEATHS OF SO MANY OF THE BEST OF THEM, AND IN THE HOPE THAT ITS UGLINESS AS AN OBJECT WILL FRIGHTEN THE CHILDREN SO THAT THEY GROW UP WITH A NATURAL HATRED OF WAR AND THE BRUTAL MACHINERY THAT ACCOMPANIES IT.

But such inscriptions are part of a dream that has vanished. Every nation seems determined to fight, if not in the immediate present, at any rate as soon as they have the armaments with which to do so. Our position is the old one of: "To prevent the powder magazines from blowing up we must have the biggest one". The higher branches of the human race at the moment have obviously dedicated themselves to suicide, and who is to stop them?

MODERN
TENDENCIES

LET'S
BE
ALL
ALIKE!

MANY YEARS BEFORE the war came, this tendency had begun to manifest itself, especially in the matter of apparel. From the year 1900 onward, peasants were every day discarding their characteristic costumes for the featureless clothing of the cities; every class, too, had begun to dress alike, and with Queen Victoria's death even the widow's cap had been wafted into oblivion.

Few distinguishing emblems were left. And when the war materialized, these, too, died. Because, final triumph of democracy, it revealed, at last and for ever, how all men really were equal and alike, serving one sole purpose—that of cannon-fodder: for which bank clerk and farm labourer were as good as a potential Michelangelo, Napoleon Bonaparte or Dante; except that the taller men, the finer men, the braver men, the cleverer men, were killed first. And, since the war, nature, adaptable as ever, has learnt her lesson from Mr Ford of Dagenham and Detroit, and has become only too anxious to produce creatures of uniform stature and capacity, mental as much as physical, until it seems almost possible to observe the process of levelling up and levelling down at work, so marked is it all over Europe, Asia and America. The dusky jungles of Central Africa are perhaps alone immune.

First of all, let us consider, the standardization of faces. There was a time, not so long ago, when every individual boasted an individual face; but now, for the most part, each set, each profession, each class, presents a face in common. And what faces they are, smooth, smug and unimaginative; inoffensive to an offensive degree!

No longer do we meet, even in public life, with the beak of a Wellington, the rugged, rocky face of a Sir Cloudesley Shovel, or the aggressive, inquiring noses of the Pitts, elder and younger, which survived to a later date, and in a more transcendental form, in Lady Hester Stanhope. No, now we are given, instead, the features, primly indecisive, of a Sir John Simon, or the blunted physiognomy of a Mr Baldwin.

Sir Oswald Mosley, it is true, has a face; one that is recognizable and offers a chance to a caricaturist; but for the rest, the captains and the kings no longer have the appearance of leaders of men; and should any injudicious survivor, with a real face, pass down the street, what a craning is there of uniform necks, what a rolling of Pekingese eyes, what shrill and yapping volleys of standardized laughter, what cries of "Do look!" and "How extr'ord'n'ry!" . . . How alike are they, even in their giggling; even in the meaningless phrases they employ.

And in their voices. Up till the end of the eighteenth century every class talked with its own voice. The very country squires, who—despite Macaulay—were, many of them, men of culture and learning, were not ashamed to speak the dialect of their native place. This can be seen, even, in the idiom of their letters.

Thus London during "the Season", resounded with pleasing rustic burrs and broad "a's", which imparted to every assembly a delightful variety. But alas! to-day there are only two—or at most three—voices to be heard; the modern equivalent of cockney, "refained and coulchawed", and now launched across innocent ether into countless indistinguishable homes ("This is London speaking. At naine-faive there will be a talk on waine by the President of the Toetal Ebstainers' Essociation"), and the fashionable, quacking tone and clipped words of the bars, theatres and few remaining drawing-rooms.

That is all. Never an accent or an intonation that is unexpected and itself.

Their voices are indicative of their general appearance. If you look at the young men of to-day you will see that, though graded according to their wealth, they all look the same, while the girls resemble one another still more. Further, this last resemblance is intentional, aided by rouge, false eyelashes, and a hundred other artifices. . . . More resemblance, too, than formerly can be noticed between the sexes, so that a year or two ago a certain "Colonel" was able successfully to give the impression, to all concerned, that she was man and husband.

Every class, as has been said, and every profession affect

95

an identical costume. "Good" clothes no longer consist in those a little different from the apparel worn by other people but, rather, in those that are most alike. For a woman to be in the mode, it is necessary for her to be indistinguishable from her neighbour.

Further down the scale of work, every difference has been erased in the outward aspect of the workers in town and country. Half an hour after his labour is finished the plough-boy, darting in on his motor-cycle to visit the nearest cinema, might be a bank-clerk, a bishop—except for a distinguishing lack of gaiters—or an author; for writers—poets, even, once so formidable and pungent a sect—now look alike, and, alas! resemble plumbers all the world over.

Everyone is the same; and so are the houses they inhabit. Think of Mr Everyman settling into any single one of those millions of homes, neither big nor small, dumped down on the intermediate fringes, the flanks of the great road; an Everyman's-land that is neither town nor country and smells perpetually of tar and petrol. All of these red-brick or half-timbered residences are the same, filled with cheap, but already superannuated—for each day brings a fresh invention —devices for labour-saving, though the enjoyment of living in a house lies, admittedly only to a certain extent, in the labour, much of it agreeable, which this form of habitation involves. And think, too, of the food eaten in these houses; the same food, out of the same indistinguishable tins!

Nor is the tendency toward uniformity confined to the classes and professions by nature most disposed to it. Of the sporting world I can claim but little knowledge; nor do I pretend to regret its passing. Formerly, nevertheless, it was at least full of character. To-day there is only one Lord Lonsdale, and few—far too few—costers. . . . Consider again the drama: the talent which survives is thinly spread, and far from individual; though the stage once shared with painters and writers a reputation for character.

All the wealthier, "cultured" classes, who have no need to do so, betray the urge toward standardization in as full measure. At the universities, for example, there were formerly the "swells" and the esthetes; now, though there will always be exceptions, a general level of pale refinement, slightly tinged by Communist opinion, prevails. The young, who should be falling off horses, consuming Swinburne, and revelling in the absurd and luscious, all read—and write (pardon! wraite)— the same poems; poems of an etiolated but slightly menacing despair. The ant, good Communist but no observer of beauty, is, it appears, their hero. Nor even, in their perhaps un-conscious desire for uniformity, have they any wish especially to distinguish themselves. They do not long for a particular or personal fame: a name that rings like Shelley's or Pope's. Instead of this selfish striving, they write criticism of criticism of critics; or novels in which the characters are for ever, though faintly, misunderstood. Their poems are those of disillusioned bank clerks sitting in the popular cafés.

Thus they enter that delicious, anonymous class, after which they hanker, of "promising young Oxford novelists" or "distinguished young Cambridge poets". Their work will be described by their fellows as "integral" or "austere" or "authentic", and prizes will shortly come their way. Not glittering, but comfortable, prizes; reviews, official congratulations, and fat little cheques.

The Hawthornden Committee will hover about them like guardian angels, and before long they will enter the paradise of their dreams, presided over by Professor Gordon, good Grannie Walpole, and the Great Dane.

ON
SNOBS

THE PRIGS, I apprehend, have changed less with the passage of time than have the snobs; or, at any rate, they have more successfully modernized their business. Both species are always with us, even though occasionally they alter their guise; and the development of each is equally worthy of our contemplation. Let us reflect, therefore, upon the snobbish mode of the moment, reserving the prigs for a later analysis and dissection.

How fallen are our snobs since the days of Thackeray! Titles and position, famous names and ancient blood no longer possess their former allurement. . . . Indeed, so far as the snobbishness of the Victorian Era survives at all, it manifests itself in an inverted form, causing its victims to mock equally at tradition and those whose names and behaviour recall it. . . . The true snobbishness, so innocent and round-eyed, has perished, or is only to be discovered among old housekeepers, who still crinkle down back passages in their black silk dresses, among retired butlers, long pensioned and sitting in the sun, or in the depths of such a continent as Australia, where the right of one man to be better than another is ever so vehemently and stridently denied. Elsewhere it is extinct; and even the popularity of the Royal Family seems less embedded now in a sense of snobbery than in one of newspaper values. Thus, for instance, the Prince of Wales is not only heir to the throne, not only a hard-working and esteemed prince; he is News Personified.

Then, again, the money-snobs of the Edwardian period today hide their confusion. Their temple has collapsed, while yet they were worshipping in it. Few believe any longer in the universal efficacy of money (and these few are only those who make great quantities of it with ease). Indeed, how could it be else in a world wherein the value of money varies from day to day, and many communities have already returned to barter as the medium of exchange? But the money-snobs are not defeated; they have merely changed their objective, become more democratic. They no longer wish to consort with those richer than themselves, so much as to pretend to be richer than they are, and consort with—and ape the manners of—those with whose incomes they claim equality.

Intellectual snobbery, too, albeit from time to time during the centuries it has raised its head—even in England, where, as against sport, intellect has ever been at a discount—is now dead. To be snobbish, in any sense, is old-fashioned; to be just silly, modern. Because fashion itself is alone fashionable; and Shakespeare and Einstein, equally, must make way for the typical pursuer of the pursuit of the moment.

There is common sense, it cannot be denied, in this discounting of titles and worldly goods, and of the past and future. Thrones rock, fortunes vanish, and only the day remains to Mr Everyman. This being so, the newspapers, with commendable enterprise and understanding of the circumstances, have extended the boundaries of his world, allowing him to enter an artificial paradise; if one, alas, inspired by a rather childish imagination. Thus, while at the same time the papers often proclaim officially that the Silly Season no longer exists, the reason of it is that, for a year or two past, we have all been privileged to exist in a permanent, or, at any rate, indefinitely prolonged, silly season; wherein beach-pyjamas and bottle-parties are seen to possess an equal value with revolutions and the threat of chemical warfare, wherein Sir James Barrie's canary seems as important as Petrarch's cat, and children's supplements, rather than literature, are all the vogue. Of this delicious realm—half Vanity Fair, half heaven on earth—the chat-spinners, the gossiping heirs to titles, the indigent but ardent scavengers of items, are the creators.

And they are the lions, or perhaps demi-lions, to use an heraldic expression, of our time. England is proud of them; hostesses hanker after their notice. Nevertheless, their reign may be a short one, for, as the Press yields to the conquering wireless, they will be supplanted by the exponents of radio-gossip. Indeed, I can see no reason why, in decades to come, the staff of the B.B.C. should not form the basis of an aristocracy, self-elected, or perhaps, hereditary. Even to-day Sir John Reith, it seems to many, has about him something of the ducal mien of a century ago.

Yet the day when we openly bow down before this new aristocracy, this new, it may be, hierarchy, and render homage to its chiefs as vassals, is still a little distant. In consequence, the Vanity Fair of the hour is, like all else, everywhere (and, if the truth were told, at every period in the world's history) in a state of transition. The snobs of to-day —those who, after the manner of Mrs Kinfoot and Lady Flinteye, still hunt their quarry through the diminishing perspective of drawing-rooms—no longer have set before them the standard that prevailed in Thackeray's time. Yet, though the drawing-rooms are fewer, their life is more frenzied, speeded up to the tempo of an age of motor-cars and airplanes. They must attend a thousand boring—but, if they are absent, tantalizing—functions (how are they to know that it is their *own* presence at them that makes them so boring?), where their grandmothers could be content with one, confident that it was the only occasion that mattered. Forced nowadays to climb sideways, and backward and forward, as much as up, they retire, hollow-eyed and haggard, for a short hour of nightmare rest; then again, up and at it! Celebrity-snobbishness, though on the wane, maintains a certain hold; for it is still necessary for hostesses to throw several celebrities, at every meal, to their jackal-guests. But no longer do they want to know a few distinguished persons; they *must* know everyone.

And who can set a limit to the fatigue which this everyman-snobbishness entails, or cure the envenomed wounds which she who harbours it must incur? For, in entertaining, the aim of the modern snob-hostess is not, as formerly, to ask a few friends, who might enjoy themselves in the process, to share a meal in restful surroundings; but, rather, to invite as many ill-assorted and antipathetic persons as she can press into the noisiest of muddled and criss-cross salons, to encounter one another over the luncheon table. The art of receiving guests, she considers, is to appear as late, and as hectic and frantic, as possible, and then to goad her guests into the somewhat malicious conversation which accords with her own exhausted nervous system.

But through it all, the old Vanity Fair can still be detected. Though the values of that institution have changed, and itself has for the time almost ceased to exist, its ethics have yet penetrated almost every class of the community. People in general visit their "friends", and constantly spend their time together, not so much because of any affection they feel for them, as because of the tinder-and-flint friction which they derive from it. Hate seems everywhere to have replaced love as the bond of human beings. In former days friendship implied an understanding—and consequent overlooking—of faults; but now the reverse is true, and an appreciation, and even exaggeration, of faults and of mannerisms, is the nearest approach to friendship which anyone can be offered. This, again, places a premium upon the little social art of mimicry, so popular everywhere. And the dead, even, are imitated long after they lie cold in their coffins and otherwise forgotten, in this way attaining the temporary stretch of occasional, vicarious immortality which their friendships have thus assured for them.

ON
PRIGS

PRIGS, NO DOUBT, existed in every age and in every place; in ancient Babylon and Ur of the Chaldees; in Greece and Rome; but the prig of to-day is very different in type from his ancestors. A sudden break seems to occur, for the modern prig is only a collateral descendant of our own eighteenth-century one, and can be seen to be more directly descended from the American species immortalized in the pages of *Martin Chuzzlewit*.

The reader will remember the talk therein between the two Literary Ladies and Mrs Hominy: of which it is only necessary to quote one passage:

"Mind and matter," said the lady in the wig, "glide swift into the vortex of immensity. Howls the sublime, and softly sleeps the calm Ideal, in the whispering chambers of Imagination. To hear it, sweet it is. But then, outlaughs the stern philosopher, and saith to the Grotesque, 'What ho! arrest for me that Agency. Go, bring it here!' And so the vision fadeth."

How familiar this conversation sounds! Perusing it, the names of many American writers of the early nineteenth century who belong to this sept at once declare themselves in the mind. Not least among them, rises the spectre of one who stands in the direct line of ancestry to the prig of the present day, Emerson.

In our own country a considerable prejudice has always manifested itself against the highbrow—an attitude occasionally crystallized for immortality in the works of Mr Noel ("You are bewitched, girl") Coward—and it is one I would not willingly encourage; for to the English public a highbrow signifies any person who has ever read a book of consequence. Nevertheless, the original use of the word "highbrow" did, I believe, add something, was helpful in describing the American-priggish outlook on life; an attitude inevitably bound up with the critical standpoint. Thus, I have met many authors and many critics, but I have seldom met an author—that is to say, a creative writer—who was a prig. The point of view, however, which insists that the only duty of literature is to offer a field for criticism, essentially betrays the prig, whom we find defined in the dictionary as "a pert fellow who gives himself airs of superior wisdom".

Now let us turn to more modern times; let us name a few prigs and indicate their activities for the entertainment of readers; for, though a certain amount of boredom is inseparably connected with the exponents of this genus, nevertheless undoubtedly a subtle enjoyment is to be derived from the processes of their didactic obscurantism.

The two leading prigs of the day I used to imagine to be female—two literary ladies; the gifted sisters-in-law Leavis, as I thought them, of Cambridge. But when I thus referred to them in print, a friend of theirs wrote to the paper to assure me that I was mistaken. One of them, it appears, is a man. Not for a moment must it be thought that Dr and Miss Leavis are stupid; they are not, but their minds undoubtedly betray a curious combination of silliness and intelligence. They are altogether without simplicity, and revel in a peculiar, puritan complication which, while they think it austere, in reality lacks all the qualities of natural reaction to thought.

To a poet every sound is suggestive, and about the names of these two Literary Ladies—for such, whatever their sex, they will ever remain to me—lingers something both dictatorial and aloof: Leavis—a sort of take-it-or-leave-it attitude; while, too, a hierarchic hint of the Tribe of Levi infuses it with exotic authority. Moreover, the initials of one of them, Q. D. suggest, again, Q.E.D., and carry with them an air of a problem clearly demonstrated. (It comes therefore as somewhat of a shock to be informed that the lady in reality bears the slightly frivolous name of Queenie.) I think any reader who follows the doings of this talented twain will not rue the day; for in them the prig is manifested in its newest, most choice and fascinating guise.

At present they edit and write articles for a quarterly review entitled *Scrutiny*, published by a Cambridge firm. And herein the modern American tendency of the prig is easily to be traced, for a large part of each number is invariably devoted to the works of the two leading American poets of the day—Mr T. S. Eliot and Mr Ezra Pound. Indeed, the critic whom we are now discussing, like those of the Parisian-American gangs (who ran *Transition* and papers of that kind), are intent on kidnapping the ancient body of English poetry and substituting for it a baby of American origin. For this reason it is sometimes known as the Lindbergh-Baby School of poetry.

To take a single typical number of *Scrutiny*, one issue alone contains first of all a critique of the *XXX Cantos* of Ezra Pound by Mr Ronald Bottrall, who ends a portentous examination with the remark: " . . . it would be ungracious if I did not admit that *I* owe more to Pound than to any other living poet". (The italic is mine.) Then there follows a scrutiny of Milton, in which that poor old manipulator of meaningless words is properly put in his place by the Doctor, who treats him as though he were a young writer competing for the attention of the critics (this, again, is a favourite device of the prig). "The verse of *Paradise Lost*", he tells us, "has to the ear that appreciates Shakespeare a wearying deadness about it". Again:

His strength is of the kind that we indicate when, distinguishing between intelligence and character, we lay the stress on the latter; it is a strength, that is, involving sad disabilities. He has "character", moral grandeur, moral force; but he is, for the purposes of his undertaking, disastrously single-minded and simple-minded. He reveals everywhere a dominating sense of righteousness and a complete incapacity to question or explore its significance and conditions. This defect of intelligence is a defeat of imagination.

I think no lover of poetry will dispute the quality of riotous fun latent in this paragraph? After which vivisection of

Milton, there ensues a scrutiny of examinations, a poem, and an article on economics, and it must be admitted that the Leavises seem to have no difficulty in finding others fully of their quality to write upon the different branches of life— or death. Queenie, as we should expect, is a little more lively than F. R., more playful, and there can be no doubt that in her notes, "Our Serious Weeklies", she actually attempts one or two jokes.

There are other prigs. Read, for example, a periodical called *New Verse*, which contains from time to time reviews by that most delicious and delirious of his tribe, Mr Geoffrey Grigson. I have followed Mr Grigson's career for some years. He used to write for the *Yorkshire Post* under the name of "G. G.", during which time he obtained a certain immortality, for, after a peculiarly silly review of Miss Edith Sitwell's poems, signed "G. G.", she wrote to the paper suggesting that his signature overrated the size and importance of his Pegasus, and that he should in future sign himself "A. S. S." instead. Subsequently he became a writer for the *Bookman*, where again he showed a profound misunderstanding of his subject, and an equal capacity for misconstruing that which he read.

Between the Leavises and Mr Geoffrey Grigson there is, I believe a running battle—though this, again, the protagonists authoritatively deny—carried on in various magazines of local circulation; a battle of giants over the bodies of the insignificant dead, Milton, Shakespeare and the rest. The frowning gods, Mr Middleton Murry, Mr Eliot and Mr Pound, look on—one, perhaps, with a faint smile—while the Homeric contest continues to rage beneath them.

ON ADVICE:
ITS
GIVING
AND
RECEIVING

SOME COUNTRIES, I think, are specially designed to tender advice and warnings; others, to profit by them. . . . Germany, for example, is a natural receiver of advice; and, indeed, since the autumn of 1918 until January 1933, was exposed to an absolute orgy of it. Never a day went by without her being treated to a warning on the part of France, and a few helpful, if self-righteous, words by ourselves. And much of this advice, leading in a thousand contrary directions, she took! Now, however, we are cognizant that, though we continue to offer, she will not accept, our counsel. Because Nationalism demands that advice, like all else, shall be of domestic origin: and in that clamour, perhaps, we may find one of the secrets of Hitler's popularity; for himself is disposed to be generous with this commodity.

Germany loves advice! To realize the truth of this assertion it is only necessary to wander round any German town, observing, pasted up everywhere, the amount of private notices containing exhortations, cautions and injunctions. . . . More than that, she loves to take advice, to obey—"to love, honour and obey". "She," I write of the Fatherland; for the Germans, despite their protestations, their beards, pipes and talk of Attila, are an intensely feminine race; much more feminine than the more delicate and charming French (female elephants no less than female gazelles). The French indubitably possess masculine minds, with a love of independent thought. Only because the Germans are a warlike—or, in other words, quarrelsome—race, is it supposed that they are male-minded; yet women, it is said, indulge in quarrels, even ferocious ones, just as often as men.

The Germans, then, like to quarrel, but they also like to carry out orders. And by a correlation of these two assumptions eighteenth-century England, which employed German mercenary troops, discovered a perfect solution of the German problem. After this fashion, the most warlike of the race were killed off at regular intervals and, as we, at any rate, thought, fighting on behalf of right. . . . And here, in parenthesis, I would like to inquire with all seriousness, whether it would not be possible, given the present circumstances, to find a similar solution of European difficulties to-day? Why cannot the League of Nations be given the power to employ a mercenary German army to enforce—or, in the present journalistic cant of the day, to implement—its decisions? So could the warlike German tribes, perhaps, be induced, with an added feeling of self-respect, to fight on behalf of civilization, instead of against it. . . . Alas! in these degenerate days it is supposed to be wrong to allow anyone but yourself to be killed in a quarrel picked against you; a totally modern development of honour, and one which must end sooner or later, if you have to deal with sufficiently quarrelsome people, in the loss of your cause.

However, I must not wander too far. Germany, I was maintaining, likes to receive advice. But it serves as a signal of general danger when she inclines, as at the moment, to show herself to the world as an example; to become a mentor, to guide the feet of others and to show them the way. Then it is time to seek safety, because, historically and almost invariably, the results are as disastrous to the world as to the Fatherland. Thus in 1914 Germany was anxious to take the lead, eager to give, rather than learn, a lesson. She advised Austria, admonished Serbia, cautioned Russia and warned ourselves; the upshot of all this being that, though she now denies all war-guilt, the whole of Europe became involved in war.

We English, on the other hand, as a race excel in the offering of advice; and because of our talent in this direction, indeed, have been dubbed the Governess of Europe. The sad truth, however, is that though our advice is, politically, nearly always right and sound and wise, we seldom profit by it ourselves, and, when we offer it to the Dominions and friendly nations, this altruistic national trait appears to anger them more than any of our less commendable characteristics. Only consider, in example of it, our note to America in 1932 concerning the Anglo-American debt. The French, in their plain way, merely refused to pay, and were quite willing to incur the onus, if any, which attached to their default. But we, once more, were as free with our advice as with our money. We paid in full yet again, and at the same time indited a note; a little masterpiece, in the preparation of which, it seemed, an army of clandestine governesses might have been at work for years, day and night, at the Foreign Office. It was infused with an excruciating air of "it-hurts-me-more-than-it-hurts-you", though actually its message, in this instance was, "it-hurts-you-more-than-it-hurts-me". His Majesty's Government, you will remember, was in one sense eager to pay; in another, reluctant. But this last sentiment was not as you might, after your vulgar fashion, have thought, founded on the desire not to part with the goods, but, instead, on the conviction of our rulers that the transference of so large a sum would injure the payee even more than the payer. They were, in fact, anxious to *safeguard American* interests. Financial dislocation and widespread disturbance would ensue, it was pointed out, in that great continent. . . . (And how right we were! . . . But then, if we had not made the payment, we could not have proffered such sound, if uncalled-for, advice to a foreign power: and much more gladly would we abandon any hope of obtaining a reduction of the unjust sums to which we were bound, than forgo our prerogative of proffering unwanted counsel.)

In this case, however, it might have been presumed that we had met our match; because America, having, as is widely recognized, a monopoly of public spirit and public virtue, will come forward to offer advice with—or to—any country in the world. (Europe's troubles are her own fault, because she remains heedless of the American example.) And so it was that, conscious as the Americans were of their own unselfish generosity and scrupulousness, the arrival of the English note, inspired by similar sentiments, became responsible for more consternation in Washington, and aroused more antagonism there, than would have been caused by any abrupt refusal on our part to pay.

And, just as some nations are born to receive, and others to give, advice, so it is, I apprehend, with persons. . . . More blessed to give than to receive. And alas, for myself, I am a born recipient. Never can I be alone for an instant without some kind person endeavouring, gratis, to improve my mind or manners; while, on the other hand, I notice that if ever I venture to *offer* advice, nobody takes it! But then, who thinks ever of acting on advice unless he is made to pay for it? Advice, they say, is cheap; but what of the hundreds and thousands of pounds earned by lawyers and doctors? Is that cheap? Yet it is the *only* advice which is ever acted upon. So, when next called upon for your views on a personal problem, refuse to give them, if you value your own opinion, except for a heavy fee. It is kinder to him who seeks your aid.

ON
THE
HORROR
OF
SOLITUDE

ALAS, THE DAY of the hermit is over! No longer are caves and ruins inhabited by sages and ascetics with flowing white beards and wild, fierce eyes. Yet the necessity for loneliness, for the possibility of meditation in solitude and amid inspiring and romantic scenes, makes itself felt, day by day, more than ever before. The very bungalows that clutter and litter the countryside are, in fact, a sign of it: since the inhabitants of each one of these ugly and crowded excrescences originally moved here in order to "get away"; get away, that is, from neighbours and noise and everyday life. They are thus in rebellion against the intense gregariousness of the modern world; in which people are forced, not only to eat, drink and think together, but also to eat, drink and think the same things in the same way. Indeed to-day the grave, that "fine and private place", is almost the only one left to man.

For the herd instinct is in possession of the world. To such an extent, indeed, that solitude has to many become akin to terror. "But I shall be *alone!*" one hears people exclaim in accents of despair: an attitude very opposite to that of the late Monsieur Pachmann, the exquisite if occasionally eccentric player of Chopin, who, when his hostess, having to leave him for a little, excused herself, saying, "Dear Master, I do hope you do not mind being alone?" replied proudly, "Madam, I am *never* alone: I am with Pachmann!" . . . And very good company, I imagine, he must have found himself. . . . But then the artist, though usually he feels more need for solitude, is generally a much more entertaining companion than the soldier, statesman or business man. To most people, however, this point of view is absurd, even incredible. Their conception of sociability is so strong that they are annoyed, even, if they see someone they know dining alone at a restaurant, condemn him straightway as "mad": as though —apart from the fact that nobody in his senses would dine alone, or in company, at any public place of eating unless driven there by necessity or laziness—to dine alone were a form of lunacy. Yet, though personally I prefer eating in company, there is no doubt that the way in which to appreciate good food is to eat it by yourself, undistracted by conversation. . . . Again, of all the vices, the worst one is to be a "secret drinker": and the accent is on the word *secret*. Than this, only to be a secret thinker is worse, in the calendar of social crime.

"What can he do with himself, all alone like that?" So you hear people speak. But how difficult it is to be alone; an expensive business, too. You have to travel far, to Canada or

Siberia. No longer is it possible to find solitude, as Words-
worth found it, among the Lakes. The Lake District is now
but a car-park, a bin for orange peel; and Scotland, too, unless you are in a position to buy a deer forest, offers no
shelter from the herd. . . . Once or twice in my life I have
found places where solitude seemed peculiarly pleasant; but
it was never long before others found it too, and invaded it,
filling it with whistling sounds of appreciation. Worst of all,
there are the kind people, the well-meaning, who *feel sorry* for
you *because* you are alone, and make it their business to come and
talk to you and to break up your thoughts. . . . You would
think, for example, that in a sense it would be easy to be
alone in a large boat, if you knew none of the other passengers?
Not a bit of it; they will take pity on you, sure enough! "We
thought you looked so sad, sitting all by yourself like that!"

Alas, those are precisely the people who should themselves
be alone, be made to be alone; be subjected, even, to periods
of solitary confinement in agreeable surroundings, but without any possibility of recourse to wireless or gramophone,
or conversation of even the most casual kind. For want of
time in which to think, they have become thus idle-mouthed
and slatternly minded. Even an hour of forced meditation
would help them to reconstruct a little their thoughts and
put their minds in order.

The most singular feature of this modern gregariousness,
this avoidance by people of their own thoughts, is, however,
that it has done nothing to help those who suffer from that
terrible affliction, loneliness. Indeed, the fear of loneliness—
the exact reverse of the longing for solitude—is more general
now than in any former epoch, and one with which we must

always sympathize, never mind to what extent the loneliness may have been earned in times past.

For often it has been. . . . Think, for example, of the old ladies, with that fear in their hearts, who for one reason or another congregate in those busy hives of idleness, "private residential hotels". (And why "private", since privacy is that which their inmates hold most in abomination?) Often they have been driven there by their own hardness in times past, by their selfishness and their lack of consideration for their friends. And now, by a genial stroke of Fate, several of them are collected here, under one roof, to worry and irritate— and, by means of that worrying and irritation, in the end to comfort—one another. It is better for them to form a herd after this fashion, better than to pine alone—and with them to be alone *is* to pine—in remote suburbs and refined watering-places. Moreover, for others it possesses the advantage of collecting them together in, as it were, a concentration-camp, until such time as Death shall seize them in its final and most lonely embrace.

Nevertheless, that from which they suffered was not genuine loneliness: the feeling of physical propinquity was what they desired. Real loneliness on the other hand is a disease of the spirit, and one of which the most sensitive and the most kindly seem, as a rule, to be the worst victims. Those liable to its onslaughts are no more immune from them in a crowd than on a mountain-top. Especially will it attack them if they are forced to attempt communication of ideas with un-congenial people. Thus a visit to a crowded country-house may be a dreadful penance to them; far more severe than a month alone on a desert island.

To the lonely, as to the lover of solitude, books and travel form the best companions, lessening the sense of nervous tension from which they suffer. Communal amusements, such as cinemas, are best avoided; though in the enthusiasm of a great crowd, at a football match or a bull-fight, it is possible both to lose loneliness and to achieve solitude. . . . And the stupid, when they suffer from loneliness, find it removed by a war, with its accompaniment of "mateyness": though I fancy that in the next, which we are all so busily preparing for ourselves, most of us will attain our final solitude, whether we have been seeking it or no. Humanity's next Great Beano may also be its last.

ON
THE
DECAY
OF
PRIVACY

THE TWO MOST important and expensive things in modern life are privacy and leisure, and though of the latter much is said and written, little or nothing is done to help us achieve more privacy.

Now leisure may lead to much evil, to acute unhappiness, illness or boredom; but privacy has no such drawbacks or dangers.

Every day, however, we are deprived of more of it. Model towns, for example, are built by wealthy and benevolent corporations for their workers.

What is the result? The worker has henceforth no seclusion, and is forced to live, as well as work, with his fellows. Or else he is obliged to inhabit one, perhaps, of a row of jerry-built houses or villas, in which every sound from every house is audible, so that, practically, he can be said to be living in the street. Thus the Englishman's home is no longer his castle, but either his fellow-workers' communal kitchen or else just part of his neighbours' street.

The world at large lives for the most part in public, eating in restaurants, travelling by tube or omnibus, visiting cinemas or theatres.

This makes it all the more necessary to possess privacy in your home. But only the rich can afford it, for to secure this most elusive thing you must have plenty of servants to guard you against intrusion and a few rooms at the back of the house which, like Bluebeard's secret chamber, no person but yourself is allowed to enter.

Then there are the hotels wherein we stay; a hotel is a bitter enemy to privacy. Not only is one at the mercy of every stray and idle bore who happens to be staying there, but to keep oneself to oneself, hitherto regarded as a virtue, has now become a social crime. Indeed, it is not very long ago since, in an hotel abroad, I crept away from a room where there was going to be a dance, for I was tired after a hard day's work and wished to avoid the very bad and noisy band which was already striking up; but as I left the room an American visitor approached and said angrily, "Have you no social ambition, may I ask, Sir, that you leave this ballroom?"

And on another occasion an interfering old Scotchwoman inquired why I did not give up writing books and take instead to politics?

And whither can we escape nowadays? It used, for instance, to be possible to find peace and privacy by walking down any country road in England.

Not so now; because the road, broad as the Grand Canal

of Venice, is overlooked for its whole length on each side by long rows of incredibly hideous houses, while fleets of motor-coaches and motor-cars hoot and roar down it all day long.

There were the parks in London. Therein it was easy in former years to sit under a tree in summer and read a book: but now we find ourselves in dear, benevolent Mr Lansbury's paradise, among dancing-halls, jazz-bands, carillons, round-abouts, swings, brass bands and paddle-pools; things which, of course, may be of benefit to the community in other ways, but constitute a fresh inroad on the little privacy left us.

Then chief of the enemies to privacy stands modern science. It has armed every friend and foe with the most formidable means of shattering it in our own houses. Telegrams, wire-less, motor-cars, telephones, are all ready to help the invader, not to succour the beleaguered. Formerly if a man wished to disturb a friend, he was put to the trouble of walking or driving to his house and doing it himself. Now, on the other hand, not only is the radius of his operations extended, in that he can motor eighty to a hundred miles if he wants to break in on someone, but, better still, he can do it by mechanical means at any distance—"just ring up". (And soon television will place you altogether in his power. Even your bath will no longer be your own). To talk to someone in his own house, which is what the telephone amounts to, is an undoubted intrusion; is just as much to deprive a man of his privacy as it would be to shout at him through his window as he sits and reads. But the bore and the privacy-killer are now all-puissant, can disturb the peace of almost any family in Europe, or even America, at very little trouble, though considerable expense, to themselves.

Till recently the telephone-operator was our guardian; and how often we should have thanked, instead of upbraiding, her for giving some friend a wrong number! But we never thought of it, and only now, when modern science threatens everywhere to institute the automatic dial-system, do we realize our loss.

Apart from special instruments for killing peace, there are the ordinary noises of the street, which have immensely increased of recent years in number, variety and volume. The traffic, street bands, barrel-organs, church bells, radios and gramophones in neighbouring houses—all have made privacy more remote and difficult of achievement.

For the clarionet at the street corner is as much of an interloper as a voice on the telephone, and, as we have pointed out, a voice on the telephone is as much of an interloper as a stranger in the house. And never a Sunday evening goes by but a part of the Salvation Army dances its noisy, albeit noble, way into the seclusion of our most private rooms.

What remedy is there? Only to increase as much as we can the privacy in our own home, by insisting on every member of a family being perfectly independent. No one must be allowed to be worried by importunate questions such as: "Who is your letter from?" or "Where are you going?" And the habit of such questions is fortunately easy to break; for they arise as a rule not from curiosity, not from any desire to know the answer, but simply from custom. The sole other remedy is to become rich.

ON
STREET
MUSIC

I HAVE VISITED NO city in the world which can rival London in the continuity and protean hideousness of its street music, which constitutes a species of never-ending blackmail. Palermo and Seville are noted for their barrel-organs, gay machines equipped with bells, which tinkle out the most fascinating sub-tropical tangos through the trembling sunlight; from the street corners of Barcelona the rattling of *coblas* and the wailing of *flamencos* are broadcasted all day long, and up to an early hour of the morning; in the half-built and yet half-derelict Balkan towns, from the cafés under the plane-trees, gramophones grind out the repetitive, metallic rhythms of the Near East; in Hungary the throbbing, catch-as-catch-can rhythms of the gypsy music can be heard until a late hour, and in Fez holy men sing out at night during the Fast of Ramadan; in New York the Salvation Army girls can be heard singing and bumping in the snow; in Pompeii, the dead city, odious and oily tenors warble Neapolitan songs among the cactuses to the floating, luncheon population. But nowhere, nowhere else, are there hundreds, nay, thousands of streets filled with so many kinds of funereal and horrid music as in London: marching bands, unemployed Welsh miners singing hymns, spoons rattled in accompaniment to barrel-organs, harmoniums, drums, trumpets, clarionets, barrel-organs alone, gramophones on trolleys, and electric drills; and nowhere in the world, I think, do the players of instruments betray so profound an insensitiveness to the noises they manufacture, and I recall Monsieur Diaghileff, the creator of the Russian Ballet, remarking that these sounds would be tolerated in no other city and that they, more than anything else, demonstrated to what an extent we were an unmusical people.

But how strange; for there was a time when the English loved music, and when the streets of the city of London resounded to lovely, if homely, singing and to the tinkling, agreeable sound of lutes and virginals; of this music was Elizabethan poetry born. And, at the time of the Fire of London, the great number of pairs of virginals that were rescued, and put on barges on the Thames, was remarked. But London to-day is essentially a city for the rich; and only the rich, immune from the onslaughts of the passing bands, guarded by numerous servants from such intrusions on their privacy, are secure; otherwise tranquillity is continually broken.

Pavement-artists, however gaudy and inept their crayons, seem to me to exercise a legitimate right and never to levy blackmail, but is there any excuse for allowing the streets of London to echo to these mournful and exasperating tunes;

the more cheerful, alas, in their intention, the more tragic in the exasperation they induce? It is not that I fail to mark the tragedy of these broken minstrels, purveying their unwanted parodies of mirth—the irritation they inflict on the nervous system only makes the pity of the hearer the greater, for, conscious that it annoys and pains him, he becomes angry with himself for the position in which he is thus placed—but is it fair on householders, rate-payers, tax-payers? Surely the average man pays enough to make it unnecessary for him thus ever to be reminded of the inadequacy and incompetence of the system on behalf of which he is forced to pay? How is it possible to work with all these noises in progress? They should be forbidden; and if they were, it goes without saying that the mournful, cat-voiced howling of religious communities such as the Salvation Army, each chorus in itself an offence against the names of Charity and Mercy, should likewise be prohibited.

There is, of course, a time and a place for everything—at least, we have been told so. Let all the bands of unemployed musicians converge one evening, when they are not expected, on the House of Commons, and there draw attention to their grievances—and ours—by continual brazen braying, even louder than that which takes place within the august portals, and by the percussion of drums, bands, spoons and hollow booming of voices. That, I think, might accomplish some good; let them besiege, too, the charitable institutions, but do not let them continue to expose the hearts of kindly people to this strain; do not let them, in destruction of their own interests, thus harden our hearts and susceptibility to human unhappiness.

The English used at one time very greatly to condemn the pre-Fascist Italian governments for allowing beggars to line up outside the places which they considered should be dedicated to the God of Tourism—the churches, palaces and museums—there to expose their wounds, deformities and diseases; but is it any better to allow men thus to display the spiritual wounds they have received? There is nothing, I think, more disheartening, nothing that makes you feel more keenly the innate cruelty of mankind than a journey, for instance, on a bus in the foggy hours of a winter's evening, when a group of poor, unmusical wretches, with the rain streaming down on them, stands outside, treating us to these unbearable melodies. I believe that if it were clearly understood that in future this music would be forbidden, even now, in these times, new and sufficient money would be forthcoming to find jobs for—or, where necessary, at least to maintain—these unfortunate men.

Let me quote a few lines from a story by a modern writer.

Nothing could be done about it. It was impossible to allow overcoats to be worn. Once that was done, they might as well have waterproofs and umbrellas, as well. After all, it was sense of pity, more than love of music, that they were appealing to. If they looked drier and more comfortable than their fellow-men they would get nothing for their pains. The only safe course was to exaggerate their woes, though, indeed, these needed no magnification. . . .

Their instruments were all steamy and wet, with drops of water clinging to them. It was like playing under the tap. The drum was so sodden that it might have been two sheets of newspaper stretched out, and it only made a muffled, twanging noise when it was beaten.

Perhaps all this was to the good! People must be made to feel sorry for these poor chaps playing out in the pouring wet. They were hurrying home, themselves, to a comfortable tea in front of a warm fire. There would be plenty of lights burning, and the curtains would be drawn. The damp, horrible evening would be kept away, like this, and it would be nasty to have to remember those fellows playing in the street. If they were given a few coppers it seemed, in some odd fashion, to keep them away. Even if they could be heard playing, still, it did not seem to matter so much. Giving them money was like the consciousness of having said your prayers!

A good plan was to huddle the band close up to the awning of some shop. The pathos of this attempt to take shelter made a much better effect than playing right out in the open street. Passers-by felt that the band were human beings like themselves, glad of any little help, willing to take any hand that was offered them.

I think if this piteous description were better known, there would be little difficulty in clearing up the whole situation. Yet it presents only one side of the picture. It does not allow sympathy to those who must suffer this music during their working hours.

ARMS
AND
THE
MAN

DURING THE LAST year I have visited—and lived for a
while in—many countries: Italy, Greece, Yugoslavia, Cochin-
China, Annam and China. I have travelled by many boats
and trains, stayed in many hotels, and talked to numberless
people. And everywhere, except in England, I have listened
to loose talk of war, rumours and forecasts, even praise of
war as a "way out of our difficulties"—the idea underlying
this last phrase, when analysed, being that, since the economic
crisis exists because there are not enough consumers, the way
to mend it, is to kill more of them! . . . But, however foolish,
this talk spreads all over the world: war! war! War in Europe
or war in the Pacific; until even I, previously inclined to
doubt it, since the last war is still so near to us, begin to fear
that war there will be. It seems, indeed, as if people are no
longer interested even in their own fate, but are prepared to

allow their rulers to continue planning means for their extinction without even a protest.

It was the same before the last war. We allowed the armaments to pile up, and the armies and the navies to grow. All the experts knew that war was on its way, and said so openly: only, as usual, they were mistaken as to the character of the the coming conflict. A glorious war, a dashing affair of Boer-War tactics on the grand scale, it was to be finished in a fortnight. "Germany cannot last out." . . . A soldier before the war, I was privileged on more than one occasion to hear Generals who had come down to review, or inspect the Regiment, talking in this strain to my seniors: of course I did not believe it, for I could see that the Generals were foolish fellows, and I trusted enough in the common sense of those who ruled the nations to think that they would avoid so palpably gross and silly an outcome to any quarrel. Besides, if war were so near, surely they would have warned us of it? But I was very young then; while now I recognize, on the contrary, that no brutality or folly exists of which a modern nation, and its rulers, are not capable.

Yet, somehow or other, I cannot convince myself that England by any means *wants* war: at least *she* is guiltless in this direction of any *intention* of evil, though her policy tends to promote it. But then, how is it that the nation has not risen against the foreign policy which dishonours its name and endangers its sons? Of what use is it to talk to bandits of law and order? They are already aware that what they do is illegal; but they are after the booty, and, with this end in view, will permit no sense of decorum to enter into the matter. As long as their trade pays, they will continue to be bandits; therefore we must make their trade profitless for them. Insist on disarmament: and provide the League of Nations with the necessary medium of force.

Each danger that faces us could have been checked or avoided a year or two ago, if decision had been shown. With Japan, for example, it should have been easy either to avoid offending her very proud people or, alternatively, if it was necessary, to take a firm line; instead, we denounced her to the world as an aggressor, and then, having done so, sat back and whimpered, thereby imparting to the world at large a fatal effect of weakness. All along, the Foreign Office has consistently shown that it *knows* quite well which is the right policy, but is afraid to follow it. And for not following it there are always very good legal reasons, doubts and hesitancies of conscience in the wrong direction.

It is quite easy, for example, to understand the Japanese distrust of Britain. We have treated her shockingly in the past! For years her allies, during that time we indulged in a great deal of island-talk: how we were sister peoples seated on our flowery isles, nations of simple fisher-folk, who built up great navies solely in order to maintain the peace of the world; a kind of fisher-police, as it were. . . . Then, quite suddenly, we renounced our alliance, in order to please and gain the good opinion of that other simple nation of fishermen, the United States of America; while, for us, the only result of this act of abnegation was that we were immediately asked to fund our debt, and forced to pay it back in yearly instalments at an exorbitant price. . . . Again, during these present years, we allow ourselves to be undersold in our own markets by goods manufactured in Japan under villainous conditions of labour; and all we do, in the way of reprisal, is to suggest a conference! . . . How can the Japanese, a practical people, respect any nation which conducts its affairs after this fashion?

In our treatment of disarmament, and in our behaviour toward France and Germany, is manifested the same absence of idea, purpose, and, above all, of any ruling principle, coupled with the same irritating tendency to offer advice, when it is neither needed nor wanted. The White Papers on Disarmament, for instance, are extremely generous in the number of moral hints they convey to foreign nations, many of which have little to do with the question under discussion. Indeed, nearly every country in Europe is offered advice of one kind or another as to what should be its correct behaviour in the future. . . . Alas, the time when the hints of the Governess of Europe were heeded has gone by. Only America, being self-supporting, can still afford to tell the world what to do. . . . Nevertheless, we hold many strong cards, and might, occasionally, play one of them.

But the question arises, if the war, to which such a foreign policy as we have described must surely give birth, does materialize, what, gentle reader, ought you to do, this time? Must we help the Foreign Office out of these predicaments into which it so frequently gets itself yet once more? Are *you*, in fact, going to *fight*? . . .

No! for the war, though by our egregious muddling we may have helped it on, and though by a different policy we might have contrived to avoid its happening altogether, will not be of our making. It seems that the European nations *want* another dog-fight; if they do, it is our duty to watch it and not to join in. Every single principle for which we fought, or were said to be fighting, the last war, we have seen betrayed during the last fifteen years. . . . We must not be taken in again. No war is ever a "righteous war". A righteous war is only one degree less wicked than a wicked war.

ON
SEX

IN MODERN CONVERSATION the word sex has to a great extent replaced the older, and somewhat more conventional, word love; a mistake, for such a label carries with it an infinite burden of science and pseudo-science. Thus if *Romeo and Juliet* had been written to-day, it would, no doubt, be described as "a straight and stirring story of sex-appeal" rather than as a love story. Sex psychology is the term applied to love psychology and while, no doubt, it is in the general interest that the study of love should be scientific, yet, in another mood, it seems a little to resemble an attempt to harness two butterflies to a waggon.

I suppose no one will deny that certain persons display a genius in sexual matters, just as they might in poetry or painting, cooking or generalship (the vehicle of genius is one that it is impossible to criticize)? And this quality of sex-genius enters, I believe, into that other curious quality, glamour: which can never quite be described or analysed. Certainly it plays its part in stage glamour. For instance, the peculiar sway which the late Gaby Deslys exercised over every kind of audience can only be accounted for by this kind of genius. Neither her legs, nor her clothes, nor her voice, nor any combination of these, were altogether responsible for the fact that when she appeared on the stage, it became impossible for members of the audience to look, listen or pay attention to anyone else.

As for the alleged "modern pre-occupation with sex", Hollywood has accustomed us to placarded displays of sex-appeal; but if in reality the modern world were preoccupied with sex, we should hear very much less about it. Sex chatter covers a void. Indeed only a very moral world can give birth to scandal. If the world of to-day were really completely amoral—as, for example, was the world of the Greeks —there would be no scandals and very little gossip, for no aberration would cause any surprise. Thus divorce, again, can only exist to shock us in a state of society where monogamy is the recognized institution. In a country like America, where divorce is every year becoming more and more common, soon only the long and happily married couple will surprise—and therefore ultimately shock—the community.

The frequency of divorce in America has produced two effects. Firstly, if morals have suffered because monogamy has suffered, at the same time scandals have very largely ceased to be scandals. Secondly, the fact that two persons may in every respect become tired of each other during the course of a few years has been recognized, and is now so well established in the minds of the people that it has lost its old power to arouse morbid curiosity and fester like a wound. After all, there are fashions in morality as in everything else. Twenty years ago a Turkish Pasha married to less than four wives would have shocked the Turkish nation, in just the same way, and just as much, as the man with two wives shocks us.

There are countries where the leisured, surplus female population of England, much of which lives quietly on the Riviera or travels extensively through the art galleries of Italy, trudging round the museums there when it is not crowding out the galleries of Burlington House, appals the inhabitants by its want of sexual experience; just as genuinely as the event of its seizure and subsequent disposal to a harem would shock us. The European standard of morality, then, may be just as much due to the fact that the average European is essentially monogamous by nature as to any inherent moral superiority. But this does not alter the fact that we have a code of behaviour natural to our civilization, and which it is thus useless to criticize.

From time to time it is stated that the old are shocked by the frankness of the young; but they are not half as much shocked by it as the young are shocked by their habit of muddling. They muddled *themselves* into domestic unhappiness, just as they muddled *us* into the Great War. They resolutely refused to think things out, and by their insistence on their own code of morality, often showed great cruelty.

For example, among them there still exists the extraordinary idea that parents who get on together very badly, and spend all their lives quarrelling and making their small children miserable, must not divorce, must not separate "for the sake of the children". If, in these cases, the children were consulted, I think there would be very little doubt as to their decision. Further, though it may shock the old to think so, it is just possible that their children would prefer to have round them parents who were growing old happily, if polygamously. And, finally, at their age, they should stop being shocked. It is a privilege of youth.

Meanwhile, to prophesy: this age of frankness will wither before another age of discretion. "Sex-appeal" will lose its sway over the hearts of the young and will take on a hundred romantic variations of name. It will become the fashion to disguise the sentiments just as, perhaps, once more to disguise the male countenance with whiskers. Indeed it looks as if whisker and crinoline were the outward and visible sign of a wish to disguise the inner thoughts.

PERSONAL
ENCOUNTERS

OUT
OF
SEASON

LONDON IS TOO large and straggling a conglomeration
of houses to be really much influenced by seasonal changes.
Yet even the most casual observer knows that London *has* a
season—almost as much as any watering-place or seaside
town. By no means, however, am I thinking of the summer
months, which for a few members of the richer classes still
constitute The Season: a recurrent phenomenon ever officially
heralded by the opening of the Royal Academy, an event
sufficiently depressing, one would have thought, to drive
every esthetically minded person out of the town; nor of the
tail months of the year, now christened the Little Season by
the Fashion-Plate Press; but, instead, of the month of August,
when, indeed, if only for a few weeks, London completely
alters its aspect.

To begin with, the residential streets of Mayfair and St

139

James's are deserted (though how curious that so many people should leave these regions, just when they become pleasantly empty, in order to transport themselves at considerable cost to summer resorts, just when those places become most noisy and crowded), while on the other hand the rest of London suddenly turns either provincial or foreign. Super-provincial and super-foreign, perhaps I should write, for in Bloomsbury the squares echo to the massed intonations of Bristol, Sheffield, Leeds and Glasgow rather than to the usual cultured cooing which in more ordinary times caresses the ear, and its thousand temperance hotels are a-clatter all day with tea-cups: while, in the Strand and Piccadilly, every European accent can be heard, and this, and the eager curiosity of the strangers, impart an unwonted vivacity to these neighbourhoods.

But what of the places which, for their very livelihood, depend on a brief season; places which, from the point of view of fashion, are created afresh, as it were, every first of May or first of August, only three months later to sink back into primeval nothingness? . . . These we must examine after the last lingering guest has taken his departure and when blinds have been pulled down in shops, hotels and houses. Even now, however, behind one or two of these blank windows, may shrink and cringe a belated, timid figure, aware that, according to all the laws of his world, he should have left. Since, however, he has nowhere to go to, no friends and no funds, he is forced, sad ghost, into this miserable, shy defiance, though at night he may be able to sneak out and crawl round the crescents unobserved, an uneasy spirit revisiting the places of his former mundane delight.

Certainly such towns, dedicated to one season, present in their off-duty moments the certainty of affording surprises. ... I remember, for example, spending a day in Mentone early in September, in the years before the summer-season vogue had spread so far down the coast. ... It was the most beautiful day imaginable, with a few fleecy white clouds trailing above the horizon, but the aspect of the promenade seemed most singular. The carefully kept winter lawns were brown as slabs of chocolate, no flowers were visible except one or two geraniums in the last stages of exhaustion and the palms spun their tufts all dusty into blue air. The numberless hotels which face the sea were shuttered, their windows having a kind of roll-top-desk shutter let down over them, for the sake of security. ... But, most striking symptom of all, under the *porte-cochère* of one hotel, in the street behind the promenade, stood an abandoned motor-car, looking twenty times its age; as if this were not Mentone, but Pompeii, and itself a recently excavated object of interest. What wild tale of adventure, one could not but wonder, what tragedy of missed trains and lamenting friends, lay behind this abomination of desolation? And how utterly broken, beyond mortal repair, must it have been for the members of so thrifty a race thus to abandon it!

Nothing, I think, is so melancholy as a ruined machine: yet human relics approach it in being pathetic. I had deemed myself the only foreigner in the town: though even then a few doubts had assailed me, for Mentone is something of a terminus; people drift there, can get no further without crossing the border (which requires initiative) and at the same time cannot return home. It has, moreover, ever been a

favourite resort with the English—and, indeed, apart from
San Remo, remains the best place in which to study English
hats of the seventies, eighties and even earlier; hats comparable, in their involved design, to those which a decade or
two earlier had so much astonished Théophile Gautier on his
arrival in Gibraltar, after six months spent in a then hatless
Spain. . . . I was turning over in my mind just what sort
of ghost might haunt these streets, when all at once it
materialized: the sad, but, at the same time, not altogether
undefiant apparition of a middle-aged English lady, obviously
economizing out of season, at a place which, alas, she could
not afford to leave, but in which there was now no one for her
to talk with—none of those lovely, impersonal, abstract, pro-
British hotel-conversations. . . . As for her dress, she had
attempted to come to some compromise with the climate, for
she was shod in *espadrilles* and, after the manner of the
natives, went stockingless, but wore one of those flowered
chiffon dresses which have now practically become the English
national costume, and was crowned by what I judged to be
her second-best winter hat; a real confection of cherries, blue
satin and pink satin ribbons, white currants and artificial
roses, but one which was plainly not too well withstanding
the onslaughts of the summer sun. Her face, which had been
vigorously painted, and her hair, which must surely have been
touched by Midas on more than one occasion, both emphasized the impression of poverty which emanated from
her. . . . I watched her. She hurried across the street to have
yet another glance at the English (Cotswold) Church, standing so stonily behind a low ivy-clad wall. . . . There was no
fresh news. The same little white notice, pasted on one of

the supports of the lych-gate, still announced in faded ink
that the Rev. Douglas Surplice would return as Chaplain on
December the twelfth. . . . There would be special Nativity
services. . . . Yes, but across what a desert of wasted Sundays
in Trinity! . . . She then recrossed the road to look into the
window of the best cakeshop in the town . . . brioches . . .
jams . . . panatone . . . crystallized fruit . . . those delicious
biscuits, all with their prices attached to them on flags. I
saw, though I did not at once interpret it, a sad connoisseur-
ship gleaming from her eye; but then I understood, for,
instead of entering, she hurriedly crossed the street again and
dematerialized into a cheap, dull tea-shop round the corner.
Alas! both body and soul were destined that day, and perhaps
on many others, to remain unsatisfied. . . .

I turned toward the promenade. The car still stood under
its *porte-cochère*, but I had already forgotten about it. Machines,
decidedly, are less interesting, however curious their history.

ENCOUNTER
WITH THE
OXFORD
GROUP
MOVEMENT

ON THE WAY back from China I travelled through Canada. Unable to stay there for more than a few days, the selection of places in which to stop during this limited space of time was not without its difficulties. I decided, however, to stay at Banff—the capital, as it were, of the Rockies—a little town nestling among white-capped mountains, bisons and buffaloes. The super-Alpine scenery offers indeed a transcendent magnificence; situated itself on a level of four or five thousand feet, the mountains on all sides tower some ten thousand feet above the town, and everywhere green snow-water flows and ripples through shrill green valleys. Here the fir-trees, usually so reminiscent of Bournemouth and of the sandy plains of Germany, lose a little of their austere horror and appear to have been transmuted to Italian cypresses. Slim and dark green, they help to punctuate the landscape, to make sense of it and to give, even, an appearance of civilization to a region in which man has so far had but little say.

The small town itself is attractive, with its display of native Indian goods and with its zoo of indigenous animals: baby black bears rattling the bars to obtain their allowance of honey, sneaking coyotes, and above all, the finest horned owls in the world. But an even more interesting exhibit was temporarily on view at the Banff Springs Hotel. This splendid hotel, built and run by the Canadian Pacific Railway Company, and set a little above the famous falls, is surprising to a European, because it has been conceived on such an enormous scale. There are, I believe, at least a thousand bedrooms in it, and it contains within its own walls every conceivable adjunct: interior swimming pools and racquets courts, a natural sulphur spring outside, while a huge park supplies the needs of golf addicts. Usually this palace remains closed until the beginning of July, but on arriving at Vancouver I learnt that it had been opened especially to accommodate the House Party of the Oxford Group Movement. Since a certain human interest was thus lent to the natural beauty of the scenery, I decided at once to spend a few days there.

The Oxford Group Movement is notoriously friendly, and so many of its adherents were staying here—some six hundred to a thousand persons, it was said, a crowd mostly American and Canadian in origin, but including also a large contingent from Britain—that the members found it difficult to recognize that I was outside the bounds of their hospitality. Whenever I sat by myself in a corner, an old lady would advance toward me, remarking, "You look kinda-lonesome!" to which I would reply, conventionally, "I am getting guidance". "Why, isn't that just splendid!" she would exclaim, turning away.

The routine of the party was rigorous. Liable to be addressed at any moment, either by business successes or by business failures (and I do not know which section is the more depressing to listen to), various groups could be seen confessing in the great halls and chambers of the hotel at almost every hour of day and night. In the afternoon they would display themselves riding, swimming or walking, while in the evening, after dinner, there would ensue a mass meeting, at which various prominent business failures or successes would again address their international audience. Two of these meetings I attended, and I had hoped to hear some interesting confessions. I had been told by a friend of a meeting she witnessed in London, at which, after some preliminary hesitation on the part of the audience, a policewoman had finally stood up and, holding up her arm as if to stop the traffic, had blown a whistle and then proceeded to favour the audience with some amusing indiscretions. But at the meetings at which I was present nothing of this sort occurred. There seemed to be, I must admit in all fairness, an absolute lack of sensationalism and of sensational appeal, and the whole undertaking seemed to be based on a political and commercial ideal: as though it were a final effort of the middle classes— now, alas, being gradually dispossessed throughout the world —to preserve their interests through a religious rather than a political medium. . . . If the workers could only be persuaded to see things from the correct angle, they would prefer prayer to wages—would, indeed, prefer—and then pray—to be given lower wages and to adopt a lower standard of life. There would be no strikes, and whenever a difference of opinion might arise as to rates of pay, the workers would engage in communal prayer with the employers.

On both occasions the enormous hall was crowded with eager, red, hysterical faces—men and women in many kinds of clothing, but all obviously possessed of a competence. There were no poor: there were some rich. On the platform was Dr Buchman himself, surrounded by American, Canadian and English enthusiasts. One or two of them appeared in evening dress. That Dr Buchman has the gift of being able to infuse an audience with a spirit of fervour is impossible to deny. But as for the confessions, they were deplorable. The most interesting one, in fact, came from a lady in evening dress, who stood up on the platform to say: "Before I joined the Oxford Group Movement I used to indulge in *inferior thinking!*"—a shocking anti-climax. At the end Dr Buchman again resumed control and the meeting ended in an outburst of communal prayer.

All over the building at odd times of the day people could be observed seeking guidance. They were for ever being exhorted to take their smallest troubles to the Deity; and indeed I think they did so. The head waiter informed me that he had heard one group, on their departure, discussing the appropriate gratuity to bestow upon him. Having consulted together for a time without reaching agreement, one of them said, "I think we had better seek direction". The head waiter seemed disappointed with the result, for, after some moments of silence in prayer, the sum of twenty-five cents—roughly a shilling—was awarded to him.

ONE
OR
TWO
LIVES

*Incorporating the Incident
Of The Lady With the
Pink Feather*

THE PHRASE, "leading a double life" always carries with it, in England, an implication of dubiety; which, indeed, mounts, as it were, with the index figure. Nevertheless anybody, it can safely be stated, who lives a life worthy even of the meanest abilities, must of necessity lead more lives than one, pursue a series of incarnations, coincident in time, but subsidiary to his chief existence. . . . And one of mine is dedicated to lecturing and speaking; a life which, though exigent, does not want in interest.

The early part of the adventure is repetitive. Lectures, in a sense, are winter fruit: and so one arrives, blue-nosed, to start the journey from any of the coldest railway-stations in England. A long journey follows, during the course of which the sort of life you are leading at the moment joins itself on inevitably in the mind to the other occasions on which you

148

have led it; so that, just as when you go home or are on holiday abroad, it becomes almost impossible, from these blue serge cushions, to recall ever having led any other species of existence. In time, one arrives and is obliged to search for that kind person, the Secretary, who has been detailed to meet the lecturer. Follows conversation, in which invariably I discover that the talkative young son of a prominent "statesman" has preceded me, as a sort of unwitting John the Baptist, and in consequence the same kind of dialogue always ensues. "Do you think he's clever?" or "He's very sarcastic", or "But he'll grow up one day". (Incidentally, "sarcastic" constitutes a stricture of the most severe kind in every circle of English life. . . . "'E spoke to me sarcastic-like.") Then comes dinner at seven—a hurried meal, which most probably, like the last meal of a man condemned to be hanged, you are invited to order for yourself; finally the tumbrel to the lecture-hall and the five minutes' wait in the ante-room; which interval, owing to the intense fear and nausea—these I am told, are the lot of even the most accustomed and accomplished speakers—mounts to a climax; and during this five minutes, now exaggerated to as many hours, several kind people choose to introduce themselves to the lecturer in order to talk to him, because they think he looks depressed. . . . (I remember, on one occasion of this sort, a lady introducing herself to me, and adding, "The name of Sitwell requires no introduction here. . . . It is famous"—I prepared a sickly smile—"in the hunting field", she continued.) Now comes the final horror: the platform, on which various persons range themselves; a pause, while you listen in detail to last year's accounts and resignations; a short introductory speech, and then one's own turn, of which oneself obtains a curiously detached impression, somewhat equivalent to the boredom of being photographed: "Try to look pleasant", one has to remind oneself, "and remember to keep your eye fixed on that unfortunate, frightened-looking woman at the back of the hall"; or "Don't fidget with your foot, and don't let your fingers rustle like mice amongst your papers". Then there are the difficult moments, such as the one when you make a joke, and two well-dressed old ladies at once get up and leave the building in, as you conceive, a marked manner; though you can never discover subsequently whether their departure was coincidental or the outcome of some deep principle which, all innocently, you have flouted.

From time to time, however, some really extraordinary event or situation is born of these occasions, and such a one I will now relate: The Incident of the Lady with the Pink Feather. . . . What a curious psychological problem she affords, as I look back: what a singular and unexampled mingling of sensitiveness and insensitiveness, cowardice and courage, wisdom and folly! . . . Will she, I wonder, if these words catch her eye, think the worse of me? I hope not. . . . It was thus. I had been asked to lecture in, let us say, Devonshire, to an institute connected with an amateur association: and my lecture had been announced some weeks previously. Several letters reached me. First of all I received a letter from the President, recalling the fact that we were cousins (though she had never previously seemed to make much of this relationship) and hoping therefore that she could rely on me to *stand no nonsense* from the Vice-President, should I meet her. She was of opinion that I should not like her: a disagreeable, interfering old woman, who needed to be put in her place. I was not to mention this letter, of course, but should I find myself called upon to deliver a few severe rebukes to the lady in question, I was to be aware that I should have, behind me, the tacit support of the President. . . . But the letter which really interested me was exceedingly long, and one which I was obliged to read over many times before I could fully obtain its gist. A diffuse letter, half frank, half secretive: it began by being concerned with nothing in particular, and only gradually the truth leaked out, only gradually its purpose suggested itself. Boiled down, the appeal was this. The writer, who bore the rare but not unsonorous name of Albinia, was a married woman and a member of the Association. She and her husband, she wrote, were great admirers of mine and of my brother and sister; took so great an interest in us and in our work that, led on by their enthusiasm, it might be that they had in some way or other, for instance by the use of Christian names when referring to us, and by relating instances of their acquaintanceship with us, produced the impression on other members of the Association that they knew us . . . well, rather better than our acquaintance actually warranted. Besides, she had only just remembered that, as a matter of fact, absurd as it might seem, we had *never* met. . . . However, the moment of trial had come, she and her husband could not bear to miss my lecture—and, indeed, if they did miss it, what would their friends think of them? Yet, if I showed no sign of this friendship which they had claimed, *where* would they be then? . . . Really, she felt she *did* almost know me. Did I feel the same? . . . She would be standing by the platform, and would be wearing

151

a pink feather in her hat. . . . Surely I would not pass her by?

As I say, the purport of this long letter, the request in it, gradually emerged. Would I, for the sake of saving two human beings from agony, claim them, though I did not know—and, in fact, had never seen—them as my friends? The request, in itself, I thought, was a compliment, for it indicated a belief, born of reading my books, that I *might* do so; that I was a person to whom it was possible to make this very unconventional and, indeed, extraordinary appeal. . . . At the same time, I decided that the letter would have been more to my taste if it had been shorter, written in the style of a confessional.

However, I decided to do the thing handsomely. The day came, I passed up the hall toward the platform, by which little knots of people were standing. I approached them, to greet the President. . . . A little way off stood a nervous but rather good-looking woman, wearing in her hat a pink feather. . . . As though suddenly seeing her, I threw my arms open, exclaimed in a stentorian voice of surprise, "Albin-ia! *You* here!" and printed a hearty kiss upon her cheek. . . . I noticed a flush of pleasure as she returned my greeting, and that is all I know of her.

ON
GHOSTS

ONLY BY NIGHT do I believe in ghosts: and then more especially in a house that lies buried in the depth of the country and in which there is no electric light. That there are *manifestations*, on the other hand, I am persuaded by day as well as by night, and if these appearances are what they seem, or if they simply produce the impression of being ghosts, will to me, for one, ever be immaterial. Whether they prove merely to be lifeless impressions, stamped upon the surrounding air in a photographic way through the strong yet surviving emotions of the persons who inhabited this room or this house some centuries ago: whether they take shape through a trick of the atmosphere or encounter us through some fault in the flowing of the time-stream—so that perhaps we give the ghost as great a fright as he gives us (that is to say, that he returns to the people of his age declaring,

"I have seen a peculiar being walking along the passage, dressed in baggy sort of knee-breeches made of cloth, and the most fantastically ugly coat") or whether they indeed be *revenants*, can make no difference to the fear with which these apparitions will always be regarded, and which no explanation, scientific or otherwise, can allay.

A great many ghosts, I take it, are the result of boredom. Just as small boys, when enduring the *ennui* of a private school, invent mysteries for themselves, and hear footsteps— or should one write the more interesting "footfalls"?—on the gravel at night, so a few people, imprisoned in the sad magnificence of a decaying country-house, may be forced to invent for themselves nocturnal apparitions. The whole of the Romantic movement (with which the modern popularity of ghosts is very nearly connected), was, I think, the result of the growing boredom then beginning to afflict the most sensitive minds of the time. Perhaps, even, the apparition which was seen by Charles I (said to be Laud, but in reality Stafford, for partisans of the King changed the identity of the visitor, fearing that it might be harmful to his cause if he had seen the ghost of one whom he had so much injured) was the fruit of the long *ennui* which his imprisonment had engendered.

Superstition is so deeply rooted in the human race, even the most civilized, that I do not know how it will be eradicated. No amount of reading of Sir James Frazer's *The Golden Bough* will ever quite liberate our minds. It will take many thousands of years before we can face the next world—or the lack of one—in any form without a shudder. Even now the inhabitants of great cities are only just freed from their fear of wild animals; to emancipate them from these more intangible terrors is altogether a more difficult affair.

Doctor Johnson, foe to all exaggeration except that of natural appearance, held the opinion that no anecdote, however wittily related, was amusing unless in strict accordance with fact. "Is it true?" was the rather astringent test which he applied to every story told him. Now, however, when most fiction is slightly falsified truth, and each biography is a neatly verisimilous work of fiction, the application of this standard would seem more than ever necessary. Certainly it has always seemed to me that the telling of a ghost story is never justified except by the good faith of the narrator: and, alas, most true ghost stories are not only pointless—which does not matter, for, in the absence of motive and clue may, indeed, consist the whole effect of such a tale—but crude and unexciting.

I know several people who have seen ghosts, and many who have been through curious, if slight, experiences. I myself have, as I suppose, talked with a ghost, or, at any rate, with someone who was not there—though I should say talked *to*, rather than *with*. During the war, at a moment when I was very over-tired, my company had to take over some front-line trenches. We arrived just before dusk. There was a rule, as most readers of then military age will remember, that the men should "stand to", with rifles on the parapet, at the moment of dusk, for it was one of the most common times of attack. I came out of my dug-out, which I had just entered, and saw a man, in the corner of the bay opposite, with his rifle on the ground, leaning against the wall of the trench. I spoke to him, saying, "How many times have I told you to get your rifle on the parapet?" and continued in the same strain, when suddenly I realized that no one was there—only a rifle leaning against the wall. . . . This experience was not in any way terrifying, but, all the same, however explicable through fatigue, it did bring with it subsequently an uneasy feeling that you could not trust your own senses, just as the man who has survived an earthquake distrusts for a time the solidity of the earth.

Another story, of an apparition of which I can no more doubt the truth, was confided to me, and is appended, under the title, "The Ghost in the Green Mask".

THE
GHOST
IN THE
GREEN
MASK

THE STORY OF Dr Goodfellow's visitation is of interest; for the occurrence, however slight, and of however familiar a type, has unusual features, one of which is the reliability and intelligence of the person to whom it happened, and another the curious insistence—seemingly quite beyond the necessities of the case—with which the apparition sought to attract the doctor's attention.

One evening I was sitting at dinner alone with Dr Goodfellow. Upstairs a relative, of whom I happened to be extremely fond, was lying ill; and this serious illness had, during the last two or three months, formed the foundation for a friendship between the doctor and myself.

Knowing, as I did, this invalid, it was impossible not to admire the combination of tact and wisdom, the tempering of firmness with intuition, which the doctor had displayed.

He lacked, too, the professional optimism of the English practitioner. He was about forty years of age, and a giant in stature; altogether he seemed a rather remarkable person.

The talk turned on the progress made recently in mental healing and the understanding of nervous disorders, and finally I inquired whether, among the many incidents of a medical career, there had ever occurred to him any event of which no ordinary explanation could be furnished?

Dr Goodfellow—perhaps because he was a little of that sceptical bent of mind which is ever unready to accept the evidences of his own senses, except when to do so fits in with the theories that it has adopted, which are by the age of thirty fixed and rigid—that habit of mind which we call common sense—at first denied any belief in the phenomena of thought-transference or apparitions.

Indeed, in these matters so great was his conviction that it seemed completely to have banished from his memory for the moment the singular event which might have caused him to abandon it.

He was silent for some seconds, and I could see in his eyes a memory trying to rise, like a fish, to the still surface of his consciousness. At last it reached him, and rather unwillingly he admitted that, once, something unusual had happened to him.

As a student, at the age of seventeen, Dr Goodfellow had worked in the smallpox hospital at Glasgow. It was at the time of that alarming outbreak which coincided with the Boer War.

To lessen the risks of catching or spreading this virulently infectious disease, it was the rule for workers among these cases to wear a special uniform, consisting of loose white coat and trousers and a green mask, with a beak-like nose, attached to a close-fitting cap. However necessary it may have been, this livery must have added a grotesque touch of further horror to the scene, dehumanising the doctors and workers as they glided in and out of the carefully shaded rooms, making them seem, in the delirium of the poor disfigured victims, rather the personification of the disease—as though the deadly microbes responsible for it had for the moment been allowed to assume quasi-human form in order to plague and torture the wretched sufferers—than what they were, courageous and sympathetic volunteers for its combat.

Working with Goodfellow was a student named Fairfax, whose most intimate friend he became. But such friendships of adolescence are apt to be volatile, and, when Goodfellow left his comrade behind in Glasgow, in order to study medicine in Paris, his letters to Fairfax, his letters from Fairfax, became more and more infrequent, and finally, after a year, stopped altogether.

Goodfellow's new life, coming at the very moment when his vitality was at its greatest, and the transforming of the scene which framed it, filled him with the intoxication of existence which comes—if at all—but once in a lifetime, and completely obliterated for him the thought of anything but the actual moment. Fairfax was forgotten, absolutely forgotten.

The young Englishman was working in the medical college which is under the charge of the famous Monsieur Blois. For a year a room was found for him in the establishment, and then he was allowed to move out into a lodging of his own.

He was singularly fortunate in the one he now rented, for it was a delightful room, the panelling of which was painted a soft, clear grey, and, what was more important, it had three wide windows looking out on to a garden.

It was the sort of room that exercises an influence, both invigorating and calming, on the mind of its occupant, however unconscious he may be by nature of his environment.

The door faced one of the end windows, and between them was a very charming mantelpiece. The bed stood with its head against the other wall opposite the chimney, but there was a considerable space on each side of it.

The only drawback that Goodfellow found to his new lodging was the absence of electric light. But this deprivation was in the day-time fully compensated by the light which poured in.

Here the young man lived for some years; during this period he never heard from Fairfax, nor could the latter have been aware of his present address.

One night, during his fourth summer in Paris, Goodfellow came in about eleven o'clock. The windows stood wide open, and from the garden below drifted the warm air of May, scented by the pale, Persian shapes of the lilacs as they were fanned by their gentle slaves, the winds.

The room was drenched in moonlight, so pearly bright that it was as though daylight were being filtered through deep, clear waters.

A sense of rest and contentment seized on him, and, puffing out the candle, he swiftly fell asleep.

Out of this peaceful but heavy slumber he was wakened

suddenly, and with a feeling of disturbance. What had happened? . . . The clock struck two, and he looked round.

In an armchair by the window, facing him, and very distinct in the milky light, was a motionless figure in gleaming white clothes, and with a green beaked mask; an unearthly Punchinello, it seemed. Even apart from this sad, fantastic uniform, the build and poise of the visitor proclaimed it as his forgotten friend, Fairfax.

Goodfellow knew that he had locked the door before going to bed. Fairfax was certainly ignorant of his address, and in any case would hardly call on him, in the middle of the night, clad in the garb of the Glasgow smallpox hospital.

The figure remained there motionless. His friend called him by name, asked him what he wanted; but he sat on there under the moonlight without moving.

Fear overcame Goodfellow; he could not find the matches, and the figure sat on. He feared that it was a hallucination, that he might be going mad. He buried his head in the blankets, and turned over toward the wall. It was some minutes before he dared open his eyes.

When he did so, the figure was opposite him once more, had moved to take up its position on a chair by the wall near him. There the masked creature sat, again rigid and immovable. Goodfellow fainted: but when he came round his visitor was no longer with him.

The next morning he made sure that his door was still locked.

But the concierge complained, when he came downstairs, that a funny, stiff figure in fancy-dress had knocked him up in the middle of the night and asked for the young Englishman upstairs: so that the apparition was able, evidently, in the illogical way of ghosts, to enter only certain rooms without human aid.

Goodfellow was so perturbed by the whole occurrence that he contrived to sit next to Dr Blois at luncheon—for the head of the college often lunched with the students—and confided in him.

The old Frenchman inquired laughingly what he had eaten for dinner, when, just at that moment, a telegram was brought informing Goodfellow that Fairfax had died the previous night, shortly before two o'clock.

Under the will of the dead man he was appointed executor. Could he return to England as soon as possible?

Fairfax had died of pneumonia, following on influenza, and had left behind him a wife and child of whose existence the new executor had been ignorant. But why had he adopted that strange, ominous uniform for his appearance; why had he not spoken?

Dr Goodfellow had never had an experience of this kind before, and has never had one since.

HOLIDAY CONVERSATIONS

On the Extinction of the Strong, Silent Englishman

ONE DAY A Spaniard asked me if the "strong, silent Englishman" really existed? . . . Rushing to the defence of my country, I replied, "Of course he does. But he prefers to stay at home, or else to travel imperially. He can be strong and silent to his fill in the open spaces of Empire, or, it may be, on the Sussex Downs and the Wealds of Kent (though, even there, lady-novelists in search of copy are apt now to break in upon his silence); but he never visits the Continent. Only the weak, talkative Englishman does that." Yet I did not succeed in convincing myself. . . . Is he not, I wonder, merely a myth, surviving till lately in the imaginative minds of foreigners? And is not the origin of this myth entirely due to our public schools, where languages are so badly taught that, in after life, the Englishman must perforce for ever keep his silence in front of all foreigners who do not talk English?

Greville in his diary records a fine instance of laconic English. At Waterloo a well-known general in attendance upon Wellington lost his arm from a cannon-ball, while standing quite near the Duke. "By God, your Grace," he exclaimed, "I've lost an arm." "Have you, by God?" replied the Iron Duke; and there the matter remained. So that many people might infer from this, and from other stories, that the great Duke of Wellington was the supreme instance of the strong, silent Englishman. On the contrary he was witty, garrulous, and, as all readers of contemporary memoirs are aware, very easy to approach, very easy to talk to. In fact, he loved conversation. Moreover, he was Irish, not English—a common fault among great English generals.

Then, where to look? Certainly, one imagines, among the soldiery.

But the better generals, I apprehend, are seldom silent. Henry V, according to Shakespeare (who usually relied on tradition), was most talkative, and as full of patriotic "back-chat" as any old gentleman in a club during the last war. . . . Cromwell, Marlborough, Peterborough . . . all were inclined to be "chatterboxes".

In times past, of course, many *lesser* generals have been silent (thank goodness!); but were they strong? Now even those have failed us; for to-day they all write books of memoirs to explain away errors which it would be better for them not to mention, or, perhaps, merely to show that they can read and write. In fact, two very good new rules of life are:

1. Avoid serving as a soldier under a literary general. With the exception of Julius Caesar, the results have always been fatal.
2. Never read a book by an author who pretends to enjoy war.

From soldiers let us pass to politicians. In the past, we have been famous for our politicians. Silence was never in them. Foreigners dread the ordeal by oratory; but almost any strong, silent Englishman can speak in public, if called upon to do so: though, as a rule, for far too long a time. There is no country in the world, except America, where after-dinner speaking is so popular.

May we not then, conclude that the strong, silent Englishman, if he ever existed, no longer survives; that the palm has passed to other races; that the exquisite mingling of heavy chin, silence and "swank" is to be found elsewhere at the present day? . . . The Italian, once so loquacious, has become strong and silent. The American, again, who was wont formerly to dwell upon the battle-strewn history of his nation, now says nothing but sets his chin. Indeed the "American Prosperity Chin" was, before the Slump, a recognized feature. Mothers encouraged it in their children, and the habit of chewing gum reinforced it. Russians, too, are strong and silent nowadays. Lenin, who is said to have lived much in England at one time, was a typical strong, silent man.

And alas! if the type is extinct in England it is hardly likely to recur, any more than the Diplodocus or the Giant Sloth. We live in an age of chatter. In cities we have to shout above the incessant lion-mouthed roaring of the traffic to make ourselves heard at all. He who shouts the loudest is able to talk most; he who talks most, is thought to talk best.

Even to-day, however, there are false strong-silent Englishmen, who will trap you, by pretended silence, and then drown you in a torrent of talk. Unlike railway conversationalists—men obviously prone to chatter—they have no

special axe to grind, such as the probable end of the world
on next Tuesday, the certain identification of the Welsh people
with the lost Ten Tribes of Israel, or some other topic equally
modern and to the point. No; their talk roams. . . . Take
them on at their own game, bore and exhaust them! If they
want conversation, let them have it; but it is not obligatory
on you to be gentle with them. You are allowed, by the very
rules of the game which they are playing, wherever possible
to puzzle and confound.

For this purpose it is necessary to develop a special technique, as complete as their own, in opening and carrying on a
conversation. You may deceive them, too, to a certain degree:
for themselves carry deceit far beyond any lawful bounds,
each of them trying to pass off on you the idea that he
is that extinct monster, the "strong, silent Englishman",
but only so that he may all the better waste your time
later on.

Let us place the scene in August, in a typical south-coast
hotel, so that the talk is entirely ungoverned by any sense of
time or surroundings. It is neutral ground. There is a dusty
palm tree in one corner of the room. For some days I have
noticed a tall, angular, long-toothed old gentleman smoking
a pipe. During all this time he has betrayed me into a false
opinion of him by saying never a word. Occasionally he rises
to his feet, takes his pipe out of his mouth, and taps it im-
pressively upon the wooden tub from which springs the palm
tree. Indeed, this bird-like, woodpecker music was the only
sound he had produced so far.

Then, all at once, one afternoon, he dashed into conversation. A friend and myself were discussing the rival merits

of Turkish and Virginian cigarettes, when suddenly he approached us. The following talk ensued:

OLD GENTLEMAN: "Excuse me, but were you talking of Niagara?"

SELF: "Not that I am aware of. But why?"

OLD GENTLEMAN: "Because I was there soon after Webb was drowned. You know! The man who swam the Channel."

SELF (*remembering Miss Mercedes Gleitze*): "But that's rather a woman's game now, isn't it? Last time I crossed the Channel it was black with typists."

OLD GENTLEMAN: "But Webb was a man, not a woman. Tall fellow with a beard."

SELF: "I know, you mean Lord Passfield—the husband of Mrs Sidney Webb. I didn't know he had ever swum the Channel—still, of course, boys will be boys!"

OLD GENTLEMAN: "But the man who swam the Channel is dead, I tell you—drowned. *He* couldn't be Lord Passfield."

SELF: "Oh, I'm sorry."

OLD GENTLEMAN (*intent on continuing his talk*): "Amazing country, America; but all the same, give me Australia every time. The wild flowers there are a sight."

SELF: "Yes, I've heard of them—Botany Bay——"

OLD GENTLEMAN: "But they were *convicts*, not wild flowers. No wild flowers there."

SELF: "You surprise me, sir! but I was sure I knew the name in some connection or other."

OLD GENTLEMAN: "Rather curious thing. The ship we went to Australia in had been to the bottom. They had managed to refloat it."

167

SELF: "Good gracious. Was everything very damp?"

OLD GENTLEMAN (*judiciously*): "No-o-o, not really—considering."

SELF: "I'm always terrified of damp sheets, aren't you? They are so dangerous. One can't be too careful."

OLD GENTLEMAN: "You'd have to learn to rough it, if you were going there."

SELF: "Well, I suppose damp sheets *are* better than wet-blankets. But tell me, had the rats left the sinking ship?"

OLD GENTLEMAN: "I can't remember. But I know that I noticed a mouse."

SELF: "How pleased it must have been to see you. I hope you talked to it? They're such dear, affectionate little creatures, I am told."

OLD GENTLEMAN: "But there's nothing like a dog for a companion."

SELF: "Yes. There is a lot to be said for *dumb* animals. Unfortunately, the dog lacks the virtues of the kangaroo."

OLD GENTLEMAN: "The kangaroo? No, no, sir—give me a dog in a tight corner, any day."

SELF: "But is Australia as much of a tight corner as, let us say, New York under Prohibition?"

OLD GENTLEMAN: "Well, what would you want with a kangaroo in New York? Why, it would be frightened. What I meant was: 'Give me a dog if there's any danger'. A dog's more than a companion. But a kangaroo would be no help in a tight place."

OLD GENTLEMAN (*resuming after pause*): "Interesting things, animals. Now, when I went to the Boer War, I was in command of a whole shipload of mules. They got pleuro.

168

Terrible thing, it was. The mules simply died like flies. Had to shoot twenty of 'em myself."

SELF: "Have you ever done any other big game shooting?"

OLD GENTLEMAN: "Only antelope."

SELF: "But mules are bigger than antelopes, I should have thought?"

OLD GENTLEMAN: "Yes, I suppose they are, if you think of it in that way——"

SELF: "You've never shot a wild mule, have you, sir?"

OLD GENTLEMAN: "But there aren't any. How could there be?" (*Pensively*): "Excuse me asking you; are you Scottish, too?"

HINTS

ON THE
EFFECT
OF
MINDING
ONE'S OWN
BUSINESS

I WAS PRESENT, SOON after the rise to power of Herr Hitler, at the first night of a play, in which the famous German actor Herr Werner Krauss made his first appearance on the English stage. The occasion was rendered memorable, not only by his fine performance, but, in addition, by the remarkable scenes which took place in and outside the theatre. As soon as the curtain went up, to show an English actor and actress together upon the stage, a shrill propagandist yapping of female voices and loud, insistent, rather guttural bellowing of male, broke out from the gallery, demanding that the English stage should be reserved for English folk, while at the same time showers of anti-Hitler pamphlets descended on the familiar crowd of first-nighters in the stalls and boxes; people showing us, as the late Ronald Firbank described it, "such *Tatler*-tainted little faces". The curtain had to be lowered, but the uproar was continually renewed whenever it rose for a moment, until such time as finally the police could be called in to deal with the interrupters.

For one, I found myself wishing that people would mind their own business. Why should they carry their politics into the theatre? . . . Yet, however disgraceful the scene, perhaps the interrupters were in the right. . . . (Of course, I would rather they had interrupted a bad play because it was bad: but, alas, it will be many years before an audience in England learns, or dares, to attempt this meritorious feat.) At any rate they were not "minding their own business"; an occupation which gives rise to untold trouble and cruelty, but one, fortunately, for which most people have neither the aptitude nor the inclination—otherwise we should never have reached even that level of humanity to which we have attained. For example, to hear the screams of children in a slum, and to report their disgusting parents to the Society for the Prevention of Cruelty to Children, is but another failure "to mind one's own business". And, what would happen, further, were doctors and hospitals to mind *their* own business?

Nevertheless, to this day we meddle too little. In country communities, for instance, the starving or ill-treatment of animals can still continue for a lengthy period, so great is the fear that, if the facts transpire, the guilty will blame their neighbours for repeating them. "They will think *I* told you", plead the innocent and by this remark implicate themselves in the guilt.

Moreover their attitude is hopelessly entangled with the respect for property, "an Englishman's home is his castle", and other such sentiments. Thus I have heard a young collier, when told to stop beating his dog with an iron bar, reply: "It's mine; and I can do what I like with it". . . . In this outburst we can see very plainly how resentment of any interference emphasized in his mind the sanctity of private ownership. With men, too, who beat their wives, the act is often a challenge to the law to interfere; a black eye constitutes a badge and symbol of property, of personal subjection, similar to the branding mark on cattle.

At this point it will be seen that *minding one's own business* is neither so simple nor, in all cases, so virtuous as it sounds. The truth is, I think, that the people who advocate it seldom have any business to which to attend. On the grand and international scale the failure of the principle of non-interference is as marked as in the sphere of domestic affairs. If you mind your own business too thoroughly at the outset, you will have to spend the rest of your life attending to other people's. Thus the late ("Great") war was the fruit of a too austere minding of our own business, just as the war itself was an instance of unnecessary meddling. If, in July 1914, we had announced that England would defend France if she were attacked, there would have been no war . . . but we sat still and minded our own business—with the result that we now have a very reduced business to mind. The proper attitude to have adopted was, surely, either to have prevented the war or to have taken no part in it? But when the possibility of war approaches, people become hysterical: "You can't have the Germans at Calais", they used to protest. But the French were there all the time, and a much more formidable, because more intelligent and logical, foe they would constitute.

As a result of the war we created the League of Nations, an instrument (God bless it!) of interference, if ever there were one; but, frightened at our own common sense in this matter, we have failed to arm it, so that it has no power. It can threaten: but it cannot execute. We allow it to interfere by word, but not by deed. Yet, if we were logical in our attitude, there would be no police: for the police seldom mind their own business; and if they do, what an outcry follows! For while we arraign the meddlers and the busybodies, opinion is equally enraged should a passing policeman fail to interfere unarmed in some ferocious street-fight. And, still more hypocritical, what of the wretched man who, during a quiet walk by the seashore, observes that recurrent "bather in difficulties" (to walk there has become positively dangerous now for a man who knows how to swim), but continues to mind his own business, and walk on? What does not the coroner say of him subsequently; what curses and oaths dance round his photograph in the paper! But if an Englishman's home is so much his castle, then, logically, his little plot of ocean is equally his own.

And so it is, too, with writing. Therein, the man who minds his own business achieves nothing. What of the novelist with little curiosity as to human behaviour? He is a dull dog. Moreover, the writer who minds his own business is of no interest to posterity: only the gossip—but by this I do not intend to indicate the gossip-writer—holds its attention; the man who notices the tricks, virtues, failings and follies of his neighbours and notes them down, after the manner of John Aubrey, or Pepys, or Horace Walpole. Yet none of these were gossip-writers in the sense in which that term is used to-day. For, to be interesting, gossip must be written for one's self or one's friends; not for a public. . . . What a loss it would have been, you will agree, if Walpole, for example, had minded his own business! But then, the qualities, the behaviour and inclinations of his fellow-men, were *not* his *business*, while they are the business, emphatically, of Lords Castlerosse and Donegall.

ON
ENGLISH
FOOD

ENGLISH FOOD AS served in English hotels, especially
those that lie upon the course of a great motoring-road,
constitutes the most evil and deleterious thing which this
country has ever offered to the world—worse, even, than its
shoddiest Birmingham goods. So bad, so unpleasant, so un-
nourishing, so unsavoury, so dirtily served and disgustingly
cooked is it, that an hotel in this country which offers even
tolerable cooking obtains quite a reputation.

And here, before dealing with the main subject, it can
be said that English food does much to weaken the constitu-
tions of England's inhabitants. The great difference in the
influenza statistics between London and Paris, and in the
incidence of the disease, is said to be due to the fact that
every French workman demands a healthy and well-cooked
meal; a meal, indeed, of more than one or two courses. I have

myself heard two workmen at the top of ladders discussing food, and one shouting across to the other, "Hier j'ai mangé un ragoût tout à fait ravissant"—a conversation it would be hard to parallel in England. But it must not be thought that bad food is here a speciality or prerogative of any one class. It is a thing which, as a race, even if we do not like it, we must yet endure.

Let us picture the scene on arrival at a typical country hotel. Tired out and cold, you enter the inn. The landlord turns round and stares at you in an offensive and unfriendly way. You sit down at a table in a room which is, owing to the English mania for fresh air, either unhealthily cold or horribly hot. Its very smell of tainted old food and unwashed dishes is enough to discourage you. All round are tables at which people sit silently, remorsefully chewing with the ox-eyed solidity peculiar to our race when enjoying itself. Several belated flies and tardy bluebottles, elsewhere exterminated in this red-nosed season, linger comfortably on the window-panes, buzzing and sleepily crossing and recrossing their wings. On the table lie a few dirty plates, some forks and knives that have not been properly washed, a stained table-cloth, spotted glasses and a square bit of dry, uncompromising white bread, the sides of which have been for so long exposed to the air that the whole cube has become as monumental and hard as the Cenotaph.

After twenty minutes of anxious expectation, a tired and very stupid-looking waitress lounges up with a menu. Until this moment she has not so much as given you a glance, and now, while handing you the card, she studiously looks away, being concerned with the people round about. Recalling her attention, you explain that you will have either roast chicken or roast beef. Immediately she takes a pencil and gleefully strikes out these two items, indicating that they were finished an hour ago. All right, you will have boiled mutton, though you do not like it. That, she explains, in a moment of sudden and tremendous mirth of which you had not previously deemed her capable, is not like the roast chicken and beef: it is a mistake; it ought not to have been there at all! There never had been any, so it would not have been worth while to cross it out! Before, she had looked extremely gloomy, but now she is still so much amused at the way you have been caught, that she goes off to whisper the news to two other maids, who each drop a plate in their merriment. "Caught 'im this time; fair caught 'im!"

Making an effort at control, she returns to you. "No 'am." Mr Blither, the landlord, finished it just now while you were ordering that boiled mutton. (An inward shaking seizes her.) Eventually you obtain a cold slab of sea-green, iridescent and altogether tasteless beef. Then you have your choice of tinned pineapple cubes, or stewed prunes which look like last year's blackbeetles, or Canadian cheddar accompanied by soft cardboard biscuits (and biscuits, to be obtained in any grocer's shop, are rightly one of the glories of England); a tepid cup of coffee, which tastes as if, in the same way in which Cleopatra dissolved a pearl in her goblet of amber wine, the presiding waitress had dissolved in it an iron dumb-bell, concludes the meal. And the all-in charge for the meal, not excluding a glass of water flavoured with dishcloths and seaweed, is five and sixpence.

Dinner is a similar sad meal, except that the flies are by

now asleep, so that, instead of their aerial manœuvres we are privileged to watch the more terrestrial adventures of one or two cockroaches, which crawl slowly across the linoleum floor. In addition, a discouraging white slab of turbot with some rose-pink sauce is thrown in, for an extra one and six; and, if you are supremely fortunate, you may be rewarded with some trifle.

Trifle, alias tipsy-cake, whenever it is mentioned, deserves a paragraph by itself. The most ill-flavoured and excruciating of national dishes, it stands for all that has given English cooking its reputation. I have often wondered who thought of its nomenclature, of which each version is as unsuitable and incongruous as the other. Trifle, indeed—this solid, mountainous mass, compounded of many rich and disgusting materials (typical, too, in that it proves, as one had suspected in spite of contradiction, that English cooking is not, as so often argued, simple, but an exceedingly complicated art. To make all these horrible things requires infinite hours of labour). Its alternative name of tipsy-cake can only mean that anyone must be tipsy before daring to attempt it. I cannot do better than quote a description of it by a modern writer as "the symbol of England's gastronomic empery, a confection composed of bits of old sponge cake that had been out all night on bad port wine, and intensified by the presence of a pretentious custard which, with good fortune, might pass itself off as cream that had taken the wrong turning". This, however, is almost equalled by a recipe which has just been shown to me in a daily paper. It reads:

TRIFLE.—A simple and inexpensive trifle can be made from six sponge cakes, soaked in a little warm milk, fruit juice, or alternatively, warm milk flavoured with vanilla essence and shrouded in a pint of custard will serve from eight to twelve people.

Yet though a meal, of the kind that we have attempted to describe, inclines us to wish that Napoleon *had* in the end conquered England, so that French chefs could have reformed our food, it may be that we ought not to complain or to require any alteration. As a race we dislike foreigners; and certainly our food keeps foreigners away. Would it be unfair to attribute to our culinary reputation that freedom from invasion which we have for so long enjoyed? Can it be that our food, rather than our fleet, has defeated the foreign foe?

Further, it can with certainty be stated that our daily food formed the basis of our colonial empire: it is, whatever its faults, the food for a race of empire builders, who, unable to eat at home—and too obtuse to realize that, wherever their race goes, the same food will follow—perpetually roam the world in search of better fare and, as a fulfilment of some dream, breed in the distant corners of the earth innumerable flocks of mutton and herds of beef, destined one day to appear at such English tables as we have described.

ON
HEALTH

It is Professor Haldane, if I remember rightly, who, in a witty, informing and persuasive essay on health, confesses that he never sleeps with the windows open, at any rate during the winter, because, if ever by chance he does so, he immediately contracts a severe cold. Similarly, unless my memory is at fault, Mr Norman Douglas urges, with his accustomed force and originality, that with the bedroom window open it is impossible in the winter to obtain really *healthful* slumber, since during that season there occurs a deficiency of nitrogen, which man is then designed to supply for himself; whereas incoming air defeats all this skilfully contrived machinery.

Many people, I fancy, could draw for themselves similar conclusions, had they the necessary individual power of thinking: but the weight of inherited medical superstition is too heavy for them to shake off. To the open window, as to the cold bath, there attaches in many minds an almost moral compulsion, something inherited from their sturdy (why are they always "sturdy"?) Puritan forefathers which removes any possible dispute about them from the realm of health into that of ethics. . . . Yet, as a layman, I would counsel that inclination is the true guide: if you want a cold bath in hot weather, or a hot bath in cold weather, take it, and if you do not want one at all, refuse to be bullied into washing by nineteenth-century public opinion; for no one ever washed before the Napoleonic wars. (And here I may say, in order to avoid unnecessary correspondence on the subject, that I always sleep with my window open and am horribly, slavishly dependent on at least one hot bath a day.)

But let us enumerate other instances of inherited superstition. I remember the epoch when to eat more than *one* orange a day was considered a folly which must inevitably end in disaster, and when, too, pineapple was inveighed against as a prime cause of indigestion; yet now doctors have discovered that these fruits are two of the principal aids to health; and, further, that a pineapple will digest almost any substance, except iron bars, with which it is brought into contact. . . . Then, again, how many times are we not solemnly warned against "eating last thing at night"; a habit which, personally, I seem to find most conducive to health; that is to say, that if ever I wake up feeling particularly well, I remember that I went to bed the previous night rather late and directly after supper? . . . What, too, of the exercise habit, against which so many people dare not rebel; are frightened, even, to hear a word spoken in disparagement of it, as though this were blasphemy? Yet many of its addicts die over young, and most of them are under-equipped mentally. . . . In this instance, let me mention that a famous writer on economics, whose health, happily, is as good as, and whose brain is much better than, the average, told me once that all the exercise he found necessary to keep him fit was to have breakfast in bed; which entailed much more muscular effort than an early riser would be willing to admit. . . . And what, finally, of the old fever, which had to be starved? Now every fever, and especially typhoid, must be fed. In the old days, when typhoid patients were only allowed a little milk, hardly a single case recovered, while, on the contrary, now that they are crammed with food much better results are obtained.

It is well, then, for us to draw our own deductions concerning our health, at the same time keeping abreast of modern scientific opinion, but always remembering that we are the victims of sins of omission as much as of those of commission. We have been brought up to do things that were bad for us; and also not to do things that were good for us. . . . Consider the question of food: when, for instance, I was young, I entertained a great distaste for salt; and, because of this, was compelled to eat it on every possible occasion, until I had acquired the salt habit. Yet now, I believe, this condiment is acknowledged to be a powerfully toxic agent, only to be consumed with good subsequent effect in very hot countries, where the human body sweats so much that it constantly demands a fresh supply of salt. (Hence the importance of the salt-tax in India and the odium which pertained to it.) . . . As for food, the "healthy nursery food", on which the children of all parents who could afford it were formerly brought up, has now been abandoned, with a coincident decline in the infant mortality of such homes. The particular combination of milk pudding and stewed fruit, which used to be forced down infant throats at every meal, has been proved, I am told, to be virtually a poison.

As for adult foods, it is easy to form a mental list of things of which to be cautious. Tinned foods, of course—and, as for that, bottled ones—should be avoided like the plague— or, rather, like botulism: all, that is to say, except certain foods—sardines, olives or anchovies—which seem only to have been created in order to be tinned. Let your palate guide you. Potted meat is an almost ideal breeding ground for germs: and tea, except China tea, and especially as drunk in England, is a very potent poison, and when consumed over a long period will kill a man as surely as will white bread. The cakes of professional "confectioners", especially those leaden sponge cakes, which take forty-eight hours to digest, are nearly always, when not actually fatal, guaranteed to make you indisposed. And then, too, eschew all English "plain food"; by which we signify the most complicated and diabolical ingenuities, each one concocted of custard powder, jam with wooden splinters in it instead of pips or seed (once I ran a strawberry-jam seed into my finger and developed blood-poisoning), old bits of bread, nutmegs, cloves, choco- late, coffee-beans, tea-leaves, tinned pineapple, lemon-peel, suet, vanilla flavouring and sultanas, and, generally, anything else to which a cook with an emancipated mind can take a fancy, all combined together according to the recipe for the particular day: (and these materials, indeed, will furnish during the week an infinite variety of taste). . . . Food cooked in fat, again, is in no sense healthy, even though it constitutes our national medium of cooking; it should be varied, if expense allows it, from time to time with dishes cooked in olive oil.

Ponder, too, on early rising and early to bed: especially if you suffer from insomnia. Usually the later you—or is it only I?—go to bed, the better you sleep; and five hours of good sleep are of more value than seven of bad. And then, never *try* to sleep. People who sleep with difficulty insist on making an effort, spending agonized hours lying rigid and unrelaxed upon their beds, instead of reading until they have to hold out against sleep, and then allowing it to conquer them. . . . If you wake up in the night, do not wait miserably in the darkness, but read something amusing, light and yet sleep-making: (a new article by the Leavises, an article on them by H. R. Williamson, or anything else which, though funny, will, for the time, take you to another and non-existent world). . . . And how much sleep is really necessary? . . . Remember that night-porters, who only sleep a few short hours—and those during the day—seem to be a particularly healthy and happy race of men.

But the thing which, after poverty, causes the chief injury to health is to lose one's temper. I was born with a violent temper as my birthright; but though often, on moral grounds, exhorted to try to abate it, no one, when I was young, ever urged me to do so for the sake of my health. Yet had I been told what I subsequently found out for myself, that apart from the remorse or satisfaction which an outburst might entail, it would poison my blood for three whole days, making me feel wretchedly ill, I should have been then, as now, more wary.

ON
GARDENING

Landing suddenly in England, the first thing that would strike a stranger—as, indeed, a native returning after some months' absence—is the quantity of gardens; endless lines of small, ugly gardens, full of laurel, rambler roses, red geraniums, fox-terriers and virginia creeper. And every garden that is large enough enshrines a tennis court.

Evidently, one would say, the English are very fond of gardens, or, at any rate, of flowers, for the cultivation of which they evince a genuine talent. And, indeed, in our climate flowers, I suppose, are a necessity, for we are a practical people. The laurels, besides being ornamental, are planted in order to hide the next house from our angry individualist gaze, while the blossoms constitute a natural clock by which to read the seasons. The summer of 1934 will be for ever memorable because of its beauty; for its lovely, honey-coloured lawns and hard, baked earth as much as for the actual weather it brought with it; but as a rule these things are governed differently in England, so that it is difficult to tell, without the aid of flowers, which season at the moment may prevail? . . . You look out of the window, forgetting which month it is. Green grass, rain, grey sky and a few red berries tell you that it is winter; green grass, rain, grey sky and a daffodil proclaim the spring more clearly than any frisking lamb; green grass, rain, grey sky and an arch of Dorothy Perkins sufficiently indicate full summer; green grass, rain, grey sky and Michaelmas daisies signify autumn with all its mellow joys. (And, for this reason as much as for any better one, I object to horticultural novelties; dahlias which blossom in the spring and narcissi in the autumn; thus placing one wrong, if only for a moment, in our map of the year.)

In other climes there is not this particular need of flowers, neither to indicate the season nor as clumps of colour with which to comfort ourselves in a grey world. No; there must be, instead, rippling water to cool the air, and fluttering branches to shelter these waters; but light, except where it pierces the foliage to make most intricate patterns, and, above all, colour, must be excluded from these sighing and odorous paradises. The temperature, the feel of the air, inform us of the time of year and the masses of colour which a garden needs are there provided by the skies, azure with purest white.

For these reasons, I think no English garden is as lovely as a foreign one; the flowers, our flowers, are much more beautiful, incomparably more developed and understood. But flowers should be confined to a flower-garden, another conception altogether; whereas, to us, a garden has come to mean a flower-garden. . . . Yet I believe one secret of the most beautiful gardens in the world—such creations as Villa d'Este, Caprarola, and the Villa Lante in Italy, or the Generalife in Spain—is that they show as few flowers as possible; are, indeed, almost flowerless. Thus Marvell writes:

> . . . Annihilating all that's made
> To a green thought in a green shade.

Green is the clue to creating a garden, and not the possession of all the hues in the rainbow. We find, therefore, that the gardens we have mentioned depend for their beauty on tree and stone and water, and on the prospect which their terraces frame. And nowhere in them do you see a tennis-court, though you may see a bathing-pool, because these gardens are created for rest in cool surroundings, for idleness and sauntering and imaginative thought, for love and a sense of mystery, but never for a show of tinkling tea-cups and hoarse cries of "love all". Physical action is inimical to the green lethargy which we seek, and sweat is a mighty foe to peace.

Flowers, I have written, should be confined to a flower-garden: but, even there, they should form only the borders to long, rolling waves of sea-green cabbages and be interspersed with the purple pom-poms of the artichoke, with the knobs of onions and the scarlet flowers of the bean. They should be edged, too, with fruit trees. There should be myrtle, verbena and bay trees, and, above all, no attempt at a daring herbaceous border.

Moreover, the few flowers you have, should be very

specially chosen, selected for their beauty in dying and in death as much as for their beauty in the full unfolding of life; that is to say, one should be as much influenced by their habits of growth as by their blossom. For what is life, except a long process—varying individually, it is true, in its length— of death? And just as the Greeks used to maintain that no man could be happy or fortunate until he was dead, so can no flower be considered beautiful until it is fallen. Thus the Chinese, most wise and subtle race, allow the quality of beauty to no flower which does not maintain an exquisite form and colour even in its decay. So it will be seen that a fruit tree is more beautiful than, for example, a sweet-pea; for in the spring it is a little fragrant cloud anchored to the ground, in summer its branches are heavy with shapes carved of true jade, and in the autumn are weighed down with tinted and pleasant fruit. How dismal, as opposed to this excellence, enduring all the year, are the brown, tattered remnants of Michaelmas daisy and chrysanthemum!

And this, again, reminds me that flowers should be chosen for their scent, as much as for their form and colour; those with a noxious smell—as, for instance, the chrysanthemum— should at all costs be avoided; dank, damp, chrysanthemums whose petals give out no light but instead seem to withdraw it from the air around them: chrysanthemums, which, in their art-shades of mauve and terra-cotta and russet, smell of moths, camphor-balls and drowned sailors, or white chrysan- themums that appear to be covered with hair rather than petals, and to resemble Aberdeen-terriers and sealyhams rather than a flower; asters, too, with their quasi American- millionaire nomenclature and monstrous rosette-like flowers, have a slightly offensive odour, and so have many other autumnal favourites; while flowers which have no scent at all are best left for the enjoyment of those who lack this sense.

It is possible, of course, to offer further hints toward the beautifying of your garden. Do not, for example, hose the lawn; avoid the too-vivid green of the English sward, preferring the harvest-moon tintings of the campagna. Be careful, as well, not to rake out and root up all those charming weeds, the natural growth of which contrasts so interestingly with the formal air of garden flowers; and never scrape moss or lichen off stone surfaces. Rock-gardens, full of however many horrible little alpine flowers, should be discouraged: and above all, crazy paving, bird-baths and stone gnomes should be not only barred, but considered as unclean and taboo. Instead of shrubs, plant fruit trees.

Thus can gardens become again, not as we think of them now, those rectangles of ugly, dusty, scentless flowers, that border every arterial road, but havens of peace, small or large; for a couple of bay trees, a vine and a basin of water will suffice to create a garden, even in the neighbourhood of an arterial road.

ON
CUT
FLOWERS

IN THE LAST few pages I have advocated that flowers should only be permitted to grow in special enclosures, and should not form any portion of the garden proper. But, though this theory may be debatable, there can be no doubt, I think, that from a purely esthetic point of view they are unsuitable to a house; should be shut resolutely outside it.

Who started the fashion? . . . It would be idle to pretend that the English instigated it. They were never, so far as I am aware, addicted to wreaths, like the inhabitants of Tahiti and Hawaii; and, at a date when the Romans feasted regularly under showers of rose petals and the Hindus were already lassoing their friends with ropes of flowers as a compliment, the nearest we could approach in that direction was to stain our bodies with woad, a dye derived from a plant (was it, I have often wondered, the aspidistra; is our devotion to it so ancient a tradition?) . . . There is no evidence, even, that we are particularly fond of flowers, unless the indiscriminate pillaging of woods represents a sublimated passion for them; though to me it seems to be much more orgiastic, much more reminiscent of the action of that notorious French marquis who spent his latter days tearing up roses and throwing their petals down the drain. Yet it is still more probable that this wholesale spoliation of wood and meadow is due in part to our patriotism, to the national superstition that "there are no wild flowers in the world like there are in England"; a superstition perhaps common to every country, but certainly without foundation where our land is concerned, for—to name but a few countries at random—Italy, Spain, Portugal, Switzerland, Morocco and Greece are all infinitely richer in wild flowers, both in their variety and quantity, and boast, moreover, two seasons for them—spring and autumn—to our one.

Historically, too, it is evident that the domestic arrangements and atmosphere, mental as much as physical, of baronial dwellings would never have allowed flowers to exist therein for more than half a minute; though it is true, on the other hand, that the red-faced, lusty holly, in a sense a form of floral ornament, did preside over the wassailing activities of our ancestors. But flowers were then confined to the borders of vegetable gardens and to the altars of churches; for everywhere they have always formed part of religious cere-monial, could have been seen decorating the temples of Isis and the sacred pyramids of the Aztecs, just as to-day they scent the temples of Buddha and the churches of Christ. Yet even in these holy places their arrangement should be formal; never "artistic", as it was, I noticed, the last time I visited Canterbury Cathedral, where art-shade flowers lolled in inappropriate places out of chased copper vases. . . . Notwithstanding, even when arranged after this fashion, they looked better than they would have looked in a house.

Who, then, was the first to drag these unfortunate captives within secular doors? . . . The responsibility must rest, I fear, upon oriental nations, upon China and Japan. It is that one flower, so cunningly arranged by slim-fingered oriental hands, which has caused all the mischief, multiplying itself within our gates—after the philoprogenitive manner of that first pair of rabbits taken to Australia—until now no drawing-room or parlour of the Occident is free of the pest. And most probably this one little flower was a chrysanthemum; that wild, woolly creature to which they have remained so faithful.

It is likely, I think, that—with the modern vogue for simplicity, for aluminium furniture and glass tables, and for rooms that most resemble a dentist's dream of heaven—the single-flower idea may return triumphantly to fashion. But if it does, this is the more to be deplored; for, if you must have flowers in the house, let them be as many as possible and as strongly scented. And there is the danger, too, that this same vogue for simplicity may end in the complete extermination of wild flowers in England; for primroses and bluebells seem, to the owners of these rooms, not altogether out of keeping with steely walls. This opinion will add a new cohort to those already pledged to their destruction, since lovers of catch-fool oak beams, thatched roofs and black-wood furniture, have long massed their armies against anemone and cowslip, fritillary and wild lily. And the richer these lovers of things simple, the more devoted are they to them, so that to-day there exist certain rich people who, it is said, spend more money growing winter wild flowers, in special hot-houses, for the decoration of their parties, than it would take to furnish whole hills of exotics, and each bit of withered meadowsweet and faded wild parsley on their table costs as much as a thousand velvet-eyed, man-eating orchids from South America. . . . Still, this is merely a harmless, foolish waste of money, which does not lead to the extermination of these wild flowers, as does their indiscriminate massacre by the rich week-end cottagers of Sussex and Surrey, who wish to squeeze their delicate spoils as tightly as possible into pieces of peasant pottery and art crocks made for them by guilds of well-educated spinsters, dressed in Hungarian and Croatian costumes. And these poor, wilting blossoms look so disconsolate in the house; are, moreover, completely without effect. It is not more cruel, more silly, even, to keep wild animals behind bars and birds in cages.

The real cottage-dweller, it will be noted, prefers plants to cut flowers, encourages one or two geraniums to hold their knotted or silky faces against the tightly closed old panes; and the slum-dweller, too, of the cities prefers to see things grow rather than wither. Mr George Beaton, in his first novel, *Jack Robinson*—a remarkable achievement, incidentally—has the following fine description of street singers drawing people to hear them: "Then to the dusty windows, hung with delicate lace curtains and ornamented each in the centre with one of those smooth-leaved immemorial ferns that seem to be the repositories of the dead souls of the race, the vessels into which like Daphne into her laurel they have transmigrated

196

to find peace and congenial form at last, would collect one by one some vague lifeless faces, either reduced by long clock-like activities to a meagre nucleus or else padded out by their inanity with pasty fat". Certainly the "immemorial ferns" figure in every window: equivalent to the scratchy, dusty-fingered palms that formerly used to figure in the mansions of the rich.

As for these, the 'seventies and 'eighties of the last century were, in every sense, the palmy days. Queen Alexandra—then Princess of Wales—introduced, it is said, the fashion from Marlborough House, and it spread very rapidly round London. But even so, flowers were still rather scarce; while heavy-smelling blossoms, tuberoses, gardenias and stephanotis, were indubitably considered rather "fast" until much more recently; for Du Maurier's drawings, which depict so accurately the strange social life of the 'eighties, show us but few vases. Instead, their stiff scenes of gallantry are staged among palm-trees under which ladies in bustles recline upon sofas or sit, willowing, on settees, while moustached grandees stand above them, drawling and stroking their moustaches. . . .

ON THE JOYS
OF A
TELEPHONE
EXCHANGE,
AND HOW TO
DEPICT THEM

O FTEN WHEN, TRYING to obtain a number, I hear instead a conversation in progress at the telephone exchange, I try to surmise what frolicsome scene is staged within those mysterious walls: for though one hears so much, one sees so little! What are they like, these goddesses, and what palace shelters them? How would you, reader, picture a telephone exchange; in the style of what artist summon it up?

Italian primitive masters, I apprehend, would not be able to render the essential robustness, as I see it, of the scene, neither would Van Eyck, nor those Flemish artists who came immediately after him. Titian and Tintoretto would have likewise failed, and Watteau would have found but little inspiration in portraying those whom he could not refine into the velvet-coated denizens of mysterious woods; for Ingres, again, the work would have been insufficiently classic. No impressionist, either, would be suitable for translating into terms of paint these flamboyant halls; though Rubens, on the other hand, might well have given us a picture of the vigorous life within them, and so might Franz Hals; much, also, is to be said for the brush of Alessandro Magnasco, who revelled in depicting Witches' Sabbaths and the meetings of Quakers in otherwise deserted and ruined kitchens. Devils, too, he loved to paint, at play in the refectories of old, ruined monasteries and many other effects of grandeur and inspissated gloom. But, of all the artists, Goya would have made most use of the delicious opportunities which the scene would have afforded him, and even as I wait, hopeless and bored, hanging on to the telephone, I try to imagine how this *capriccio* would have materialized. What satyric and gloomy fervour would have infused it! Rowlandson, again, with his mordant pen, would have done justice to the subject, and Daumier, with his swift comprehension of human fallibility and make-believe, would have taken a certain pleasure in its rendering.

Certainly, if I were a modern painter, instead of writer, I would choose to depict scenes (and curious, abstract conversation-pieces they would make) in the interiors of telephone-exchanges, rather than any other sketches of contemporary life; for there is something romantic about them, and about the secluded vestals who dwell within them, yet whom one never sees. At times, indeed, they seem like the veiled women who used to inhabit the harems of Turkey. Nevertheless, if asked to turn my brush to this purpose, I should, rather, seek to depict them as rosy, robust and good-humoured, touching the wrong switches out of *joie de vivre*, just for the sheer fun of the thing, while they set the room shaking with full-blooded Flemish laughter. In these sad times elsewhere there can be no offices where such mirth is invariable, where never a dull moment ushers itself in. . . . It may, of course, be argued that the automatic telephone has a little curbed them, curtailed their opportunities, but, even with these disadvantages, endless openings still remain, not only for jollity, but, too, for social intercourse. And how high, how sustained, how informed, are the fragments of conversation we are privileged to hear, and, though in those long talks that intervene while we are trying to get a number, hats, cosmetics, dress and new plays—musical comedy rather than Shakespearean drama—seem as subjects to prevail, yet where else in London would you find conversation, not only of this quality, but of this length?

Moreover though its matter may not be highbrow, it would be wrong to presume that, in order to enjoy this kind of life, no study has been necessary. It may, for all we know, be no easy matter to get five people speaking on the same line. A beginner, perhaps, can only score two or three. Further to produce those sudden screams and roarings, those howlings, as of lost and disembodied spirits, floating and quarrelling in the nethermost regions, is probably in itself no easy matter. Then, too, the joy of inventing new sounds ranks high; a list issued a little time ago described what various sounds signify, such as: "When the called subscriber is being rung, a low-pitched 'burr-burr—burr-burr' (the ringing tone) will be heard in the receiver"; and again, "If you hear a high-pitched 'buzz-buzz—buzz-buzz' (the engaged tone) it indicates that the number dialled or the connecting apparatus is engaged".

But what, for instance, can that sound of galloping horses portend; what that neighing which later accompanies it? What is the meaning, moreover, of that sudden ear-splitting shriek, or, as it seems, of those cats singing in endless nights?

What telephonic sounds or what questions, I wonder, are, from a telephone-exchange point of view, most successful? Let us offer a hint or two: to me nothing is more irritating than, when I have long been demanding a number, to be asked at last by the exchange, "What is *your* number, please?" Because in the course of Nature I have known this many years. Only slightly less exasperating is the habit of waiting till five minutes after you have dialled a number, and then inquiring of you what number you want; for at that stage of impatience it is usually impossible to remember.

I imagine, too, that a lot of fun is to be obtained out of inventing new numbers, and substituting them for the old. The subscriber asks mildly for a number which has long remained in his memory—which, indeed, he has called every day. A ten-minutes hold up ensues, and then an angry voice demands, "What number are you calling, please?" The subscriber repeats it and is then told, "The-number-has-been-changed-to-Blank-double-O-double-O". But the next day the number will be back again. . . . There is also the question of the telephone voice. No one who does not habitually pronounce "five" as "faive" is ever likely to obtain a number of any sort, except through the dial system.

What remedies are there, you will ask? None perhaps; but I can offer one tip. If you are in a hurry it is often a help to call the operator and say gently, "I have not got much time;

you can give me the wrong number later on; but would you mind giving me the right number now?"

Sometimes, again, I see these girls, not as Flemish boors or Dutch burgesses, but as goddesses who sit secure and immune from disaster, presiding over the destinies of mankind: impersonal and abstract deities, now preventing one from obtaining all-important news, here frustrating a valuable business deal, there causing an engagement to be broken off, or even (by making it impossible—or as for that, possible— to call a doctor) a death. . . . No idea of their deep unpopularity affects them, and I shall never forget the surprise of one of them when, on a certain day, in a frenzy after an hour or two of abortive effort to get into communication with my friends, I rang her up and asked her if she realized that the people who would suffer first in a revolution were not the rich, but the telephone girls; that on them the popular rage would be focused? "Do you really think so?" she asked, in a frightened voice. But just as, before the French Revolution, the aristocrats were dancing, we are told, on the edge of the abyss; just as the first officers who went out to the war took their evening clothes with them; just as the Tsar and Tsarina were still occupied in their peculiarly futile little religious observances the very day before they were deposed, so, even as I write, that hearty and Gargantuan laughter still reaches me over the telephone, rolling in great gusts through the receiver. . . . What jests and what frolics are in the air!

WORDS
AND
THEIR
MEANING

ON
A
COMMON
COLD

COMMON, INDEED!

A cold may be common: but it should not for that reason be despised. Many common things partake of the nature of a miracle; and a cold is protean, amazing in its diversity. What an inventive germ must lurk behind its malevolent manœuvres, behind these sneezings and coughings and red noses, these pains in the teeth and in the roots of the hair, these sore eyes and achings in the limbs, this difficult breathing, these voices, husky and grating, or speaking out of hearing somewhere, as it seems, in another dimension, from mouths that open and shut to no accompanying sound.

Common, indeed! Why, a common cold alters the very existence of him who suffers from it; not only, I mean, his mode of life but also the appearance and feeling of it, so that passing events, the very view from the window, are now seen by eyes that have not looked upon such things before. Pathos, together with a slightly hysterical humour, suddenly invade every accustomed act of our everyday existence. The very pleasures of life are transmuted as at the touch of a witch's finger: cigarettes become at the best tasteless, at the worst a torture of burning brown paper, emitting suffocating fumes; food holds no interest for us, and our animal appetites, if we are wise, become entirely centred on hot-water bottles and hot punch. . . . Oh! the joy of those cloves and that lemon infusing the steaming glass, and of the steam itself, which, so pungent and fragrant is it, can, even now, just faintly titillate the sense of smell. Boredom, again, holds no terror for him who now only wishes to lie down, or better still, rest in bed, bookless and untalkative.

But most of all does the *common cold* alter the spirit, the very nature of the person it attacks. Those who have many friends are no longer eager to see them; while, on the other hand, the friendless, and even the unfriendly, at once become genial. If in dead of winter your telephone bell rings to ask whether Mr Snooks, whom you have never liked and have hardly ever met, and who, you are aware, harbours for yourself a feeling of very acute, though, as you are inclined to think, unjustifiable hostility, may come to see you by appointment, suspect the common cold! I even remember an old and distant cousin of mine, who in all her life never troubled herself at all about my existence, calling on me as she was driving down to Ascot Races. Why had she thought of me, I wondered; no race-meeting could remind anyone of *me*, for never have I attended such a function? For a moment, until I saw that black-velvet nose, I was at a loss; but then I at once realized that this extraordinary feature really constituted but one more manifestation of microbic malevolence.

Other persons, again, usually of a lonely temperament, become of a sudden gregarious and pleasure-loving, afflicted with the desire to visit theatres, lectures and concert-halls, where for a brief hour or two they may splutter and sneeze to their hearts' content. But these people you can distinguish at a first glance, by a certain look of self-importance, an air, too, of subtle triumph, which marks them off from the healthy of their tribe. Even those who, when well, present a forlorn and meagre appearance are invested with a certain strange radiance.

In addition, it must be borne in mind that persons undoubtedly exist to whom a cold is an obvious, a positive pleasure. One or two of them occur in every community, however small, and in a household they are apt to form a reservoir of germs, which though dormant may at any moment enter upon hostile activities. Such persons you should compel to be inoculated, not because of any particular belief in the virtue of this operation, but because the pain of it serves as a powerful deterrent, and acts as a valuable moral lesson; they will be more careful another time, will think twice before attempting to launch a new series of germs. After this manner inoculation, however inefficacious in itself, forms a useful weapon in the armoury of hygiene to-day.

Of trades, those most addicted to colds as a habit are hairdressers and waiters, to both of whom their work affords various and splendid opportunities of spreading infection. Clergymen, I must say, run them pretty close—so that most country churches are, as it were, to be considered as refrigerators, in which germs can be preserved fresh and healthy during the week, until next Sunday the time comes for them to renew their attack. And next after them, in the strange and awful order of precedence dictated by bacillic virulence, follow the lady-novelists. Oh, those pitifully blurred consonants that fall from eminent mouths at the P.E.N. Club meetings! But, above all, if you wish to avoid catching a cold, never enter an English chemist's shop: for these shrines are centres of pilgrimage to the infectious, and he who is gifted with vision can see, when he stares into its windows, whole cohorts of germs dancing round the huge bottles filled with coloured water, and pressing their blue and eager noses against the glass panes in their hurry to be out and at him. Doctors, again, carry the infection into your own house; and, before summoning a general practitioner to the aid of any member of your household, it is well to read the passage in Marcel Proust, wherein a doctor is described in the act of opening his black bag, which property the author compares to the bag of Aeolus, for as he opens it he releases all the battalions of bacilli, which are to be seen whirling out of it, rejoicing to escape from their captivity.

A common cold! Why, even the history of this germ is interesting enough to rescue it from the possibility of any appropriateness in the application of such a term. Indeed it boasts a descent of incomparable length. Long, long ago a horrible and sudden plague afflicted mankind, then in an early stage of development, decimating the race, leaving only here a man, there a woman, who was able to resist its ravages. So numerous were the corpses of even the chieftains, that the survivors could not dig barrows quick enough to bury them;

but from the survivors, whose children, again, were attacked, though somewhat less savagely, by the children of these same germs, are we descended; and from the germs, too, are descended those which to-day are causing me—and perhaps you—such hideous discomfort. A long and evenly balanced battle through the ages, at the end of each era the weapons of the opponents have varied. In the Elizabethan Age, poetry itself entered into this wintry warfare; for "Roosemary", we read, "is good for palses and for cowghs and good agaynst colde and for the fallynge syckenes. Rooses be a cordyall and doeth comforte the herte and the brayne." Later, no doubt, the patient was bled, as for every other disease; and now, in this age of steel, stacks of dead germs are pumped into our arm to feed, so the theory goes, an invisible but beneficent host which inhabits our body. All these remedies, I suspect, are possessed of an equal value.

And the cold, too, has played a noble part in world events; fighting, as you might have presumed, for ever on the side of England, its favourite habitat; since our climate is the best, most loyal, and most abiding ally which this affliction possesses. Thus the Emperor Napoleon typifies, I suppose, the arch-enemy of England: he was defeated finally and for ever at Waterloo, by a common cold. Not the Duke of Wellington was his conqueror, neither Blucher—but this despised and altogether underrated bacillus. The Kaiser, a biographer tells us, on being informed by his doctor that he was suffering from a "little cold", replied: "It is a great cold. Nothing about me is little." Herr Hitler, though we hope no enemy, is another very notorious sufferer. (His cold at the time of the proposed visit of the English Secretary for Foreign Affairs was a much more historic one than the Kaiser's. Further, he has, several times since then, suffered from hoarseness.) . . . Caesar's troops must have sneezed their souls out. And, in addition, the common cold has often helped-on English arms by knocking out one of our own generals at a critical moment, rendering him unable to speak the fatal word of command, which would have ended in the massacre of our poor troops. . . . *Common*, indeed, with such a history!

ON
WORDS
AND
THEIR
MEANING

THE FRENCH ARE in many respects the most thrifty and prudent people in Europe. Something of Chinese wisdom and providence seems to attend their management of both private and public affairs. They are *so* sensible; they can, on the one hand, run their trains punctually, without the necessity of having a frowning and menacing dictator to preside over them, as in some Latin countries; nor, on the other hand, do their Governments find it necessary to torture or banish all those of whom they disapprove. Their judgment in public affairs is, at the same time, determined and defined; they act with courage and swiftness. Thus when Mr W. R. Hearst, a visiting American newspaper-baron, offends them, they ask him to leave the country: a thing we should never dare perform in England. Again, when they can afford to pay America no longer, owing to the increase in the price of gold, they do not argue for months, or, it may be, years, before making a decision; nor do they indulge, even, in the luxury of governess-like, it-hurts-me-more-than-it-hurts-you notes; they simply refuse to pay. What is more, the result of their actions in no way injures them; on the contrary they gain still further the respect of the more barbarous nations and individuals with whom they are forced to deal.

And one aspect of—or perhaps one reason for—their refined civilization is the manner in which they use their language, with its eloquent, if thin, vocabulary. Certainly it is incapable of the richness to which ours is heir. Nevertheless, the French mean, to a much greater extent than we do, what they say. If they speak of a great poet or painter, they *mean* a great poet or painter: not a mediocre versifier or a sugary, incompetent portraitist, as these terms so commonly denote in England.

Similarly if, for instance, we take French journalism, we shall find many neat and amusing examples of the precise and scrupulous selection of words which they affect; and of their thrift, too, in this respect. For they assign to each word its exact value; a word is allowed to parade itself, neither at more, nor less, than its proper worth; and this leads to a heightening of meaning and an intensification of personality.

Thus, recently the *Matin* reported three police-court cases. In the first of these a young Armenian had shot and wounded his sister. Giving an account of this affair, in reality one of little consequence, the journal announced that "the police asked themselves the reason for this gesture".

In the second a workman threw vitriol at four persons, but fortunately missed his targets. This constituted an incident of greater importance; no longer did the police "ask *themselves*" a question; nor was this ill-intentioned act allowed to masquerade as a gesture. No! this time they asked—presumably of the world in general—what was "the reason of this *demonstration*".

Finally, third instance, a man was discovered in a state of alcoholic exaltation in the Place de la Nation. On this occasion the Parisian police, courteous as ever, "invited him to calm himself". Alas for Bacchic wisdom! The invitation—never, alas, destined to be repeated, which they had, after their fashion, so politely extended—was refused by him. Their next invitation to the errant one proved to be that he should accompany them to the police-station.

I fear that in English newspaper-reports of such police-court incidents we should find but few examples of this scrupulous explanation and description. Probably each would have been described as a "police-court drama".

Foremost amongst the dangers to which cheap literature and sensational journalism expose us is this threat to our rich, full-blooded language. True to our national character, we allow them every day to throw away, to squander without thought of the morrow, the inherited riches of our speech; riches accumulated during centuries of poetic exploration.

Sometimes, under these unfortunate influences, words are drained of their vitality, become pale and anaemic; sometimes, on the contrary, inflated and unnatural. Such words as "wonderful" and "magic" no longer bear any significance at all, while often the meaning becomes stunted, dwarfed and crippled; as in the word "tragedy". In the past this term was applied to the work of the Greek dramatists, or to such stories as those of *Othello* and *Macbeth*; but now it is used indiscriminately of any death as the result of a common orgy (in itself a devitalized word), of any over-indulgence in narcotics, or of any squalid murder in which neither victim nor murderer has any hint of greatness; in which neither could ever be hunted by the Furies. The difference, again, is the difference between Mycene and a third-rate—or, as for that, first-rate—night-club; between the bee-loud tomb of Agamemnon and the grave of a rich manufacturer in Aberdeen or Sheffield.

Then there is the word "romance"; originally applied to the deeds of chivalry and of the high love that inspired them; later used to describe *Romeo and Juliet* and the story of Perdita. What strings of poetic memory formerly vibrated at the very mention of this word, now used to designate any trivial coincidence—the marriage, let us say, of two people who met for the first time through a collision of their standardized motor-cars—or the meanest and most sordid of vulgar divorce-court episodes!

Countless other words are equally abused. The word "beauty" stands now, at the best, for prettiness—and often for ugliness itself. The word "literature", again, is applied to the accumulated rubbish sold on railway bookstalls.

The result of this is not only the debauching of our language, but the debasement of our values in life, so that people in general have no longer any knowledge where they stand. Mr Noel ("Poor-Little-Rich-Girl") Coward, for example—a competent but incomparably boring writer of musical comedies and revues—became a playwright, poet and musician (Shakespeare and Beethoven must make way for him when the time comes); whilst the lady who so adequately stages his work becomes a "great theatrical artist". Actually Mr Coward has less musical talent than the late Mr Paul Rubens, whose name is now no longer remembered; less talent for lyrics than the late Mr Adrian Ross; less talent as playwright than the late Henry Arthur Jones. We must not allow ourselves to be blinded by the fact that he does three things rather badly, instead of one rather well. Equally, Mr ("If-Winter-Comes") Hutchinson is a "great" writer: while somebody else is a "great" golfer or "great" spillikin player. Such are the values of the newspaper words of to-day. And, of course, nearly every actor and actress is a "great" actor and "great" actress.

To prescribe the exact remedy for this state of affairs is difficult. I suppose a constant reading of the classics would enlighten anyone as to the comparative merits of various writers. As for the stage, perhaps the best course is to read Shakespeare, and then if you are fortunate enough to find a play of his running at one of our West End theatres, to see it acted. Nobody, I think, can accuse the work of Shakespeare of being better off, than on, the stage. The reason that we prefer to read his lines is, then, because they are so often badly acted and spoken. On the other hand, to see a performance at the "Old Vic" or "Sadler's Wells" is always a pleasure; for there we find no pretence; there, at least, words still have their meaning.

ON THE
BELITTLEMENT
OF THE
GREAT

THOUGH THE MAJORITY of fashions scarcely outlives the span of a year or two at the most, yet at least one still prevails, and continues to give signs of growth, which started fifteen years ago or more: the vogue for belittling the dead— that is to say, the dead who, either through their own abilities or by virtue of heredity, occupied great positions of trust, respect and responsibility, in their lifetimes. Dig up their faults, show up their weaknesses, rootle about in the dust of ages for those things they hoped forgotten; at the best, let them appear to us, in our plus-fours, the funny old pieces of upholstery that they were, with their wigs and velvets! This seems to be the attitude of the writer of to-day toward the past. . . . And, in a sense, it is easy to understand, being the result in part of that very justifiable disrepute which the still living generals and statesmen have earned for themselves by their repeated and signal failures. Since the laws of libel compel the author to suppress the truth about the failures and oddities of the living, instead he exaggerates or invents those of the celebrated dead.

The methods of posthumous belittlement are numerous and diverse. One of the most successful, however, is the adoption of a spurious familiarity, by which the writer puts himself, and every reader, on Christian-names terms with the subject of his book. It is a kind of *"tutoyer"*-ing through the centuries, the style of the gossip-writer applied to history. Just in the same way as in the Villa of the Knights of Malta, outside Rome, the architect has arranged for visitors peeping through the keyhole of the front door to obtain a magnificent yet intimate view of the dome of St Peter's, so these modern historian-biographers only require the reader to look through the keyholes with which they provide him, to obtain an intimate view of the love affairs of King Henry VIII, the writhings of King Louis XIV in the grip of that singular indigestion to which he was victim all his adult life, or the *accouchement* of Queen Victoria. King Henry, it goes without saying, is always referred to as "Hal", the Roi Soleil as "Lulu", the Queen as "Vicky". Indeed, this type of writer deserves the classic rebuke which I once heard delivered by a worldly old lady to a young man inclined to this same sort of misleading reference: "Mr Merely, how different we are in our outlook. I notice you always address the Duchess of St Dodo as 'Duchess', but refer to her in her absence as 'Muriel'; whereas I always call her 'Muriel' to her face, but, when she is not there, refer to her in front of other people as 'the Duchess of St Dodo'."

In this particularly intimate writing, as in so many other directions, America originally gave us the lead; but only too readily have we followed it. Almost the worst instance is the book of an American author, an incredibly bad book which purported to be a life of that genius, the first Duke of Marlborough, and in which that great soldier and statesman was referred to throughout as "Jack", as though he were a boon companion whom the author had met every night in a speakeasy. Indeed, the Duke of Marlborough seems to be a favourite for such treatment (which doubtless was one reason for Mr Churchill's decision to write a life of his ancestor and show that interest could be maintained by the inherent wonder of the life and vigour of the writing, without any such artificial aids), for pages can be taken up entirely with his supposedly treacherous character. And even if some of the alleged facts were true, what do they amount to, and who cares? It has been charged against him sometimes, for example, that he accepted money from King Louis XIV, receiving it as a bribe to allow himself to be defeated, and then, instead, defeated the French King. . . . And what action, let me ask, could be more patriotic: a double defeat inflicted on a rival and hostile power in the realms of both finance and battle; much more patriotic than rout in battle alone? Only the ghost of King Louis XIV ("Old Loo") has the right to complain.

To return, though, to belittling by means of names, it is one thing for Ben Jonson to refer to "Will Shakespeare" and quite another for, let us say, Miss Clemence Dane to do so (for some reason "Ben", though familiar, is a necessary distinction). And what of "Kit" Marlowe? Then, again, there are those who love to refer to Chaucer as "old Dan", under the delusion that "Dan" was his Christian name, instead of being a misreading of "Dom:", which probably indicated his position as a great man at Court. Indeed, this method is so popular, in the writing of both biography and romance, that even the title of a book must hint at it. . . . Thus we are given, as a robust belittlement of Queen Elizabeth, the title "The Tudor Wench", although, on the contrary, other knowing writers have recently insisted that the poor Queen was in reality, all the time, a man dressed up as a woman!

Biography is, admittedly, a difficult medium, and one which many, too many, persons—some with misused ability, and some without any qualification at all—attempt. When writing a life, the author must remember continually that it is the subject of his book, not its author, which will make that book interesting. Biography, except autobiography, should never be selected as a means of self-revelation and interpretation; for no sensible reader wants a personal or modish view of a great man. Who wants to know Mr Snook's view, fashionable author though he be, of Dante, or Mr Sydney Solomon's of Nelson? What, even (though the book was not by any means his worst), can be the interest of Mr Philip Guedalla's opinion of the Duke of Wellington; though, as I have written elsewhere, I can quite conceive that the Iron Duke's opinion of Mr Guedalla (to my mind, a lesser man) would be, were it obtainable, concise, instructive and epigrammatic? How *dare* they do it?

But one sin in which all modern biographies, even the more competent ones (such as those of Messrs Guedalla and Harold Nicolson), indulge, is that of oblique reference. This was initiated—together, indeed, with the rest of modern biography—by Lytton Strachey. In his essay upon Gordon in *Eminent Victorians* that delightful author suddenly switches off on to Rimbaud's journal, the effect being one of surprise justified; for though some persons hint that the document is a forgery, the quotation which follows does, at least, contain reference to the General. But in the end, and in the hands of lesser writers, the use of this method becomes horribly tedious; as tedious as *Romola* with its dovetailed "Who's Who" of contemporary Florentine celebrities. The recipe, as now practised, is roughly this: write a biography of Marie Antoinette and give a description of her at the age of ten; then let it read, "But four hundred miles away, in a little house outside Paris, in very different circumstances, the infant Robespierre is on hands and knees, cutting off the heads of dolls with a rusty knife; and further off still, in an old island in the Mediterranean, in Corsica itself, a mother is crooning to a little son; a mother who is afterwards to be known to all the world as 'Madame Mère'!" . . . Let Parliament decree a close season of ten years for the ghosts of the great.

ADULT
FRANCHISE
FOR   *The Sad Case of the Pig*
DOMESTIC
ANIMALS

IT IS QUITE time that certain wrongs to the animal world
were remedied. The English, a race essentially of animal-lovers
(for, though they kill more members of the animal and bird
worlds than any other nation, they are surely—except in the
case of the fox, the badger and the stag—kind to them until
the tocsin sounds for their official massacre), yet display, in
the abusive or playful phrases that roll off their rather un-
practised tongues, the most profound misunderstanding of the
various, even dumber, tribes that inhabit the English and
foreign countrysides.

The horse, by far the most imbecile of God's creatures,
and one which, apart from its brutal bad temper, stupidity,
and annoying habit of holding up street traffic, contrives to
give any sensitive person brought into close contact with it
an attack of hay-fever, is, of course, our acknowledged pet;

with the dog, so well described recently as "dirty and immoral", ranking a good second.

I do not object to such favouritism, such horrid injustice, when it errs, as in these two instances, on the side of kindness; but that the goose, which, as every motorist recognizes, is the only intelligent biped on the road, should be cruelly libelled, grieves me. "You silly goose", indeed! The goose is wise, decent and economical in its private life, and has a beauty of speech rare in the animal world. "You silly chicken" would be a much more apt description of a pedestrian who refuses to clear out of the way.

Who again has given the donkey, a favourite animal with painters of all schools, and an animal full of spirit and intelligence, its bad name? And then there is that pathetic poor relation of ours, the monkey, in whose behaviour—inquisitive, inventive, playful and humorous—we can trace every virtue, as well as every vice, of the human being. The monkey, it seems, is blamed for catching fleas; yet surely it is to the credit of our little cousin that he should strive after this almost unattainable and very clean dexterity?

But, rather than for all these, would I put in a plea on behalf of the cleanly and almost puritanical pig. A more moral, more thrifty animal has seldom existed. The tragedy of the pig-world lies in the fact that this creature is ever carefully and slowly saving up for a winter that never comes. Originally intended for hibernation, like a thrifty housewife, she accumulates her winter stores—only inside herself rather than within the household cupboard. Thus, as some would hint, after the fashion of a good Christian, her whole earthly life is regulated with a view to a future state which never comes to pass. Nevertheless, a devoted wife, a good mother, the pig is possessed of every peasant virtue, in addition to every instinct that makes the capitalist so beloved in modern Europe. Yet even in France, a thrifty country, the word *cochon* carries an unpleasant significance. Why, then, in the name of justice, should "pig" be a term of reproach, when the camel, notoriously self-indulgent, and equipped for gluttony with seven stomachs instead of one, is allowed to move amongst us free and uncensured?

Moreover, if the names of animals are thus to be taken in vain, why also are they not sometimes used as terms of commendation? Why, for example, do we not say, when we wonder at some mother's devotion, that she is "a perfect kangaroo of a mother"? Has there ever been a better parent than a kangaroo, with all the ingenious fool-proof equipment for carrying her children; a machinery evolved, no doubt, from hundreds of thousands of years of acute maternal love and anxiety?

Finally, as a fervent democrat, I should like to advocate the granting of adult franchise to domestic animals. And of all these fine beasts, the backbone of this great country, not least of them could the pig be trusted to register an intelligent and cautious vote. . . . And I think that I, for one, know which statesman would have the support of the porcine tribe, loyal, affectionate, ever willing to return devotion.

ON
FOGS

THE SOUND OF the word "London" is magnificent; no better name could be found for a great city. Its simple, re-iterative syllables evoke all the thunder of modern traffic, and there pertains to it a ponderous and exquisite dignity. Nevertheless, to most foreigners the word "London" is merely synonymous with "fog": a fact about which is something peculiarly appropriate, for, after all, the power of Britain blossomed from her coal, and fog is the aerial manifestation of this force. To them England lies in a murky mist, floats on the ocean, a heavy and impenetrable cloud of smoke. Foreign eyes can hardly pierce it, but, if they do, they find a strange country, peopled by inhabitants who seem as different from the Europeans as are the Japanese from other Asiatics. Something romantic always clings to islands in the minds of continental peoples, and from the time of

Caesar to that of Casanova there is continual comment on the strangeness of the life to be found here. And just as the Japanese are inevitably pictured under the snowy cone of a volcano, with the falling petals of plum, peach and almond flickering down over their golden faces and slanting eyes, so to others we remain subtle, inexplicable and morose, only just discernible through the dark and sinister screen of smoke poured forth from every chimney.

As we know, Continental nations can never comprehend us. To them our actions and the processes of our minds are as much enshrouded in mystery as the kind of lives we lead; we are a rich, proud, perfidious and intensely subtle people. Our Foreign Office, staggering from blunder to blunder in the past century, has achieved undreamt-of successes owing to the Continental inability to understand our lack of logic: the fact, for example, that our diplomats really say what they mean, though they often change their minds. Even now, with few diplomatic triumphs to our credit during the past three years, it is still supposed that we pursue a policy, ingenious and diabolically subtle, and that all this is connected with the fogs through which we move and in which we exist.

Every Englishman, I think, loves fogs; both of an atmospheric and of a mental variety. The first memory of many a child is often of a fog; of walking, for example, through Kensington Gardens when the trees could only just be discerned, looming up suddenly, and the Palace was altogether hidden. All my life, indeed, fogs have been my friends. At school a black fog would occasionally visit us and supply a whole holiday; one was told that the railway lines attracted them, and certainly they rolled down them as far as Barnet. In this dark, delicious moment, games became impossible, and fortunately it was still more impossible to be made to watch them. When I was in the army a fog, again, prevented parades; and the centre of fog-land still seems to me to be the Tower of London, in which my battalion was stationed for some months during the winter of 1912. It was my introduction to soldiering, and there was something very impressive about the havoc that fog caused to the military system. You might have thought that where so much mental fog prevailed, a little more of another, more material kind would not have made much difference; but this was not so. All parades had to be cancelled, bugles sounded out in the darkness, and the barracks became hives of light and gaiety as the word went round, while the Tower of London itself seemed to be a lighted beacon in the centre of this enormous circle of fog which surrounded it for miles and miles in every direction.

During the war the fog was a firm and very valuable friend. The white Flemish mists that hung, like cotton-wool, above the little dark pools and muddy fields made life more difficult, and yet easier, for both sides. They prevented sniping; but, on the other hand, any broken tree that showed itself suddenly was liable to look like the figure of a man, and fog seemed to invest these still things with movement. Sounds in the fog, too, became magnified and therefore more alarming; yet on the whole fog was an ally to friend and enemy alike. . . . But I imagine that the authorities did not approve of it, for anything that tended to check the pursuit of hostilities, and thus to make life more normal, was unpopular with them. Thus I shall never forget the rage that inspired our Staff when, during Christmas week, 1914, the Saxon regiment opposite my own put up placards with "Why should Saxons and Anglo-Saxons fight one another?" and, in consequence, the men began to fraternize. It became quite obvious to those in command that if the rival troops found that they liked each other and the artificially manufactured enmity waned after this fashion, the war might end: and then where should we all be? . . .

Of course, there are different brands of fogs. There is the almost tangible, white fog which fills the streets of Florence and the neighbouring Tuscan cities in the winter. From the top of one of the mountain ranges, indeed, I have seen the whole of Tuscany, though I stood in bright sunlight, lying engulfed beneath the frozen waves of this mysterious sea, out of which, every now and then, there rose a hill with a castle on it, standing up as though it were an island. . . . But to the Londoner, fog means either a yellow fog or a black one; a Dickensian fog, a fog which creeps up from the river and hides all the black wharves and mean streets, a fog in which the criminals can pursue their business unhampered; bringing the sort of night on which Fagin would have chosen to go out on one of his nefarious errands. And indeed, fog takes you to another world, the sort of locality and age which Dickens describes in *Oliver Twist*:

Near to that part of the Thames on which the church at Rotherhithe abuts, where the buildings on the banks are dirtiest and the vessels on the river blackest with the dust of colliers and the smoke of close-built, low-roofed houses, there exists the filthiest, the strangest, the most extraordinary of the many localities that are hidden in London, only unknown, even by name, to the great mass of its inhabitants.

227

Over such regions ever broods a fog, just as it always fills the offices and rooms and the Court of Chancery in *Bleak House*.

Some find a black, others a yellow, fog the more interesting. It is a matter of temperament. If lazy, you will prefer the black: for London can turn bright primrose yellow, and yet retain a certain semblance of itself, because a fog of this kind —not so much a blacking-out as a darkening, or rather, dyeing of the atmosphere—enables the life of the city still to retain its shape; whereas a black one closes down every activity. Eternal night seems to reign, and in it you lose your identity for other people, just as they lose their identity for you. It imparts a strangeness to every street, and, if you have a good sense of locality, an additional pleasure to walking, for it alters all distances, investing the town with more than its usual enormous proportions. It would be possible, it seems, if you had the strength, to wander through streets, on ordinary days familiar to you, for hours and hours without reaching their end or being able to identify your surroundings. . . . And it is to the vast blackness of this wonderful yet nightmare city that the minds of foreigners turn, at mention of the word *London*.

TRAVELLING

BY
TRAIN

UNLIKE THE MAJORITY of my friends, who seem to be for ever regretting that they were not destined to live during the reigns of Cleopatra, Caesar Augustus, Queen Elizabeth, Louis XIV or King George IV, often I repine at having been born into this world too soon. But, whereas the reasons which govern their nostalgia for past epochs are usually vague and indefinite (though not seldom founded upon a suppressed sentiment of self-importance, a belief that their talents would have guaranteed them a greater respect and position in ampler days) my desire for a later birth is, at any rate, in its foundation, simple and precise; prompted by an overwhelming hatred of railway trains.

For one who likes travelling—to whom, indeed, travelling is a necessity, almost a mania—this prejudice is unfortunate. Easy, you may say, to charter an airplane or hire a car; but airplanes are fortunately still expensive as well as dangerous (fortunately, because you can attribute your neglect of them to a love of economy, rather than to a morbid fear for your own personal safety), and motor-cars, too, cost a great deal of money to hire. Trains, on the other hand, are supposed to be quick, cheap and comfortable; while, moreover, quite a number of places—desirable places—are still inaccessible save by rail or on horseback; and however unpleasant may be the idea of a railway-carriage, the thought of even one hour spent on—or off—the capricious back of Nature's most ridiculous creation is yet more distasteful.

Trains sum up, to my mind, all the fogs and muddled misery of the nineteenth century. They constitute, in fact, so many slums on wheels. Think, first of all, on their dirt! No mere question of personal vanity instils in the wretched passenger his dislike of arriving at his destination disguised, apparently, as a collier or dustman; for, while no reasonable being can entertain any objection to fancy dress in appropriate surroundings, who, on the other hand, would wish deliberately to arrive at one of the large stations of the metropolis, where friends and enemies may be in waiting, with a face blacked like that of a nigger-minstrel? Or is it, I sometimes wonder, only myself who suffers in this manner? This may well be so; for, as the fields whirl themselves past into the distance, and the telegraph poles dance by with ungainly hops to the rhythm of a nightmare polka ground out by a discordant jazz orchestra, every scrap of dust, perhaps long treasured, every speck of soot and, worse still, every fragment of cinder, finds its way into my eyes, nose and ears—until I am blinded, choked and deafened—and the residue smears my face and enwraps my hands, the while I sit, enviously regarding from bloodshot eyes the clean and untired countenances of my companions.

And what of the noise, so far scarcely touched on? The engines of automobiles have been subdued to a gentle purr, a little soothing, even, in its monotony; the roar of the aerial engines sounds far overhead, a brave and leonine roar; but, even apart from the jolting thunder of its naturally ungainly and stilted movement, no train can ever either start or stop without an agonizing bump accompanied by a fiendish scream. Why, we demand, this convention of hooting and whistling, when the noise alone of an approaching train is sufficient to herald its arrival? Perhaps this sound is due, again, to that prevalent sin of our time, an "inferiority complex". Certainly the smaller the engine, the louder the screech; and I suspect that, as trains become more and more supplanted by other forms of locomotion, they will yell more loudly yet.

Then let us examine the problem of Hot or Cold. . . . In England, it is true, the question seldom arises, because in the winter a train is never allowed to be brought to a higher temperature than just above zero, unless it contains a restaurant-car, which is then scented with a sickeningly vivid smell of cabbage, bad Virginian cigarettes and stale smoke in tunnels, and brought to a steady temperature of 90°. In the summer, too, the really clever railway can always arrange for a train to stand for several hours in the sun before starting on its stifling journey. . . . But, on the whole, the compartments are cool. . . . On the Continent, however, it is otherwise, and I have been almost unable, sometimes, to discover

233

a waiting train owing to the dense clouds of steam encircling it, but, having at last fought my way through this atmosphere, so painfully reminiscent of the last act of *Götterdammerung*, I have finally found myself in a torrid zone of overheated red plush, reeking with stale tobacco, while every cubic inch of so-called air is laden with the most lithe and vigorous of germs, which after the manner of the hosts of Midian, prowl and prowl around, alert and waiting for new victims.

And what would you have me say of travelling companions? In the days of coaching they appear always to have been either delightful, intelligent and considerate, or conspicuously, interestingly sinister; but the railway-chatterers stand high on the list of public bores and liars. Only with long experience can be acquired the technique of dealing with them, for which it is necessary to develop an admirable terseness of retort. In example of it, a famous professor, now, alas, dead, who was an expert in the use of words, when questioned by a fellow-traveller as to whether there had been snow where he had come from the previous day, countered with the enigmatic reply, "I did not come from anywhere yesterday", leaving his interlocutor puzzled and silenced.

On the other hand, but only with rare luck accompanying, the entire life-history of a fellow-traveller, or of some friend of his who must for ever remain unknown to you, may be laid at your feet. Thus it was Mr Max Beerbohm, I think— or at any rate one of those very few other fortunate persons to whom all good stories are attributed—who was privileged to be present at an occasion of this kind. Travelling in his compartment was a couple, man and woman, who remained silent all the way from London, until, as the train passed

Malmesbury, the man looked out of the window and remarked in an intensely meaning voice: *"Poor* Mildred! She had reason to remember Malmesbury", and then lapsed into silence again for the rest of the journey. . . . As to liars, I was once on my way to London in a crowded third-class compartment, when the talk turned on the murdered Tsar and Tsarina. The general feeling was with them, until a mean, cringing little individual in the corner suddenly looked up from his paper and said, "If you people only knew what *I* know about the Tsarina you wouldn't feel a bit sorry for her; but I'm pledged never to tell." This speech produced a temendous impression and the Tsarina at once lost the sympathy of all those present except myself.

BY
BOAT

FIRST OF ALL it must be understood that by the word *boat* or *liner* I in no way seek to indicate those series of floating Mappin-terraces, the pleasure-cruisers. Let them sail on, without remark from me, displaying rival herds of purple-faced, seal-like old gentlemen and thin spinsters sunning themselves on their different levels, of red-faced, shouting boys and sweating young things playing their deck games by day and night, to their various ports of call. A Sunny Day in Old Spain, A Morning in Colorful Morocco, An Hour in Gracious Hellas—thus is the language of showmanship, formerly only applied to freaks in a tent at a fair, now smeared over the holy places of our civilization. And yet, before we leave these sun-baked ledges to approach the subject of boats proper, consider for a moment the remarkable spectacle continually afforded to the inhabitants of the more remote and "backward" parts of Europe, by this human cargo of the pleasure-cruiser, unloaded every morning, dumped into charabancs, to be paraded in front of startled fishermen and peasants! There, by the side of the road, stand the peasant women in their dignified traditional dresses, wide skirts and high, braided hair, regarding these phantoms, the curious by-products of city life, which we materialize even in the mountain passes of Albania and the green, tinkling vales of Arcady. Strange restless phantoms: Mrs Smith, the widow from Huddersfield, in that purple hat with fading clematis clamped to a half-transparent brim, above a mauve-coloured, perspiring face; and Mrs Jones from Eastbourne, that overgrown giglot with a suppressed tendency to jazz. Every day such people embark on one of—as my charwoman remarked to me—"these 'ere crusades".

No, by liners I do not intend to signify the floating homes of these extraordinary, if temporary communities; nor, indeed, the luxury liners, which for huge sums continually waft backward and forward across the Atlantic the ruined million-aires of America, but rather those ships which follow regular routes, and are bound at stated intervals to serve the convenience of permanent communities overseas; boats which voyage constantly, and as a matter of course, from England and France, Germany and Italy to the Americas and Africa, to India and Japan.

When they are English, these boats often manage to combine a maximum of red tape—and, though on the sea, of semi-military discipline—with a minimum of comfort and consideration for the passengers. Italian and German boats, for example, cater on modern lines for their guests, but the

English ones, with a far greater tradition behind them, pay ever so little attention to their needs and wishes. In seamanship, which is, of course, the main thing—though one less obvious—we still excel; but the life of a traveller on an English ship is far from pleasant. Hurled into every meal, at a ridiculously early and unsuitable hour, by the sound of a bugle, he is then regaled on the stalest of stale, and, if possible, the most tinned of tinned, foods. The coffee which brings these meals to a longed-for conclusion is compounded, it seems, of curry, iron-filings and bovril, and rivals that of any English inn or railway train. Deck games, again, are, as you might have surmised from the public-school atmosphere which prevails, practically compulsory; while at night it is essential to wear evening clothes, eminently inappropriate to your surroundings. After dinner a terrible, organized hilarity reigns for a few short hours; sad jazz and, at the worst, fancy dress.

French liners are very different, always full of bearded missionaries and holy women sitting in medieval clusters upon the decks, reading their tracts with a sweet-faced impassivity, while the captain can be seen from time to time drinking a care-free glass of the latest absinthe substitute. Here the meals are better, but, on the other hand, far from the sound of any bugle echoing over the lives of the passengers, an almost painful and entirely perilous lack of discipline obtains. These boats nearly always catch fire in the Red Sea. No French liner passes through it without trepidation. Passengers are requested to put out their cigarettes in special ash-trays provided for the purpose and, oddly enough, made of wood. Moreover, travellers of Latin origin, whether Italian,

French or Spanish, are possessed by an intense notion of correctness, of appropriateness; when in Rome, do as the Romans do, they seem to advise, and, in consequence, they wear yachting caps and go in, after a much more business-like fashion, for being seasick even on the calmest seas. Perhaps they are persuaded, as was Dr Johnson in his day, that otherwise they will derive no benefit from their long voyage. Then, again, on Latin liners children abound, to stamp their way, singing, over your head, at six in the morning—*les pauvres enfants!*

There are certain things, though, that all boats share: a tendency to over-decoration and a morbid love of stained glass. The passenger is not now even allowed, as formerly, the brave feeling that he is "battling with the elements" but, merely, instead, that he is sitting in a mad hybrid apartment, half overheated conservatory and half cathedral, which ever rocks to and fro, backward and forward and from side to side. Further, the personnel of all boats, manned by whatever race, and however lax or however strict the discipline, invariably betrays a quite prodigious ignorance of geography, and incomprehension of time. How often is it repeated that travel teaches geography: yet no sailor, no steward, when you ask him, is ever aware whether the island a mile off is the Isle of Wight or the Isle of Man, Sardinia or St Helena, Formosa or New Guinea; and, moreover, though these men constantly perform the same journey, and therefore should be accustomed to the changes of time—an hour or half an hour a day—which their shifting of position regularly entails, not one of them can even inform you, either what the time is at the moment, or to what extent you must alter your watch during the night.

Such matters hold for them, apparently, no interest. Whether they are off the coast of Greenland or of India is of no consequence to them: but the mere sight of a piece of dimming brass, and they are after it with rag and polish, eating their very hearts out over it. Peeling paint, again, constitutes an agony of soul to them: after it, in all haste, with sandpaper and brush and paint-pot; and, in consequence, it is impossible to accomplish a single sea-journey, however short, without becoming involved with wet paint.

And I believe that the sailor's mania for unnecessary cleanliness remains with him to the end. During the war ("Late Great"), Robin Hood's Bay, in Yorkshire, became one of the richest communities per head in England; for it was almost entirely populated by retired sea-captains, whose savings were invested in shipping-companies, and the artificial restriction of allied shipping output by German submarines had sent the shares soaring. In consequence, many of these dear, fat, bearded old men were temporarily in receipt of incomes running into thousands of pounds a year, yet would never allow a single day to pass upon which they did not conjure their very considerable bulks up slender ladders, to spend an enjoyable hour or two in scrubbing, polishing and painting.

AMERICA
BEFORE
THE
FALL

THE FIRST, OBVIOUS impression of America stamped out on the mind of anyone gifted with sight, must be the extreme, unearthly beauty of New York as you approach it—a clustered citadel of fantastic, thousand-eyed skyscrapers, bathed in the flat yellow sunshine that belongs so essentially to this city. A hard yellow light prevails against a deep blue sky; the river, too, being deep blue, while on it huge liners look like toy vessels against the mountain range of buildings on the island. The smoke from these steamers, and from the buildings, is very typical, nowhere else to be seen: white and soft as cotton-wool; perhaps the result of floating upon this pure and sparkling air.

The shock of New York to the stranger consists, not in the size of the Woolworth building (for which one is prepared) but in the multitude of high, slender towers (of which the

Radiator Tower is the most beautiful, built in black and gold), that make it, on a vaster scale, comparable to one of the old towered cities of Italy, such as San Gimignano.

And the second impression which the foreigner receives on landing is caused by the extraordinary intelligence, kindness and courtesy of the American newspaper reporters. Why and where have the English derived their ideas as to their crudity and brutality? In no New York journal would you find adopted that tone of silly rudeness towards modern art and artists which has become so marked a feature of the "chit-chat" columns of the more uninteresting English daily papers. But then, the average American approaches intelligence with an instinctive respect, rather like that with which we approach games in England. He has, too, an almost German reverence for expert opinion, and would never consider himself free, as the Englishman would, in the presence of an expert, first of all to admit his entire ignorance of the subject, and then to lay down the law about it.

The third impression that an Englishman receives is the most surprising of all. In England so much talk exists of blood being thicker than water that he almost expects to find himself at home. He imagines the language to be the same. It is not, and neither the porter nor himself can understand a word of the other's queerly accentuated syllables. He feels, suddenly, an Englishman, a European, an alien.

America is overwhelmingly foreign. The difference between Europe and America is greater than that between Europe and China. Now I can understand how a Chinese feels. But with America the whole level of thought and consciousness is different, and escapes me. I do not mean to say "better" or "worse", but "different". And the Englishman not only feels English, he feels Canadian, Australian, New Zealander, and above all, European, to an incredible extent. A word against Monaco or Montenegro, and he is willing to shed his own or someone else's blood. Greek, Latin and Teuton are much more his own kith and kin than these American cousins, grafted on to a redskin soil, with their innate, unconscious un-Europeanness, and their own ready-made, synthetic institutions. That is why the understanding between the two continents must always be imperfect, and neither should be encouraged to interfere in the other's affairs.

The American, however, has a very real respect for England; and here I should like to suggest that an attitude of cringing humility toward America—social, political or financial— is pointless and unbecoming. It is taken as an acknowledgment of what the American himself suspects to be untrue —that the dollar gods are the true gods.[1]

The idea is gaining ground in the States—and in Europe— that England will put up with anything, from the Debt Settlement, or the coal strike, down to Mr Baldwin. Such not being the case, it is a pity to spread this impression. There seems no reason why we should adopt as our attitude during the twentieth century one of apostolic abnegation. It does not suit the essentially just, and yet buccaneering, English spirit.

The kindness, lavishness and extent of American hospitality are incredible. Nowhere else will people, out of simplicity and kindness, take so much trouble. They even allow their guests to express opinions—except on certain subjects upon which they are touchy. Steam-heating is one fetish

[1] Written in 1927, five years before the American collapse.

243

of this sort: the Englishman may, if he is uncivilized enough, abuse every major institution in the States, but directly he mentions steam-heating a shiver of horror at his blasphemy passes round his audience. In return, the Americans draw a horrible picture of the Englishman crouching all the winter in a damp, icy-cold cellar of a house, possessing no light and no heat, and thus obliged to drink heavy wines, such as port and brown sherry, in order to aid his circulation and, indeed, preserve his life.

There are other curiously sensitive zones in the American soul. Directly a word is said about the American pride of plumbing, directly a certain ignorance is confessed as to the aims and personality of the late President Theodore Roosevelt, or a mild word of defence is put in for President Wilson (whom one day they will acclaim as they now acclaim Lincoln), you run the risk of severing the friendships of a lifetime. Again, frivolity in humour is taboo in the foreigner. One well-known English lady, with a reputation for wit, was asked, very solemnly, what had interested her most in America, and replied alliteratively: "The drains and the dancing". Her name is now anathema.

Speaking personally, I was disappointed, frankly disappointed, with plumbing in the States. The first night I arrived off the boat, longing for a hot fresh-water bath, I turned on the tap in a frenzy of European expectation. The hot water proved too hot to get into, so I turned on the cold water. But the heat of the hot water was as nothing compared to the scalding, scorching hotness of the cold water, and, like Narcissus, I was forced to remain gazing at my own image through the steam, unable to lave toe or finger.

"The pipes got a bit mixed up, Doc., that's all", the plumber confided in me; but two whole days passed before the matter could be put right. . . .

(Incidentally, I much enjoyed the experience of being addressed as "Doc." and "Cap."; courtesy titles conferred on tall strangers.)

Owing to the extremes of comfort to which my hotel in New York exposed me, it took me at least three times as long to get up and dress as in London. And here we come to an interesting point. Time races in New York. The tempo of time (if one can express it like that) is inherently different—a problem for Einstein to investigate—and the hurried, harried American, though for ever on the rush, is yet never able to accomplish in the day half that the quiet Englishman does easily. Similarly, it requires a super-heated and super-lighted skyscraper of rushing, telephoning, shouting Americans, working (let us say) as publishers, to get through the work done by one old-fashioned English publisher, supported by a secretary, an office-boy and a cat, in a cold, dark, London office.

Yet this enormous output of unnecessary work, and the effort which this skyscraperful represents, are in reality the secret of American success. The American habit of doing more unnecessary work, and getting less actually accomplished, gives more employment. It enables more people to spend the same money; and the great American discovery is that "nothing pays like expenditure".

To have a large nation earning and spending, to spend your money and get a share of the spending of other people's money, to keep your money moving, and not in stockings—

that is the secret of American success in finance and trade. Thrift (how pleased our government would be if they realized it!) is a thing of the past and dead.

As for the dancing in America, it is magnificent: the typical and splendid recreation of a people whose civilization is not static, but a thing of movement, a constant journey from class to class and place to place. The American man moves from poverty to riches, and back from riches to poverty, in as many years as, formerly, it would have taken centuries. In his lifetime he can revolve the full circle which it would have taken a European family in the old civilization seven centuries to build up and then to dissolve. He will travel, and think nothing of it, from end to end of his continent; and, next to dancing, his favourite recreations are travel and motoring, all typical of a mobile, high-spirited civilization.

Dancing remains the supreme sign of the vitality of America and of its new knowledge of world-domination. It is also the first thing he has been able to "put over" into Europe. American trade will one day again follow American dancing, as English trade used to follow English missionaries. And, with apologies to elderly polka-lovers, there is nowhere in the world where dancing is so beautiful.

Yet no one knows the sheer joy of *being* in Europe or being European until he has visited America.

ABROAD

THE CHIEF DELIGHT of travelling at this moment consists in the emptiness of the hotels. All the big hotels everywhere in Europe, except in London and Paris, are vacant, void of life, and the wistful quietness of them and the affability of those fallen gods, the tail-coated directors, amply compensate the traveller for their melancholy. It is, of course, a very expensively staged tragedy; but one well worth seeing before the curtain falls on it. And fall it soon must.

Some of the causes of this emptiness are interesting. The Americans, for example, insisted with all the weight of their dollars on having a bathroom, and a basin with running hot and cold water, to each bedroom. The dilatory Europeans waited several years before they realized the necessity of these things. It was only an autumn or two ago that most of the large hotels in France and Italy were reopened, fully equipped after this style. Alas, by that time the American dollars had melted, and their owners were forced to remain sitting round their own electric firesides.

Even before the slump, however, our cousins had done much to make difficult the lives of the proprietors of the smaller hotels in the smaller towns. For, while never staying in these, they would rush on them like a swarm of locusts for luncheon. Three hundred strong they would rocket, screaming up, from their charabancs, devour in one brief hour all the food in the neighbourhood, pick all the flowers, shake down all the oranges off the trees, and then drive away again. This habit compelled the proprietors to maintain a huge staff, out of all proportion to their ordinary requirements, in order to cope with such hurrying, occasional crowds. It was bad, too, for the staff; which, demoralized by days of idleness, would suddenly be worked to death for a few short hours and left utterly exhausted and discontented.

But the hotel proprietors are as much to blame for their present position as anyone else. I was last here in Sicily at that dramatic moment, about seven years ago, when in a few days the Italian exchange moved up (or should one say down?) from the neighbourhood of one hundred and thirty lire to the pound, to that of seventy. Now Sicily shares with the Italian Riviera the privilege of being the Governesses' Paradise. Many poor, oldish ladies had saved up for years to stay at a pension in Taormina, let us say, and there execute a few water-colours of "picturesque old bits". It was difficult to imagine, looking at their honest British gaiety, what privations over the course of years had gone to the trimming of those straw hats, with their trailing wreaths of artificial poppy and cornflower; but so it was. Thus the sudden movement of the exchange against them at once inaugurated a pathetic panic among the *pensionnaires*. (It bore particularly hardly on those who had not paid their bills for a week or two.) Peasant pottery and, I regret to say, monastic liqueur-bottles of a mottled majolica, were hurriedly thrown into green canvas trunks, there to lie among bits of quasi-Saracenic embroidery, paint brushes were tearfully put away, and the lids of these boxes, the coffins of their hopes, were shut. Day and night long, sound English walking-boots could be heard marching softly, sadly through the dust to the railway station.

Hearts of stone, one might have thought, would have been melted by this exodus. Not so the hotel managers, or even the people at large. The *forestieri* again. . . . *Everything* was their fault. Touched at the plight of my countrywomen, I dared to approach the manager of the hotel in which I was staying and to suggest that now the lira had jumped in this way, he might consider the possibility of reducing his prices? Drawing himself up haughtily, he replied: "Our prices will always remain the same". This attitude of superb hauteur has now borne its fruit.

Another cause for the scarcity of visitors, and especially, I imagine, of English ones, is the growing habit among continental peoples of referring to us as "the Tourist Industry". For several years it has been impossible to pick up a newspaper in a French or Italian hotel without reading some reference to the "Tourist Industry", and many magazines, left tactfully lying about in lounges, are entirely devoted to it. Speaking as a free-born Briton, I dislike being treated, after this fashion, as a robot-unit, to be treated as are pigs in

249

Chicago, passed through the machines of the hotels, deprived of my skin and shillings, and then packed, and sent home empty. And I am sure many other people must feel as I do.

The obnoxious phrase originated in the United States; where, indeed, the guest is made to feel that he deserves its application. (I remember asking for a glass of water to drink in the lounge of a very well-known hotel in New York, and being informed that such a proceeding was forbidden. If I wanted to drink water, or anything else, I must do so in my bedroom.) And it is in that great and enlightened country that the most amusing hotel-magazines are issued. In Spain last summer I found a delightful one which afforded the reader quite a fresh snake's-eye view of the hotel dining-room as seen from below stairs. All the same, a guest cannot but be deeply humiliated by studying these publications. . . . There are, for instance, the veiled instructions to the waiters to treat the guests like lunatics. . . . Humour them, let them always imagine they are in the right. Don't let them see that you despise them. . . . For some reason or other the creatures *like* their food to be clean and hot, so remove any dead insects that are lying about first, before you serve the dish, and then put it down on the table with a sudden, jingling clatter, as though it had burnt your fingers.

But best of all the features of this paper were the two columns I found devoted to the qualities to be cultivated by the "official hostess" or "hotel receptionist", as the more typical phrase goes. This lady should aim at "a gracious, old-world manner, welcoming, but not over-familiar, as of one who for many years has moved at her ease at Court and maintained her own among the European nobility". She should have "grey hair, and a quiet, educated voice", and, above all, she must be able "to impart an air of culture, travel and distinction, and to move like a gracious presence through the hotel". Poor thing, she must be ever apt and ready. Just as the unfortunate guest is trying to find his key, or the lift, she must move up "like a gracious presence", and slap out at him a stirring quotation from Longfellow, or a dreary old platitude from Emerson or Wendell Holmes. Or she should, again, draw his attention to the large, coloured reproduction over the lift of the Sistine Madonna, and favour him with her impressions of Dresden and Rome, or a little spoken essay, easy but convincing, on the comparative merits of Raphael and Michelangelo. Thus she would distract his attention from the noise outside in the street, where armoured cars are no doubt rattling on their way to the banks and a pitched battle is taking place between bands of rival gangsters. Very medieval. . . .

TRAVELLERS'
TALES

FOREIGN TRAVEL, ONE used to be told, broadened the outlook, and it must be admitted that it seems to make various people, at home unused to any such foreign practice, indulge in "thinking". Sometimes one is even privileged to overhear them express it in speech, and so to take a part oneself, passive though it may be, in the process. . . . But laudable as the effort must appear in anyone, it is nevertheless a thing not always to be encouraged. There are certain persons who *never ought* to think; not only individuals, indeed, but whole categories of labour and even entire nations.

Servants should never think, for example. With them it spells trouble for others, leads inevitably and at the least to the losing of collar-studs or the breaking of valuable china. ("I thought I'd put it somewhere handy for you, Sir", or "I thought to myself, what it wants is a good dusting; so I just took it off the shelf, and before you could as much as 'ear it smash, there it was, lying on the floor".) Professional soldiers, and generals in especial, should never think—and very rarely do. It can only lead to their unhappiness. Musicians should not think overmuch. They should feel a good deal, and their thinking should be done in terms of music. And I am inclined to think (if this is permitted to me after what I have been saying) that it was a mistake for the Russians to begin "thinking"; for it was thinking that made the revolution, which, after all, is an attempt to rationalize an irrational nation; one ever better at feeling than thinking. And now, through some terrible and gigantic perversity, the Russians, who by nature are the only genuinely religious and absolutely unpractical people in the world, have adopted a purely practical and material creed. . . . The English, on the other hand, have always thought more as a nation than as individuals: it is time we began to think again.

Travel in Mediterranean countries appears to distil from nomad Anglo-Saxons the finest aroma of their civilization, and in my travels of the last few years, two questions have been addressed to me which I shall never forget, for they seem to sum up the whole of the post-war world.

A rather rich widow came to stay in Florence. She had led a fashionable life, and was now advancing in years. It was her first visit to Italy, though, as she said, she knew "the French Riviera well". Italy puzzled her. She felt no enthusiasm for the yellow stone palaces and monuments, and referred, almost at once, and quite without malice, to the chief street in the city, a mixture of Bond Street with the entire history of the Renaissance, as "the slums", saying to me: "Why do all

253

these well-dressed people walk about in the slums?" But finance was her chief subject. I knew this in advance, for once I had met her coming away from the "Rooms" at Monte Carlo, and when I inquired, "How have you done to-day?" she replied: "Oh, I never have much luck now, not since dear William died. You see, I know it's old-fashioned of me, but I never can remember which are the *odd* and which are the *even* numbers." This I had considered an interesting remark at the time, and it made me wonder whether all the Edwardians, of whom she had been a prominent and typical member, had shared this same old-fashioned idiosyncrasy? For aught one knew, it might have been that very inability to distinguish the odds and evens which had been responsible for the policy that led up to the "Great" war. Who knows? . . . However, as was only natural in so original a mathematician, during her visit to Florence she began to take a great interest in the then minute variations of the Exchange: and one day she said to me, prophetically[1] (it must be remembered that she draws a fixed income): "Of course the Italian exchange is good, but not so good as the one in Paris and on the Riviera. Do you suppose *our* exchange will ever be so good?"

Last spring I journeyed on an Italian boat, largely peopled by Americans. We had been cruising round the Greek islands, the names of which were unfamiliar to all the passengers except a few Greek scholars or historians. But at last we were approaching Rhodes; a place, thank heaven, that we all knew, at least by name. The deck facing the coast of the island was crowded with passengers explaining to one another

[1] This occurred a year before England abandoned the Gold Standard.

where the Colossus had stood, or examining the machicolated walls through field-glasses, as though they were sea-horses. There was an air of growing excitement as more and more grey walls came into sight: for we of the Anglo-Saxon race dearly love stone walls, so long as they have no present use and have never boasted any beauty apart from the supreme one of being ruined. At last an American lady who stood near me, unable to bear the suspense any longer, demanded loudly, in an ultra-modern voice that seemed composed, like many of her own skyscrapers, of steel, glass and reinforced concrete, "Do tell me . . . where *used* this to be?" "Do you mean in classical times or before the war, Madame?" I replied. After the manner of all eager questioners, however, she did not heed my answering query.

The problem she posed undoubtedly expressed the American pre-Great-Slump view of European life. ". . . One never knows where anything will be next and things in Europe are not what—or where—they used to be." But during the last few years Americans have altered. Nations do alter, I think, more rapidly than most of us allow.

Thus one result of the war, and certainly its only benefit, was that it changed for a time, if not the heart, at least the voice of the German people. Before the war they were apt to be very harsh, throaty and spluttering in public. Museums and galleries constituted their place in the sun, and here the halls rang with hoarse shouts and loud grunts of wonder. . . . But later, until the advent of Hitler, they cooed like doves, had very nearly the most beautiful of all European voices. That amount of comfort we derived directly from the war. Similarly, the Great Slump of 1930 has hit so many English people hard, that we must draw comfort where we may; the effect, then, on American subjects of the richer sort has not been wholly maleficent. Poverty is no longer confounded with original sin: but, more than this, it has made them talk quietly. You can hear a pin drop (if you want to) in the Sulgrave Institute. That abandoned, Lord-of-Creation shouting, which used to make life in hotels abroad such a misery, has stopped.

How much of your income, reader, would you have given, at one time or another, to achieve this purpose? If an angel had appeared to you in the night—after you had been trying all day to write, but had been prevented by the rise and fall of steely accents outside your door—and had said to you "Lo!"—for men of God and holy beings always begin their earthly communications in this rather intimidating manner— "Lo! I will soften the voices of the Great American People: but first thou must yield up a tithe of thy earthly possessions, which are but dust and ashes", would you have accepted the offer? Personally, I should have considered it a bargain. . . . But when I try to console in this manner rich Englishmen, who have lost much of their wealth "on margin" in New York, I notice that the idea does not appeal to them as much as to me.

FORTUNE
TELLERS

DURING BOTH DAY and night Peking is profoundly quiet; peace reigns, in spite of the more minute sounds; sounds such as you will discover, perhaps, in no other large city in the world. In the day-time there reach you, of course, the shouts and cries of coolies running, their bodies shining like copper in the noonday sun, and, in addition, the more diminutive and insect-like notes which compose the symphony of Peking life; a composition orchestrated on the grand scale. Indeed, a thousand castanetted sounds, clangings and drummings and cicada-like crepitations, vibrate through the golden air and every now and then there will be wafted to your ears the gentle beating of a gong—not such a gong as summons all true Britons to their most hideous meals, but a sound that holds in it something tragic and not of this world, a mournful tintinnabulation. This signifies, to those who have become acquainted with the streets of Peking and with this kind of sound-hieroglyphic, that a blind fortune-teller is making his way through one of the numberless lanes, pausing every instant to lean on his long stick, the while he disengages his other arm and sounds the gong which he carries in his right hand. For in Peking those who cannot read the signs of the day before them, who can hardly tell dark from light, can plainly discern, it is believed, the course through the years.

The Chinese, indeed, are intensely superstitious, though they would hardly admit this, since they prefer to regard their practices as scientific; and, moreover, their superstition has often genuinely benefited science, for the fact that they possessed the earliest astronomical instruments in the world is actually only a by-product of their ancient reliance on superstition. Marco Polo, most accurate of historical observers, tells us that in his time there were in the city of Kanbalu (or Peking, as it was subsequently called) "amongst Christians, Saracens and Cathaians, about five thousand astrologers and soothsayers. . . ." (To-day there must be almost as many, only instead of "astrologers" we must read "fortune-tellers".) The Emperor, we are told, provided for them, so that they could spend their time in the constant exercise of their art.

Marco Polo also informs us that they had their astrolabes, upon which appeared the signs of the zodiac, the hours and their various aspects for the year. The different schools of astrologers examined their respective tables every year, in order to discover the course of the planets in relation to each other. From this they could forecast the weather and natural phenomena for each month of the ensuing year. "For instance," he says, "they predict that there shall be thunder and storms in a certain month, and earthquakes; in another, strokes of lightning and violent rains; in another, diseases, mortality, wars, discords, conspiracies". The predictions were recorded upon "certain small squares" and sold to the public, and those astrologers with the largest number of correct forecasts to their credit were, very reasonably, ranked the highest in their art.

The early astronomical apparatuses used by the Chinese have many of them survived to this day, though some have been moved from Peking to Shanghai because of the fear of Japanese invasion. But you can still see the shapes of these beautiful instruments outlined against the sky above the Eastern Wall. Two of them, originally designed for Kubla Khan, now at Shanghai, were taken to Berlin after the Boxer Rebellion in 1901. Referring to these, Bertrand Russell, in *The Problem of China*, says: "I understand they have been restored (to China) in accordance with one of the provisions of the Treaty of Versailles. If so, this was probably the most important benefit which that Treaty secured to the world."

Though these bronze machines for reading the heavens are no longer used, no Chinese to this day will decide on any project or undertake any course of action without acting on auguries, and many different methods of fortune-telling are, of course, in existence; such, for instance, as the temples of the Three Hundred and Sixty-Five Worthies; each of these represents a day in the year, so that you can tell what your fortune will be from the appearance of the worthy under whom you were born. . . . I remember being much impressed by the fact that my Chinese chauffeur, on inquiring from the custodian the identity of his tutelary guardian, was shown a great golden face so identical with his own that, unless he had moved, it would have been difficult to tell one from the other.

At every fair, too, there are those who divine by pouring sand on to the ground before them, and others who tell fortunes by an arrangement of beans or nuts. The blind, again, tell from the feel of the hand. But the oldest of all these methods, so its exponents claim, is that of telling the fortune from the lines of the face. And this art is not one to be lightly undertaken, since ten years of intensive study are needed for it. Those who practise this style of prophecy are men of professional repute, called in for every wedding of wealthy people. The fees seem high. Though life in China is inexpensive, to have your fortune told by this method costs at least a pound, while if called in, following on a marriage, to foretell the birth of children, the charges of the soothsayer mount still higher. Women being still despised, if he forecasts the birth of a daughter the charges will be reduced; but a prophecy of this nature is so unpopular with any but the most freaky parents that he would scarcely venture to make it.

You can imagine the scene. It is a hot day, and so we are sitting in the courtyard. The painting of cornices and doors and windows—the cornices in bright blues and greens, the doors and windows in the shade of red lacquer—glow in the spring sun, the light of which attains a particular brilliancy in this country. The doors stand open on to the quiet street beyond, guarded by a devil-screen which protects you from visitors both earthly and aerial. The trees, maple or lilac, send a flicker of shadow over the intent face of the diviner and record their shapes on the paper windows, which gleam with a slight translucence. The man regards you with a pitiless stare; no line in your face escapes him. He begins at the forehead and reads down. A Chinese servant helps him by translating his forecast, but this is not so easy, for a simple fact may be of considerable portent. When, for instance, I was informed that in ten years' time I should grow a moustache —and this, indeed, was to be one of the central events of my career—I did not at first realize the political importance which is attached to such an embellishment in China. Only a person of power would dare to indulge in those few drooping and sparse hairs. . . .

The idiom of the language, too, is often picturesque. The fortune-teller prophesied the birth of several male children of my impending marriage. Though they would eventually attain success in life, there were difficulties ahead; when, he prophesied, I told them to go to the east, they would go to the west.

THE
DELIGHTS
OF
FOREIGN
COLONIES

SELF-IMPORTANCE DIFFERS, I think, from conceit; which is a much more amiable, because imaginative, failing. Poet, painter, musician and sculptor, cook and gardener, if good at their jobs, are liable to be conceited, existing as they must in a world which they create for themselves, just as the silkworm, living for a time in the golden shroud which it constructs for itself, remains in all probability very much aware of its own virtues and beauties and inclined to turn a deaf ear to the murmured merits of artificial silk. But the business man and politician and lawyer, the gamekeeper and tradesman, unless they dwell upon such imaginative heights as Cecil Rhodes or Disraeli, are not conceited, but, instead, are given over to self-importance. They continue to exist in the real world about them: but, owing to their egotism, it is invested with such a nightmare quality of humdrum and ponderosity that its *clichés*, accompanied by the appropriate grimaces, its tergiversations, mounted with so noble a gesture, have less in common with reality than have the airy pinnacles of the artist's imagination. . . . But worse, far worse than this personal self-importance, is the clique self-importance which sometimes informs a whole group, the "social and artistic sets" of Mr Chit-Chat or, even, business communities: those Anglo-Saxon microcosms, those parasitic bodies floating in the blood-stream of foreign countries from China to Italy, from Bolivia to France. . . . Though, of course, I do not include in this category the swollen, cosmopolitan associations that now litter the whole Mediterranean coast of France; alien growths that have little national feeling, but are composed of those who, having money but being too stupid to spend it elsewhere, come here willingly to be milked by the expert Riviera tradesmen and hotel proprietors.

The English may possibly make good colonists, but certainly they make very bad foreign-colonists: and so do the Americans. They remain intensely narrow-minded and national, while priding themselves on an enlightened breadth of view denied to their countrymen at home. They boast of their freedom from moral prejudice, but no people are more unsparing in their comments on those who appear to have transgressed the Anglo-Saxon code. . . . As for recreations, in China they drink Ceylon tea as a protest against the country in which they live; and everywhere they play bridge and quarrel. . . . And, having been away from home for so long, they are a little afraid of being *out of it*, especially where books and the arts are concerned, and so tend to wish you to know that, because they reside abroad, it does not mean that their opinions are not as important as those of any Englishman or American alive. Consequently they are determined to make you notice the idiosyncratic force of their personalities, actually often meagre and commonplace; they envelop you in them, smother you with them as though they were—what they often are—so many wet blankets.

Directly they meet a visitor from Europe, they seek to impress upon him that they and all their friends are interesting; "different" from the people he has encountered elsewhere. And contradiction is almost their one method of emphasizing this point; for, while the artistic conceit which, for example, I possess in full measure myself, makes me sometimes too proud to argue, unless convinced that he who seeks argument is one whose point of view it is worth while to combat, the self-important man, on the other hand, believes that by flat contradiction—which to him seems the beginning and end of all argument—he necessarily proves himself to be clever, possessed both of learning and originality.

And these communities are invariably composed of the same types: one or two characters, old men of violent opinion and gay life (they are the best, but will not mingle with the others, remaining, a menace and defiance to them, outside the circle); and a few disappointed and repressed University professors, precociously bald and grey but still fox-terrier-like, who were, ten years ago, considered to have promise, but who are now forced to rely for their expression of self-importance upon a faintly distilled communism and a complete misreading of the younger poets. (These, also, always speak the language of the foreign country in which they reside with so pure and exquisite an accent that no native can understand them.) Then there are a few literary ladies, serious but winsome, who overload their talk with allusion to other famous literary figures of whom no one else has ever heard—the sort of literary ladies whom the B.B.C. would call in to arrange their music-hall programmes—and, of course, the local novelists, male or female, of the particular place, much courted, however boring and incompetent as writers, and very fractious and on-the-look-out, jealous lest, since you are a writer too, you should have come all this way to steal their local colour from them, miserable theft that it would be! Inevitably, too, there are a few American ladies, very old, though no one knows their precise age, but very spry and never-say-die, willing in deepest winter to stump out to lunch or dinner. Their figures are lean and they shiver all day long, as though consumed within by some terrible, internal ice-age, but really because of the number of cigarettes and cocktails they consume: while their wrinkled faces, much made up, seem to have been smeared with the juice of cock-tail-cherries for rouge and dusted with the ash of Virginian cigarettes for powder. Something sad hovers about them, though they are not aware of it, for they have no life, good or bad: they have always lacked the reality even to be evil. They have no relations and no background and have drifted here for no purpose; equally, though one day they will suddenly go away, there seems no purpose in their drifting anywhere else. . . . A few business men, and those who "run the club", make up the colony.

These people, then, dine together constantly and lunch together day after day. They play bridge together and sit on the same committees, and every action and every saying of each one of them is comprehended by the rest to the full, so intense is their hatred and understanding of one another. Yet some of their conversation is impersonal: they are fond, for instance, of seasoning it with tags, brought in in a vague way; so that nearly every fragment has attached to it as a label, but introduced with an air of great knowledge of men and books, some such phrase as "Who was it said, 'Hair is a woman's crowning glory'?" or "You remember . . . 'Tis better to have loved and lost than never to have loved at all'." Then they join in witty badinage which, though painfully without point, is yet, if only one were familiar enough with them to detect the hidden sting, infused with venom, and, after an hour or two of it, turning to you, with a suspicion that you have not seen them at their best, ask "Do you think you are beginning to 'get' this place? . . . It's quite *mad*, as you see for yourself. . . . We all admit that . . . but it's such *fun*. . . . There's no place like it."

Of course there is a pathetic side. Most of the residents in reality hate and loathe the country of their adoption and its inhabitants, and are bitterly unhappy. . . . And then, too, foreign colonies, wherever they are, tend to the same practices. Many members, even the most respectable and respected, are commission-hunters, taking a humble five per cent on almost anything that is sold within range; and this secret of their commerce is one they all hold in common, and of which each, when absent from any gathering, is accused—and justly—by the rest; for a degrading and grind-ing poverty often lurks under the surface of their gentility, and this, again, places them more than ever on their dignity.

266

THE
SUMMER
PALACE

IN 1860 THE allied armies destroyed Yuan-Ming-Yuan, the most romantic and beautiful oriental palace in the world. At the head of the English detachment rode Lord Elgin, who, having some years before removed from the Parthenon the marbles which now bear his name attached to them, having further contrived for a time to lose them at sea, was now bent upon other artistic achievements; and indeed, at the end of his visit, hardly one stone was left upon another. And yet to this very day, as you wander through the desolate courts, now the property of farmers, a faint perfume of the former palace still lingers in the disposition of the gold-lacquered fields and hills, and in the artful windings of the stream. For the rest, there remain one or two smashed bridges and a plumed arch or two bearing the remnants of Jesuit rustication; but while you pass, the little children in their padded winter coats, which resemble eiderdowns, are hammering at them for their amusement with huge bits of stone or logs of wood, far too heavy, you would have said, for their years.

After the destruction of the palace it was three decades before the Empress Dowager faced the question of a new summer retreat; but eventually even the garden courts of the Forbidden City, even the pavilions of Coal Hill, that artificial mountain raised in the middle of Peking, failed to compensate her for the delights of country life, and, carefully choosing the situation, she decided to build the new Summer Palace on a hill between the Jade Fountain and the ruins of Yuan-Ming-Yuan. At the back of it there still existed, almost complete, an abandoned Summer Palace of the Ming Emperors: and this, no doubt, influenced her, both in her choice and in her designing of it. It is the fashion among many people to deride the Empress Dowager's creation, because of the late period of its building, but, in fact, the palace and demesne are as national in style as anything of an earlier period, and while a certain vulgarity is to be observed in the detail, I can at the same time confidently assert that nowhere else in the world at that period would it have been possible to evoke so beautiful a home. As for the grounds —lakes and peony-terraces, as well as streams and bridges— they are lovely beyond criticism, quite as beautiful as anything made five hundred or a thousand years before.

Of course, the Summer Palace cost an exorbitant sum of money, and money at that time was not easy to get, for China was already in course of being exploited by the foreigner. The Empress Dowager, resourceful as ever, decided to create a great fleet to meet the threat of the Japanese navy. Having announced this, and having obtained a grant of the necessary money, she then quickly appropriated it for the building of her Palace, and provided no ships at all. The Chinese incline, in patriotic moments, to bewail this fact, but the truth is that, even had their fleet been built, they would certainly have lost it, just as did Kubla Khan, against the Japanese. . . . (One day, perhaps, the Chinese armies may prevail against the Japanese, but never a Chinese navy.) It is well for them to avoid naval battles, especially against islanders. And even had they won, even had a few rusty cruisers and battleships survived, these would offer little of interest or beauty now, while the Summer Palace, which since the fall of the dynasty has always been open to the public, lies within easy distance of Peking and provides a pleasant day's picnicking for those of the population who can afford it.

The particular beauties, as I have said, of the Summer Palace are its waters and its bridges. The Camel-back bridge is one of the most beautiful in the world, and every now and then it seems as though the Empress Dowager had been inspired by the famous Royal Park of Pei-hai—once the pleasure-ground of Kubla Khan, and later adapted by one of the Ching emperors to the pleasures of eighteenth-century life. It seems, indeed, a development of the same themes of lotus pool and marble balustrade. Herself a great gardener, the chief pleasure of the Empress Dowager, as an old lady, was to wander among the flowering shrubs.

But the Chinese conception of flowers, which she shared, is a very different one from the European. The great national flowers of China are the peony and the chrysanthemum. Of the chrysanthemum I cannot speak, for I have never seen it bloom except in Europe; but certainly the peonies, balancing gaily upon their special terraces, beneath an awning to protect them from the fierce sun of the Chinese summer, attain to a hitherto undreamed-of perfection; especially the tree-peonies. In colour they range through every shade from lotus-pink to so deep a purple that it is known as black. The buds have been cut off here and there, and a great art has inspired the whole of the growing of the tree, while the terraces enable the onlooker to view it from a thousand different angles; for that, indeed, is part of the Chinese theory of gardening. Thus a blossoming tree must always be viewed from above, as well as from beneath and at the side, and for this purpose are constructed those miniature mountains of rock which, at times when the trees are not in flower, seem so meaningless. But who that has seen it can ever forget the flowering of a cherry tree, when viewed from this particular unusual altitude? For it reveals a vista of winged life at which, before, one could only guess from the deep murmur inhabiting it. From above, as the blossoms lie displayed in the sun, you can watch the going and coming, the endless journeying of the bees and the fluttering of the swallow-tail butterflies.

The cultivation of wistaria, too, has attained in China a degree of excellence unknown here, and the blossom is treated in various and original ways. Sometimes an old vine is hung through a lattice, so that each drooping head is framed in a square; sometimes a stout tree has its serpentine branches supported by painted props of wood which look as though they were fashioned of coral, or, again, it is encouraged to writhe over a shallow pool so that it may be mirrored the better. And in these pleasances are found to perfection the natural stones which, in a Chinese garden, so often take the place of statues. Indeed, for a well-shaped, honeycombed piece of natural limestone rock a Chinese connoisseur is willing to pay the most extravagant price.

But it was the peonies, I think, that were the cause of my seeing the grounds of the Summer Palace at their best: for the Mayor of Peiping—as Peking is now called—is a very important person politically as well as socially, and has his residence therein. Suddenly he decided to give a party. One day a large and beautiful envelope was handed to me, with a huge card inside, on which lay sprinkled a delicate inscription in Chinese. I induced my Chinese teacher to translate it, and his translation runs as follows:

Everything in the old capital is a fairy place with nice plants and flowers. The old Palace was a place for amusement in the springtime, and whoever went there was glad to be alive. It is that season now. The air and clouds are very nice, cold weather has already left, the trees are in leaf and the birds sing. Everything causes the spring to smile. The whole demesne of the Yi-ho-yuan, the Summer Palace, was an old Palace for amusement. It has many good and famous things still remaining. Surrounded by hills, it is surprising how high the temples and buildings seem. The fragrance of flowers clings to our clothes and a nice lake ripples before our eyes.

So now I intend to have a party on the 6th May. Both foreign and Chinese high-class officials will come. When you arrive you will have the same pleasures as those who came in an earlier day. Furthermore, there are good trees everywhere, so that it is not necessary to roll the screens for shade. You will find kitchens in every place, and it will not be necessary for you to bring your wine with you. I am having this party as was done in olden times. It is just the same as the good party given in the Sung dynasty.[1] I hope every friend will bring his family. You had better bring your handkerchief for sitting on the rocks when you wish. I can provide you with a jar of wine, and we can sing after dinner as we think of the past and contemplate the future. On that day you will give and get happiness, and we shall take a picture for a memory which you might like to see afterwards.

I beg your pardon for writing such a short letter, but I shall be much pleased if you will give me your company.

MAYOR YUAN LIANG OF PEIPING.

And the Mayor lived up to his word. Although afflicted with severe toothache (which was said to be the reason for his wearing a bright blue tie with his frock coat—evidently it made the pain more bearable), he was to be seen everywhere, instructing people to take photographs of the company. Many great marshals and generals, who now in reality govern China, had come for the occasion, and at every point you could obtain tea and wine, as well as many varieties of cake. Boats floated on the lake, boats with awnings, painted boats and plain boats; the yellow China roses and the peonies were in full bloom, and down the long-roofed, open corridors, decked in gay colours, walked the Chinese ladies, with their small feet and elegant robes, observing the flowers and watching the dragon-eyed goldfish performing their veil-dances in standing bowls of water.

[1] A.D. 960–1279.

THE
ANIMAL
CREATION

DOGS

IF YOU ADMIT to—or, it may be, boast of—a dislike for dogs, then, in England, it is inevitably assumed that you favour their being treated with brutality. Many people, indeed, hearing you indulge in such a confession, would demand your immediate impeachment by that fighting body, the R.S.P.C.A. . . . It becomes necessary, then, to remind yourself from time to time that you cannot, as yet, be prosecuted for an aversion from, but only for cruelty to, animals.

Therefore consider, and condemn, dogs and their ways. In them, very few virtues of the animal world are evinced. They are dirty and dishonourable, immoral—not amoral, as some suggest—and yet, teetotal; enemies, too, of beauty, of silence—in itself enchanting—and of all lovely objects from Persian carpets down to foxes and pheasants. They have no sense of humour, only a vacuous and rather cruel grin. Above all, they are cynical, supremely cynical: the very word cynic is derived from the Greek word for "dog", for cynics were supposed to "grin like dogs", and, indeed, the dictionary definition of "cynic" as a "sneering fault-finder" fits all dogs to a tee. Finally—and this, too, is a serious objection to them —they are not even good to eat. . . . (Let me interrupt my dissertation here, to assure nervous dog-owners that I have no wish to eat their pets; but that, were I to do so, they would have no remedy. To eat an animal is, in English law, neither cruel nor illegal; though I, with no great fondness for brutes, should have deemed it both.) . . . They are not good to eat, I was saying, except to the very cultured palate of the Chinese; for it is stated that the word "chow", which is the formal title of one of the proudest and most detestable of canine breeds, means "good", merely in the sense of good to eat.

But worse, far worse than any fault that I have cried against them, worse even than their unappetizing in-edibility, is the fact, plain for all to see, that they do not *know* when they are disliked: unless, perhaps, the explanation is an opposite one, and they do know it and revel in it? . . . In any case, they delight in adopting me, in following me on what I had intended to be a lonely walk through the country-side, disturbing my train of thought, tripping me up un-aware, panting hotly after, so as to make me, too, feel hot and out of breath. . . . And then, any sign of wild life in vale or woodland, and, however fatigued they have pretended to be, they are out, hot-foot, to destroy it, snuffling, fussing, growling and yapping. And this brings another objection in its train: how ugly are their voices, whether gruff in anger or wheezy in contentment! Yet, in their self-conceit, it is plain that they think them tuneful, pleasing to all men. "What can I do to comfort my master, for he is nervous and ill at ease to-day", they seem to say, and reply to themselves, "I will bark". . . . Nor can man, his master, be altogether acquitted of lending a certain encouragement to this point of view.

Yet, though dogs, it may be, are popular to-day, were they always regarded with such approbation? Is this alliance between man and dog in reality such an ancient one, to be traced back, as the archaeologists have told us, to far times when, together, these two creatures were hunted, through lands which are now seas, by the sabre-toothed tiger? . . . Perhaps the idiom of our language, a frozen repository of knowledge of such a kind, can help us toward a conclusion on this subject.

The dictionary, certainly, informs us of no innate liking for dogs in our ancestors. To begin with, it defines the meaning of dog, when applied to a human being, as "worthless or surly person" (and, in support of it, I may own that often, when reading some particularly stupid and ill-tempered review of a book, the description "beastly dog of a reviewer" has risen involuntarily to my lips). Again, "to go to the dogs" was wont, formerly, to be considered no desirable journey; "a dog's life" was no good thing, "dog-days" were days to be avoided, nor was a "dog's death" an end after which to hanker. The baboon, called "dog-faced", does not derive his name from the beauty of his countenance, neither is the "dog-fish" a pretty object; nor, as far as that, is the word "bitch" generally used in any sense even of empty compliment. And

I notice, in the dictionary once more, that "Dog-Fennel" is a name applied to "Stinking Camomile".

Of course the explanation of so much dignified dislike and contempt may be that dictionaries are compiled by literary men, and that authors, as a profession, must be hostile to dogs (George Moore, for example, was a noted leader of the anti-dog campaign), since many are the books, good and bad, which dogs have prevented being written, many are the poems in embryo which their insensate yapping has strangled. . . . Yet it looks as though this antipathy rested on a firmer basis. Why, then, you may ask, are dogs, their names formerly a term of reproach, so popular in modern England; who has conspired to give the dog a good name? . . . In modern England alone, for foreign races, more kind to children, are less kind to animals.

The reason, I apprehend, is because the dog is by nature dumb, inexpressive; incapable of speech and gesture, or the thoughts which these things transmit. . . . And this, of course, appeals to the Englishman, often in somewhat the same way himself. Babies, too, are loved in this our land until they grow old enough to be sensible, when, indeed, they lapse in favour; for, as a race, we loathe reasoning, or, as we call it familiarly, "answering back". The dog cannot answer back. . . .

In Latin countries it is quite otherwise. Parents adore children; children love parents. There we find never any need for a society to prevent cruelty to children. But animals certainly need protection. . . . Thus I remember sitting at breakfast on the terrace of a hotel in South Italy. The concierge, talking of animals, pointed to a waiter, and remarked, in a congratulatory manner, "Michele is very good with animals". "You mean, kind to them," I corrected, "very kind, no doubt." "No, Sir," he replied, "I mean, he can kick them very quickly, and as if by mistake, without attracting the attention of their masters." . . . Now therein Michele goes too far for my taste: though often I, too, make horrible, frightening faces at these pets, when their owners are not looking.

To sum up, dogs should be neither seen nor heard; they should never be allowed to enter a house or city; nor should they be permitted in gardens, but only in parks and meadows. . . . From this proclamation of outlawry I would alone except the Pekingese, that arrogant but quiet race of palace-dwellers, and my personal friends. For I have friends in the animal world; and Carlos, who pants beside me as I write, is one of them; a fussy, woolly, self-important friend, but a friend none the less.

ANIMALS
VERSUS
CHILDREN

LET US NOW pass on to an examination of the British attitude toward other animals beside the dog: which brute, together with the horse, this strange race worships, as surely as ever the inhabitants of ancient Egypt ritually adored hawk, crocodile and cat. Essentially a people with a tendency towards favouritism, out of all the animal world, horse and dog are the only two beasts to whom they grant immunity from the consequences of the rites which they term "sport". Thus a continual public clamour is raised against the traffic in worn-out horses, which are carried over to Belgium to be made into meat—though, leaving altogether out of consideration the point of view of the gourmet, why, you will ask, should it be more wicked to eat a horse than to eat a sheep? . . . Again, the practice of vivisection is intensely unpopular because, firstly, a dog might be injured in the process, and, secondly, the results might be of benefit to mankind.

Yet, for the English, all other animals only exist "to offer sport". Fox and stag and otter and hare must, once their tracks are discovered, be pursued for panting miles, and, at the end of the run, if possible, be torn to pieces. (It is held, I know, that stags and foxes *enjoy* being hunted, but the instance of the stag which swam up the channel as far as the Kentish coast constituted, surely, a disproof of this statement?) Bigger animals, elephant, lion and giraffe, were created only to be shot, just as the purpose of the wild pig is to be "stuck"—in whatever that unpleasant process may consist. Thus in our free land, so long as it does not involve the two national pets, very little objection is raised against cruelty to animals. It is just sport. But directly a really magnificent and tremendous sport, like bull-fighting, is mentioned, some English sportsman will at once protest: "But don't the poor *horses* run some risk of being injured? I think that is terrible." Notwithstanding that "poor foxes" are injured after every successful meet.

Yet we are apt to boast of our fondness for animals in general, blinding ourselves to our treatment of them. In order to avoid a plain statement of our feelings toward the animals we eat, we have adopted the equivocal practice of using two names for them; one when alive, the other when dead. And so, skilfully facing both ways, we are kind to cows, sheep, calves and pigs, but devour those doubtless synthetic victuals, beef, mutton, veal and pork. The French and Germans, more logical and more blunt, care for these animals *because* they eat them: we pretend, when we face the matter at all, to eat, because we love, them. Nevertheless we expose our cattle, before they are killed, to the most horrible, nerve-racking

281

ordeals in our slaughter-houses, the conditions of which are, for the most part, much more cruel to the victim, and dangerous to the consumer, than those prevailing in civilized foreign countries.

And yet, I believe it to be really true that we are fonder of animals than of children. . . . Especially, I think, would a visitor from another planet, were he to visit our country, conclude from the evidence round him, that the wealthier classes were possessed by a morbid dislike—or, perhaps, fear of—their children. (And, indeed, antiquaries inform me that this was always so; that in medieval times the young nobles, pages in the castles of the great, were much more ill-treated, and made to lead a much harder life, than the children of the villeins—those Saxon untouchables.) The moment the poor little creatures are born, they are handed over to the fond attention of a succession of ill-educated and morose half-wits, to be trained by them during their most impressionable years.[1]

[1] During the war, I remember marching one morning down Sloane Street, at the head of a Company, preceded by the drums of the battalion, when I noticed a nursemaid wheeling along, in a gaily varnished and delicately balanced perambulator, a nicely dressed infant. She did not look where she was going, but stared in an adolescent trance at the men, gaping at them with rolling eyes and mouth wide open. In consequence, she did not observe the curb-stone which she was approaching, and upset the poor mite, henceforth destined to be cripple or idiot, on its head upon the hard pavement. But in no way taken aback by this accident, she just paused to pick up the little creature, its cries drowned, mercifully, by the drums, swung it back into the perambulator, and continued to accompany the troops, her face still exhibiting a look of rapt, round-eyed complacency. Certainly, when she reached home, she failed to inform the parents of the misfortune which had befallen their child; she had not, really, taken it in at all.

Further, they are treated in the most extraordinary fashion in several directions: given horrible food to eat—sago, tapioca, rice and greasy meat; hushed whenever they talk—though talk must be their medium of learning; hurried away, whenever possible, from the living-rooms to the nursery; and, finally, sent to bed at six of a summer evening, by far the most healthy and agreeable hour of the whole day. This, of course, is defended on the assumption that it is *good* for children to go to bed early. But who is to decide, save their Maker? In Naples, they are taken to the Opera, which continues until two o'clock in the morning, and you can hear them playing in the hot, summer streets of Barcelona until the small hours. Yet are there less of them, fewer survivors, than among our downtrodden, less lively children? . . . Abroad, too, they receive better food, and are not forced to drink barley-water and the like. They are nurtured on wine and water. . . . Thus an old Italian woman once remarked, "I think it dreadful to give wine to very young children. Personally I never allowed one of mine to *touch* it until he had reached four years of age!"

Finally it must be acknowledged that, as soon as the male child of prosperous parents has attained an age when his elders can be certain that by so doing they are not rendering themselves liable to a prosecution for cruelty to children, he is got out of the house altogether and dispatched to a preparatory school, where a prison-like system of life and discipline obtains.[1] Henceforward the child is never seen again except during a paltry three months of the year.

Would fond, or even humane, parents consent to being

[1] See "On Private Schools", *ante*, p. 7.

thus parted from one whom they love, at such an early age? They must know what schools are like; especially since most fathers have been to school themselves. Usually, however, they comfort themselves with the argument that material conditions have improved since their time; there is more jam, less dripping; more play, less Latin and Greek. But they know, surely, that human nature changes slowly, and that small boys, while often delightful and intelligent as individuals, are, in the mass, most barbarous and brutal?

LEWD
SING
CUCKOO

NOW, WHEN SPRING has transformed itself into the full-leafed silence of summer, and every bird but the wicked cuckoo has become mute, is the appropriate time to ponder on our national partiality for all things feathered, so long as their gifts are not, as in the case of the parrot, too exceptional, nor their plumes, as in the case of the peacock, too fine. Let us compare our attitude, of admiration, with that of other countries.

A mere glimpse of a bird on a branch serves to move the stolid Englishman to poetry. Devoted as he is to dogs and horses, a thrush or sparrow yet stirs even higher feelings; to him, angels were not given wings for nothing, and something sacred attends all winged things. Rich old women, who seldom think of their fellow human beings suffering cold or hunger, will evolve the most elaborate plans for the protection of their favourites, robin and sparrow, in a fall of snow, until fragments of coconut and old toast litter the white ground. . . . Indeed, on occasion, the evincing of a similar passion by the head of a foreign state has so moved people as almost to affect our policy; and no other deeds have, for example, so endeared to us the Fascist system in Italy as the Duce's reported action in providing airplanes to convey weary and stormbound swallows from Switzerland to Venice, and his subsequent decision to proclaim the island of Capri a bird sanctuary.

Now the choice of swallows was a particularly happy one: for the English love the swallow and the lark above all other birds. The announcement that a cargo of cuckoos had been landed at Venice would, I imagine, have caused less gratification here; for the freedom of their domestic life did much to injure them in the public esteem during Victorian times, and though in these days of easy divorce the abhorrence in which they were held formerly has no doubt a little abated, a certain prejudice against them is still to be observed; so much so that I remember an elderly gentleman, with whom I was walking one spring day in a garden, suddenly, on hearing that wonderful liquid call to evade parental responsibility, pausing to remark to me in an irate manner, "The cuckoo, I regret to say, has a most *unpleasant disposition*".

As for the bird-sanctuary, if birds are to survive at all in Italy, such a refuge is certainly a necessity: for, to the Southern Italian especially, a bird is a creature without poetry. To him the feathered songster represents merely an edible commodity, in the obtaining of which a certain primitive pleasure is also to be procured; or less—let us amend the definition—an edible commodity than the only edible target which his country offers. Indeed, to the members of all southern races, with their unsentimental outlook, a bird in the oven is worth twenty in the bush, and no amount of sweet singing will afford immunity. Even the nightingale, which poets of other nations besides our own have lauded, even the beloved *rossignol*, survives there in such multitudinous numbers more because of its shyness than because of its musical virtuosity. Yet, in spite of their devil-may-care response, the Italians have surpassed all other European peoples in artistic achievement; and the poetry of Dante— though utterly, I think, lacking in the swallows—was not inferior to that of Sir J. C. Squire and his band of Georgian choristers at their very best.

Even English people, however, when transported to a southern climate, seem to adopt a different attitude toward birds: the sun affects them as much as the birds themselves. In the glades and groves of Tuscany, pointed with dark cypress trees, the nightingales, who make an appearance in Italy before moving on to England, practise all day long, as well as all night, just as do Italian prima donnas before they journey northward to make their debut at Covent Garden; and, during a sojourn in that country, I have known the kindest and most sympathetic of Anglo-Saxon bird-fanciers moved to such sleepless fury by this continual clamour that, stealing softly to the window at two or three o'clock in the morning, they have hurled stone after stone at the songsters, just discernible in bright Italian moonlight; though without obtaining any success, either through maiming them or through frightening them into silence.

To speak for myself, I love the music of the nightingale, and it never becomes too familiar to me, for, hailing as I do from the north of England, that bird is never to be heard in my own countryside; yet I am bound to admit that I find the full-throated chorus of the frogs in southern countries no whit less beautiful, interesting or stimulating to the imagination. How resonantly it rises, that age-old chant from the mud, in praise of sun and water. . . . And then the sight of some of the smaller and more quietly coloured birds which haunt the English lanes and dells is often very repulsive to me; a spectacle, I imagine, only in reality appreciated by those to whom, having been brought up in cities, it comes with all the shock of novelty. . . . What can be more horrible than the sight of a nestful of wide-eyed young birds, their greedy mouths gaping for food? And, again, the glimpse of a bird darting through the branches after its prey is often alarming, for in its sudden movements, in the motions of its neck, and in the sinuous, if brutal, strength which one of these drab and shabbily plumed creatures will all at once manifest, it demonstrates so plainly its near kinship to the serpent; just as, in the glance and movements of that super-bird, the South African ostrich, there yet lingers a quality which, however much one may admire the panniers of biscuit-coloured, rococo plumes in which it indulges, remains unpleasantly reptilian.

As for the music of birds in general, some races, not content with the natural variety, have devised means for its improvement. As, at this very moment, I sit writing in my room in Peking, a most mysterious, mournful but beautiful sound reaches me; a music, one would say, a little menacing, though harmonious and inspiring. It is most certainly, one is aware, a sound from the sky and caused by birds, and yet very unlike any booming of . . . is it the bittern? . . . ever heard before. . . . The solution of the problem is that the Chinese, who, for thousands of years, have cultivated great flocks of pigeons for this very purpose, first strap whistles of various utterance to their fluttering bodies and then release them into the air. Children are employed to wave flags at them, and, by thus scaring the birds, they keep them in continual flight and sound, so that, as they wheel and sweep above rose-pink or grey walls and blue lakes, this strange and noble music varies but never falters. . . . After a time, of course, they are allowed to land. Yet I feel sure some reader will raise the cry of cruelty. Is it, I would ask him—save that it has the attainment of beauty as its object—more cruel than the use of scarecrows in England, or than the common massacres of birds in which all true sportsmen delight?

BOOKS
AND
AUTHORS

PORTRAIT
OF
LAWRENCE

THERE MUST BE many who suffer from an identical inhibition: the difficulty of reading a new book! Not for a moment do I mean to suggest by this that a single one of us belongs to the uninterested, uninteresting, and effete band of readers who preen themselves, saying, "Whenever a new book comes out, I read an old one", thereby assuring to themselves a Bourbon-like renown for learning nothing and forgetting nothing; but that, undoubtedly, I, for one, find it easier to read a book a year or two after it has come out, when the banging of critical big-drums or the ejaculation of critical cat-calls has a little subsided, and literary clubmen no longer assault the unwary with: "Have you read Muggins's latest? Do read it, and then let *me* know what you think of it." ("Why should I?" one would like to reply.)

But alas! death, quite apart from its other drawbacks to an

author, lengthens these processes. Moreover, in the case of D. H. Lawrence the bad treatment of his work by several newspapers in their obituary notices of him caused a very violent championship of this writer among his worshippers: and so it is that only now am I finishing *The Plumed Serpent*, though the volume was bought at the time of its publication. A marvellous book it is, too, with all its author's daring defiance—for in this instance it was a challenge, and not the lack of the quality in himself—of the English sense of humour, and with its haunting, if absurd, beauty.

Above all, Lawrence possessed the power of arousing the emotions of the reader without any apparent cause—and this, surely, is genius? For example, you are almost laughing at one of the intensely ridiculous passages describing the horrible, new-old religion, a cross between peasant arts-and-crafts and the worship of Baal, which is to oust Christianity from Mexico, when you discover of a sudden that your emotion is not laughter at all, and that the cumulative effect of the pages you have been reading is to bring you near tears—that laughter through the looking-glass.

Then, again, one might have imagined at first that his genius could apply itself only to the country in which he was born and brought up, and out of which I came, too; that country of abrupt cliffs, wooded valleys and hanging woods, with its dark-leaved old trees and gigantic plumes of smoke rearing themselves like serpents into the still and watery air. . . . Certainly one feels it to have a strange power of inspiration, this land of two populations, the white, rustic, old, stationary population that labours by day in the open air of the countryside, and the shifting masses of black-faced miners who work, day and night, under the earth. There is a beauty that broods and flowers in these desolate villages, and on the black waters of these rivers: an energy that finds its typical expression when in the late summer the pyramids of the slag-heaps flame out for a month into blazing magenta willow-herb.

But, as any reader of Lawrence's later books must see, his genius, confined as it may originally have appeared, quickly naturalized wherever he wished it. It became equally at home describing the breakdown of white life in Australia or in Mexico as ever it was in a world of tramcars, tin chapels, and backyards; perhaps more at home, for the dark, dirty gods of the native races permit their peoples none of that bantering, ribald, rather beery talk that might be found among miners. No: the dark gods were most serious when most obscene; their followers condescend occasionally to "mock silently" the white men, but they never enjoy a joke at the expense of anybody else, least of all about themselves. Similarly, when Lawrence himself is ribald, he is ribald with an almost religious seriousness that shows that his blood was not so red as he would like to paint it. . . . And often I wonder whether this preoccupation with the dark races, this belief in them and extolling of their qualities, is not, silly and superficial as such a theory may sound at first, something left over from his very early life, a reflection of the sympathy he had felt with the miners and of resentment at their lot, as he watched them, that other dark-faced and, he considered them, dispossessed race, trooping back to their labours?

I only met Lawrence once, when he and his wife were living in Tuscany. I was staying near by and they asked my sister and myself to have tea with them; so we drove through the blossoming countryside—for it was high May—to his farmhouse. This square, blue-painted house stood among gentle hills, with rather Japanese pines springing from rocks and brown earth in the distance, and with the foreground sprinkled with bushes of cistus, flowering in huge yellow, white and purple paper roses. A few cypresses, the most slender of exclamation-marks—not robust, as they are further south—orchestrated the landscape. Lawrence opened the door to us, and it was the first time I had ever realized what a fragile and goatish little saint he was: a Pan and a Messiah; for in his flattish face, with its hollow, wan cheeks, and rather red beard, was to be discerned a curious but happy mingling of satyr and ascetic; qualities, too, which must really have belonged to him, since they are continually to be found in his work. It was, certainly, a remarkable appearance. Unlike the faces of most geniuses, it was the face of a genius.

He was extremely courteous, I remember, and prepared the tea himself, doing all the work: which grieved one, for he looked so ill. The rooms were charming, simple, Italian-farmhouse rooms, with none of that broken, gold junk one so frequently encounters in the homes of the English in Italy; a great relief. On the other hand, they were hung with large canvases by Lawrence: pictures that he had just at that period begun to paint. These, though many wise people have since praised them, I thought then—and still think—crudely hideous and without any merit save that he painted them and in so doing may have rid himself of various complexes, which might otherwise have become yet more firmly rooted in his books; useful, then, but not beautiful.

Two hours, two extremely delightful hours, we spent with them, and then he saw us off at the door, standing with the evening sun pouring down on that extraordinary face: but Lawrence, I am sure, must always have been glad to be alone once more. I left Italy a day or two later, and never saw him again, so that, scarcely knowing him, I am left to fit those two hours and their impressions on to that solitary, delicate and ever so interesting figure. . . . Some of his books bore me profoundly; others seem of an inspired nature that no one can deny. Exasperating is too mild a word to describe some of his repetitive passages. His use of language can be nauseating: viz. his fondness for the words "winsome" and "dainty"; nevertheless, he is a prophet and a poet. And yet even now I think it is less in his novels that he is a great writer than in his miscellaneous books, his *Studies of Classic American Literature* for example, in that wonderful, unpleasant, and even unintelligent preface to *M. M. A Memoir of the Foreign Legion*, in certain of his poems, and, above all, in his short stories.

A
NOTE
ON THE
NOVEL

THE TERM "NOVEL" is now used to describe a thousand different things. Since its false start in the age of Elizabeth and its true start in the age of Charles II, this form of literature has resembled a snowball which gathers snow as it rolls down hill. After this manner does the novel gather to itself every variety of motive, every description of purpose. Starting with amusement as its only intent, starting in an effort to beguile with tales of adventure the dull hours of dullish people in country houses, in the course of time it has picked up every kind of moral and artistic aim. There are the novels of excitement—which still continue—short, sharp, machine-made books to while away the intolerable *ennui* of the hour's journey in the train; there are others of a very ancient order, which have in reality displaced, and assumed the position of, the old sentimental ballads—things turned out, I apprehend, for the ever-diminishing class of domestic servants. Melodrama, too, has been expelled from its original home in the theatre and installed between the pages of a book.

Yet novels of the types described, low as their order is, continue in a sense to fulfil the obligations of a novel. But, alas, the more intelligent the writer, the more confused does he become in his conception of what a novel should be. Thus, with Mr H. G. Wells it has replaced religious teaching and has deepened into a kind of scientific and political programme; propaganda which his genius as a story-teller and his extraordinary gifts of humour and foresight make it easy for us to devour. Other authors—Mr James Joyce ranks chief among them—are attempting to build up a new language for the use of generations yet unborn, and, as some critics maintain, likely to remain so: others, again, are occupied with some philosophical or metaphysical aspect, or with the actual art of words to the exclusion of all else, after the manner of Miss Gertrude Stein; others, like Mrs Virginia Woolf and Mr E. M. Forster are concerned entirely with something vague but none the less interesting—is it human relationships?— but treated with such subtlety, and written of in such quiet and exquisite language, that we accept them as story-tellers.

This mixing of roles is extremely confusing to the novelist, and before leaving the subject of such diversity I should like to examine the lowest class of this literature, detective fiction; a class showing in itself the infinite variety to which even a single branch of novel-writing alone has attained. Nor is it possible to bar these novels of excitement altogether from the realms of literature. Consider the different subdivisions: there are the machine-turned, smart novels—composed in equal parts, like modern furniture, of metal and glass—of Mr Edgar Wallace, books of much undeniable but misguided cleverness; there is, at the highest point, such a book as appeared a year or two ago, *Malice Aforethought*, in which the thrill and excitement are rooted in the psychological interest, rather than in the events described; there are the exquisite adventures of Sherlock Holmes, books which unite the delights of detective fiction with something of the quality of *The Swiss Family Robinson* in that, so to speak, if potatoes are wanted, potatoes, or a substitute for them, are immediately discovered; there are the books, in the American detective style, where, so hurried is the life of that continent, whole sentences rather than words must be read. By this I mean that each sentence is a *cliché*, and that just as the Chinese possess characters which express, not words but whole sentences, so these books are expressed in a similar way, for the untrained brain can from the first assimilate the whole *cliché* it knows, much more easily than it can receive one word it does not expect, and therefore advantage accrues to this method, in the ease and swiftness with which even a rather illiterate person can follow it and be able to grasp without confusion the import of each sentence.

Then there are the masters, Stevenson or Edgar Allan Poe, who exhibit so many levels of interest beneath that of excitement: one, let us say, in the actual fantastic interest of the plot; one in the subtleties of their atmosphere, or the intricacies of their psychology. And how well these books hold their own! Thus, the other day I re-read *Dr Jekyll and Mr Hyde*, astonished at the simplicity of its language and sureness of its touch. In the whole book only one thing could be found which at all dated it, and that was in the character of the person who was murdered—for the fact that (I think his name was Sir Danvers Carew) was a Member of Parliament caused more consternation than the brutality, even, of the crime itself, whereas, in these days, that it was a politician, rather than a more useful member of society, who had been done to death, would, I think, relieve rather than deepen the general horror.

The cause of the decadence of the English novel to-day is, then, to be sought as much in its merit as in its faults. Alas! the most perfect artists are often the most crotchety, convinced of some particular duty to the world: whereas the first duty of every novelist is the plain one of being *readable*. It sounds a humble aim, but it is, in truth, a gift for which any writer must pray. That certain authors are read many years after their bodies have perished, is, first and foremost, because of this quality. By this, I do not mean to signify a lack of obscurity; many extremely obscure writers are eminently readable. Miss Gertrude Stein, for instance, without being easily intelligible is extremely readable—that is, she is a born writer, and once the eye of the readers has lit upon any word she has written he continues to be interested and therefore to read on.

But after this, the chief aim of the novelist should be to illumine personal experience: (this, after all, is only my own conviction, and many authors, as I have suggested, are crochety in respect of their personal convictions); but surely a novelist should seek to identify himself to such a point with the reader, that the reader responds, crying, "This is I! How often have I experienced this, and now I understand it." But for the author to achieve this *is* not as easy as it sounds; for, besides personal experience not being so universal as it is deemed, even this effort to identify reader and author cannot succeed unless the whole novel is *designed*, and that, alas, is precisely where the English writers fail as novelists. They are always writing *outside* the covers of their books; adventures and ideas swarm out of the pages into the air. This love of detail, this wealth of imagination must be disciplined, and yet not so severely as to trim these books of their character. One cannot impose, as Mr George Moore has so interestingly attempted, a French form upon the English novel. The especial national flavour of the British novelist is to be discovered in his Gothic character; and the Gothic Englishman, by his nature, must be free to build his pinnacles and indulge in picturesque, if unnecessary flying buttresses; but, notwithstanding, he must construct them within a disciplined system. This alone is essential.

THACKERAY
AND
"VANITY FAIR"

I HAVE JUST BEEN re-reading Thackeray's *Vanity Fair*, pondering the problems that its former popularity raises. For undoubtedly at one time it *was* universally read, though I am unaware of the extent to which the book is read to-day, and whether it has maintained its appeal.

I had not opened its pages, though they still remained familiar to me, since I had left school, and was amazed at the inferiority of Thackeray to Dickens as an artist. And, which renders the position so much more peculiar, all the stock criticisms of Dickens, made by those who dislike his novels: that he cannot render the portrait of a lady, that he exaggerates, that he interpolates chunks of his own feelings into the story and addresses the reader in an irritating manner, that he indulges in sticky, slushy sentimentality are all of them, however untrue of him, fully justified if applied instead to Thackeray. In his drawing of character he uses a vulgar exaggeration, as it were; never the superb, the magnificent distortion by means of which Dickens bestows upon some of his characters a quite extraordinary significance, by no other method obtainable. Even the names of Thackeray's supposedly comic characters, when compared with the nomenclature invented by Dickens, prove the truth of this assertion: how weak a name is Lord Tapeworm, how good Sir Leicester Dedlock!

When he tries to depict it, Thackeray can never, it seems, produce any characters that are true to low life, and though this may actually have been of aid to his popularity in such snobbish times as those in which he wrote, it deprives the broad panorama that it was his aim to produce of some of its vigour; that sense of energy and virility which Hogarth and Rowlandson share in English pictorial art with writers such as Smollett and Dickens. . . . Further, how much more incisive are the low-life pictures of Dickens than the high-life ones of Thackeray, for which he was so celebrated. Even though Sam Weller and his kind indulge in a Cockney lingo which no longer exists and is difficult for us to read, this does not deprive them of their verisimilitude. Their talk is not nearly so extinct as that of Major Dobbin and Mrs Sedley. In addition, it seems to me that Dickens's Vanity-Fair characters, when he attempts that sort of thing, are actually better than Thackeray's; how much more alive, and of their world, are the distorted portraits of Sir Leicester and Lady Dedlock, in *Bleak House*, and of that supreme poor relation, who always has to be so gay and youthful, Miss Volumnia Dedlock, than any which Thackeray achieves in his exaggerated galleries.

What a horrible suppressed sycophancy, for example, exhales, all unnoticed by the author, from the portrait of the majestically wicked Lord Steyne; what cringing before money and position, what peeping into forbidden cupboards and furtive gleaning of old letters locked in drawers. And why should Becky Sharp, the only attractive and comprehensible person in the book, be made to drink and intrigue so scandalously, just because she has Bohemian connections and comes of Bohemian stock? How deep an importance does not her creator attach to the fact that her grandmother is discovered in the end as a person who locks up the boxes at the Paris Opera! . . . Again, Dickens surely held up a far more accurate and yet amusing mirror to the middle classes than his great contemporary: the image of Amelia's sister-in-law, the unmarried Miss Osborne, fades into nothingness beside that of Mrs Copperfield's sister-in-law, Miss Murdstone. Indeed, it appears as though Thackeray were only successful in his rendering of foreign scenes; for, directly he removes his characters abroad, whether to Waterloo or to a foreign watering-place, they assume a life hitherto lacking altogether in them; whereas Dickens abroad, as in his *Sketches of Italy*, is at his worst.

It is strange, too, to notice the extent to which Thackeray is obsessed by certain antipathies: young cavalry officers, for instance, and above all Members of Parliament. He can hardly allow a chapter in any novel of his to run its course without chucking a literary coconut or a rotten egg at the august body of poor, dead King George IV; poor sport, one would have assumed, and unworthy of an artist of any description; for, whatever the sensual faults of that monarch, he was the only English Prince since Charles I to be endowed with an interest in the arts and literature; the only English Prince since Charles II who liked to be surrounded by people of wit, such as Fox and Sheridan, rather than by the usual court numskulls. It must be remembered, too, that he was a great patron of architecture, that he caused a good collection of old masters to be formed for the royal palaces, that he helped to found the National Gallery and read the works of Jane Austen with an understanding of her worth. For all this, artists should praise him; what business is it of theirs if he was, or was not, married to Mrs Fitzherbert? Moreover, before judging him, it is well to recall the final verdict of the Duke of Wellington, since he at least cannot be accused of any undue partiality for a man who had caused him constant trouble, and who, because he knew that he could not trust his word, had in this respect earned his contempt. He often swore about the King in his lifetime, but many years after his death, when there had been time to focus the dead man in proper perspective, he remarked of him to Raikes: "He was indeed the most extraordinary compound of talent, wit, buffoonery, obstinacy and good feeling, in short, a medley of the most opposite qualities with a great preponderance of good that I ever saw in any character in my life". And this, from the stern and truthful lips of an old man who knew so much, and had read so many men, is an epitaph by no means to be despised.

In this respect, then, as in many others, Thackeray appears to have been unjust.

He is at his best, it may be, in his portraits of the British Merchants: that race of stout, top-hatted, iron-whiskered, bullying braggarts who in his time inhabited the squares and streets of Bloomsbury, now the homes of a much more pacific, cultured and mild-accented sect. . . . But, indeed, his novels suffer greatly from the way in which the scene has changed, even in the last ten years. . . . Where are the moustachioed young artists, the gorgeous, lisping cavalry officers; where the villainous card-sharpers of good birth; where the club-toadies? . . . All are under the heel of industry, commerce and the Slump. The great houses themselves have been pulled down: Lord Steyne's is a museum, Lady Kew's a club. The vast estates in the country have been disposed of, and their heirs pay 16s. 6d. in the pound in income-tax and super-tax. The country houses are only to be visited by those who, having beheld them in the advertisement pages of *Country Life*, have applied for the proper permit. . . . And yet, though Vanity Fair has changed, though the vulgar have inherited the earth and hypocrisy has been succeeded by an often revolting frankness, nevertheless Thackeray's picture of it is still recognizable.

IS
FASCISM
BRITISH?

I HAVE ALWAYS FOUND it, I confessed a few pages back, difficult to read books when first they come out. As exception to this rule, however, I can instance one book which I read at the time of its issue in 1917, and have re-read several times since with the greatest enjoyment, a volume (of which far too little has been said and written) entitled *How to Lengthen our Ears*. It is indeed surprising that it should have been passed over.

Its author is Lord Harberton, described in *Who's Who* as:

7th Visc., *cr.* 1791; Ernest Arthur George Pomeroy; *b.* 1 Dec. 1867 . . . *s.* father, 1912. *m.* 1932, Fairlie Harmar. *Educ.*: Charter-house; Trinity College, Cambridge. Formerly Lieutenant 20th Hussars, and Captain 3rd Battalion Royal Dublin Fusiliers; served South Africa, 1900 (medal). *Publications*: Worse than Scripture, or the Truth about Science, 1924; How to Lengthen our Ears, 1917.

But whatever his qualifications, Lord Harberton, I have no hesitation in writing, is a prophet, and a man of remarkable and humorous discernment, for in his book is to be isolated one of the two germs of Fascism. Further, it must be remembered that this work, a courageous and robust one, was published as long ago as 1917, in the full flood of democracy, when it was almost treason to suggest that people were fighting for any other purpose than to make the world safe for democracy; a moment when, owing to the fact that the powers fighting against us were largely autocratic in government, we persuaded ourselves to forget all about our imperial sentiments and machinations. Sons of big business and great territorial magnates, all were forced equally to fight on behalf of an ideal in which they could not have believed. Those were the days, if you remember, when statesmen and journalists used to indulge in special *clichés*, designed to tickle afresh the public ear; those were the days when they wrote of "the crucible of war", about "the fellowship of the trenches", of "the new spirit of unity", and indulged in all the rest of that treacherous, democratic claptrap which was consummated by a million British deaths.

Into the middle, then, of that perilous welter of platitude, when to speak one's own mind, if it possessed any tinge of common sense, was treason to the State, at a time when we had already lost three-quarters of a million men, and inflicted countless torture on others, all on behalf of the false gods of democracy—into the middle of all this breathed the still, small voice of Lord Harberton. . . . To-day the freshness of his theories is a little faded; they are accepted to a far greater degree than they were fifteen years ago, and, thus removed out of the battle's turmoil, the voice that announced them should prove agreeable, even to those who do not care for his doctrines. For it is a courageous voice, and one intensely prejudiced and humorous. It demonstrates, too, I think, to perfection, various entirely racial characteristics, and indicates how different, were Fascism to triumph here, would be its development from that which it has taken abroad; for, whatever the theories of Lord Harberton, there is no sign of the portentous imperial manner of Rome, which at times mars the effect of the Roman utterance, nor of the solemn, cruel, humourless, exaggerated verbiage of the Germans.

Lord Harberton is a great putter-up of hares, and swift and beautiful creatures his hares often are. Among his theories, then—for it is impossible to enumerate them all—the central theme is that public education has been a mistake. "The terms 'ignorant' and 'uneducated'", our author writes, "are only applied to those unacquainted with books. A man whose knowledge is confined simply to books is considered educated and well-informed. A man whose knowledge is confined to locks will be considered ignorant and uneducated, until he takes up books, but the man who reads books need never understand locks nor anything else, nor need he be able to do anything else except read books." And again: "A man's understanding is almost, if not quite, independent of his education, and to confuse the two has become the folly of the day". I think many fair-minded persons who have met men and women unable to read will agree to this extent, that they must have noticed their far greater acuteness and charm, for they have been forced to study mankind; to study it from nature and not from books and have thus learnt the wisdom of Alexander Pope's dictum that "The proper study of mankind is man".

Lord Harberton tells us that "Athens originated this craze about education; though the Romans were too sensible to have much education themselves, a course at Athens was fashionable". He also maintains that the educated person is the traditional guardian of false doctrines and lies; that only those who were educated enough to understand, for example, the Roman system of portents, could believe in them. He continues: "The buyers and sellers in the market-place . . . can never have believed in Roman portents quite so extensively, so exquisitely, so profoundly, so specifically as a member of the sacred College of Pontiffs, or a member of the Royal College of Augurs (yes, there was one) who had been through a course. Consequently, given the opportunity, the ignorant person was the more likely to shed his beliefs, which is exactly what has occurred over and over again all the way from Caesar to Victoria. The influence of learning has never exploded a single fable or cleared up a single superstition, but, on the contrary, has given to every old error blood, body and backbone."

Again, Lord Harberton was the first to pronounce democracy a failure, and to argue that a great modern people may demand to be governed firmly and not to have votes thrust on it; that it may not want millions of officials, nor the perilous oratory of democratic statesmen, but may prefer instead to be allowed to get on with its business, to be given a good bus service and punctual trains.

All this, it will be seen, was a foreshadowing of Italian Fascism. He must be the first writer to have pointed to the Roman ideals of punctuality and big business. On the other hand, he attacks science, whereas I am inclined to think that

Fascism would patronize it. He is the forerunner of the New Barbarism.

Lord Harberton attacks education and books with all his force. Notwithstanding, it is safe to say that himself must be a cultured and well-read man. Who, it may be asked, has influenced him in his doctrines? Certainly Schopenhauer and Herbert Spencer, while there is something of Nietzsche too. Moreover, at his best he has the blunt, shrewd, adroit style of Samuel Butler; of Butler in his *Notebooks* rather than in his more sustained works. A little class-conscious he is, too, for he advocates that the sons of the richer classes, or, as they used to be called, the upper classes, should now be brought up in a new way; that their "education" should be neglected, and that they should learn, instead of dead languages, practical trades. In this way, he urges, they would regain their lost mastery over the nation; an argument, indeed, which I once put forward in another form,[1] when I advocated that the sons of the workers should be sent to Eton.

[1] "On Public Schools," p. 12.

EIGHTEENTH-
CENTURY
DETAILS

I HAVE BEEN READING a beautifully and profusely illustrated publication, which has recently appeared from the Clarendon Press, entitled *Johnson's England*. To it the appropriate experts have contributed chapters on nearly every branch of English life during the period with which the book is concerned. And though, as a participant in one chapter, I perhaps ought not to allege this, a fascinating two volumes these make, full of information which every educated man ought to possess, and the previous lack of which he must feel, while he reads, to have been humiliating; full, moreover, of hints, all too tantalizing, of further information, of which, were he really educated, he would be cognizant; facts which lurk only just round the corner, and which, in his sloth, he may never now acquire.

Even in the man-in-the-street's realm of patriotic history, shame must overwhelm him who reads. Sir John Fortescue, for example, in his excellent essay, "The Army", writes: "After all, even now how few Englishmen realize that those" (the years 1748 to 1781) "were years of continuous fighting? How many battles are known even by name to the ordinary man who conceives himself to be educated . . .? Of Minden, one of the most striking examples of the prowess of the British soldier, of Warburg, although the elder Mr Weller's public-house bore the sign of the Marquis of Granby, of St Lucia in 1778, the most wonderful instance of success achieved against vastly superior numbers by perfect concert between Army and Navy, they have never heard, or at least could give no coherent account. . . . In India the early work of conquest was achieved principally by mere handfuls of British soldiers, serving under the command of captains, as spear-heads to small bodies of sipahis: yet that is no reason why the names of Stringer, Lawrence, Knox, Forde, Adams and Caillaud be forgotten."

And if our ignorance is thus profound concerning the historical background of the lives led by our not so distant ancestors, how much less still do we know of the miscellaneous details pertaining to them, details of social, artistic and everyday life, even of the startling events of the time! Were *you* aware, for example, of one incident during the American War of Independence, which a little illustrates the vagaries of transport in that epoch, and the difficulties with which commanders had to struggle: General Clinton was sailing from New York to Charleston, Carolina, with the force under his command, when a fierce gale overtook him, and two of his transports were blown clean over the Atlantic—one to Falmouth in Cornwall, the other to Cartagena in Spain? . . .

Were you informed, again, of the circumstances attending Captain Cook's third and last voyage of discovery; things, surely, which we all ought to know?

The great Captain, on his return from his second voyage, had, in token of gratitude, and as some slight recompense for his immense services to England and the world, been granted an appointment at Greenwich Hospital. Almost at once, however, the Lords of the Admiralty found themselves in need of more information: as to the possibility, among other things, of a North-West Passage. Aware that he was the only man who could help them, they yet did not care so soon to disturb him. When their difficulty became apparent, he solved it for them by at once *volunteering*. And indeed, as Professor Williamson writes, "being what he was he could not do otherwise. He was now the representative not only of England but of civilization, and civilization acknowledged it." And in the method of this acknowledgment there is something for this century to learn, for when, during Captain Cook's last voyage, war broke out between England and France, the French Minister of Marine issued orders to all his admirals that "Captain Cook shall be treated as a commander of a neutral and allied power", and subsequently the American and Spanish naval authorities issued similar instructions to those under their command. . . . In the last war, I fear, a special price would have been set on his head, and the enemy troops would have been encouraged to bomb him from the air and torpedo him from under the water!

Are you aware, again, of how your ancestors were buried, of the severe but costly ritual attendant on their funerals? "Hatchments were hung on the front of the house and cards of invitation, adorned with all the trappings of grief, skulls, skeletons, coffins and gravestones, were issued by the undertakers. Women, known as Wakers, sat up with the dead. . . . In memory of the departed, mourners were presented with mourning rings, some of which were of a considerable value. The pall-bearers were given black silk hatbands and black gloves, and servants in attendance received the same. The parson who performed the service was also presented with a hatband and gloves in addition to his fee, which varied with the rank of the corpse and the generosity of the relatives." Parson Woodforde, in describing in his diary one funeral at which he presided, relates how before the service there was "Chocolate and Toast and Cake with red Wine and white", and after it, again, cake and dried toast, chocolate and wine, and concludes his description, "It was as decent, neat, handsome a funeral as I ever saw"! Nor was this ceremonial spirit limited to the richer classes; among the labouring poor burial-clubs were common, and at some pauper funerals it was customary to toll the bell and provide beer for the bearers.

A French contemporary traveller, Le Blanc, observed that "the care the English take of all particulars of their burial, would make one believe that they find more pleasure in dying than living". But herein, surely, he was wrong. Londoners, we learn from the pages of this book, were able to enjoy themselves then as never since, in their own way whether vigorous or quiet. There were constant scenes in the street, so that walking was a pleasure; and, in the fine weather, there were cool places in which they could find comfort. When next obliged to slink down the burning pavements of the petrol-laden streets of our great metropolis, conscious that no place exists in which we can sit, peaceful and contented, in the open air, we shall look back with regret to eighteenth-century London. Of the existence of Ranelagh and Vauxhall, the resorts of the rich, we were cognizant; but what of Bagnigge Wells, Sadler's Wells, White Conduit House, Marylebone Gardens and Islington Spa?

The features of these London pleasure gardens, we are told, were walls, lawns, clipped hedges, shrubberies, as much ornamental water as could be managed, with a grotto, fountains and statues, vistas and views. "Within the environs of the capital", wrote a German visitor, "there is a prodigious number of tea-gardens. The happy arrangement, the order, the cleanliness, the promptitude of the service, the company always numerous and agreeable make these gardens as pleasant as they are interesting. At Bagnigge Wells, in fine weather, it is surprising to find from ten to twelve hundred people taking tea. . . . These places are frequented only by the middle and common class; people of distinction come rarely, ladies of quality never." . . . What can be said now on behalf of the sweltering London teashops, which cater for those of middle income, in a "new and elegant way"?

SOME
PRESENT
ELEMENTS
OF LITERARY
CORRUPTION

THOUGH AS YET very little plain venality exists in politics (and that which obtains is mostly of a nature more subtle, indirect, and therefore unindictable than in former ages), never, I think, since the days of the nineteenth century has improbity so flourished in the world of books.

The other day, for example, I noticed that a young lady-novelist—let us call her Miss Mink—had written a new novel. Doubtless it did not altogether lack merit (it was on the recommended list issued by the Book Society): and I saw quoted, in the publisher's advertisements of the book which appeared in every newspaper, the laudatory opinion of another lady-novelist, better known—she had been at the game for years—somewhat to the following effect: "This is a work of entrancing genius and should be read in every home. A. B. C. Smith." Now, herein lay, at any rate, a suppression of the truth; the reviewer should have signed herself "Aunt Alice": because Miss Smith is maternal aunt to Miss Mink, as I happen to know, but the world does not. (How should it?) . . . Miss Smith's husband, too, squirts ink upon paper, and I await from his direction further discoveries of the talent of his niece by marriage.

I admire family feeling, and far worse than this fond semi-ramp, it seems to me, is the "New Reviewing": which, so far as I am aware, has never yet been exposed, or explained, to the public. Its method is simple and yet bold.

Those who review novels are, for the most part, poor men, not averse to increasing their incomes, so long as the means to this end present an honest appearance: unfortunately, too, they are, in the main, simple men with an exaggerated love of books (or they would no longer be poor). A publisher, then, will approach a few of these people, the reviewers of— from a literary standpoint—several important papers, and, without any one of them being aware that his *confrères* have received identical letters, will assure each of them of the great admiration and respect which he, the publisher's representative, has conceived for the judgment of this particular critic, and will ask him if he will not act as a reader for the firm? Only a few books—for the publisher well knows how busy he is, how important his time—will be sent him each year, and these will be the ones by which the publisher sets store: and may he offer a salary of a few hundred pounds a year? It is not enough, the publisher asserts, for such valuable services; that much is certain; but it should not entail too much labour. . . . The delighted reviewers, all innocence, accept. The cheques arrive regularly: but the firm waits until a likely book comes their way, then send to each of these reviewers, retained at a fee, a copy of it, with a covering letter to indicate that this is the only book for many weeks which has been thought worthy of him. Should he form a similar opinion of it, will he inform the publishers? . . . The reviewer, in a contented mood—only one book in so many months and drawing a salary all the time—writes an enthusiastic letter back. Henceforth this written statement of his opinion pledges him. He must give the book "at least a column" when it appears: though when that time comes he will be surprised, once more, at how right was his decision in the first place, for he notices that four or five of his *confrères* award it the same place and treat it with the same flattering respect. Should he suspect the machinations responsible for the favourable impression the book has created, he must be content to face the loss of income which his rebellion must inevitably entail. He prefers not to bother his mind about it. . . . Probably it is a coincidence.

Literary prizes, again, offer a new element of corruption; of which perhaps sufficient advantage has not yet been taken, for comparatively few literary prizes exist in England. Gold Cups there are in plenty for racehorses, but none for poets, that equally famous English breed.

Nevertheless one or two committees *do* award prizes, paltry in their amount, if kindly in their intention; but these, it must be admitted, have seldom picked a real winner of whom little had previously been known. Either the old favourites romp in every time, or else outsiders, of whom nothing is heard again. . . . The Hawthornden Committee, it is true, have selected at various times Mr David Garnett, Mr Blunden and Mr Siegfried Sassoon; but all of these were already celebrated writers. So far as I am aware—I hope I shall be proved wrong—no English prizes have been awarded, to take a few names at random, to Mr Aldous Huxley, Mr Richard Aldington, Mr T. S. Eliot, Mr Sacheverell Sitwell, Mr Coppard, Mr John Collier, the late Mr D. H. Lawrence, Mr Roy Campbell, Mr Plomer or any other writers of like distinction—for alas! however worthy or even admirable the motives of the donor, it seems as though the committees which govern the decisions are invariably liable, either to fall into academic stupor, or to become the victim of some attack of fashionable hysteria, the literary influenza of the moment. . . . Nevertheless whoever is privileged to be invited to the functions in which these decisions culminate, should always attend them, so productive are they, to an almost distressing point, of unconscious humour. What mutual compliments abound upon the platform, what fanciful congratulations, what lisping and mouthing, what writhing and twitching, what sighs and hollow, owl-like pantings; how shy, too, is the recipient of the prize, ignored by all. A cheque, even when given in time to ward off starvation, seldom stops the derisive lips of a satirist; yet these prizes are not without their effect. The needy must keep an eye on their master, must learn to be good boys, not too original, not too mutinous or inattentive.

Then again—and these, being armed with greater power both in the way of spreading the jam and forbidding it altogether, keep order more successfully—there are the Book Societies, the Book Guilds and Book-of-the-Month Clubs.

The history of these nefarious associations is recent and easily related. After the manner of so many other destructive phenomena, like the philoxera and the rose beetle, they first reached our shores from those of America. At their best, a sinister manifestation of that all-prevailing tendency toward uniformity, toward a standardization of taste, at their worst they place power in the hands of a narrow coterie of critics, publishers and authors. It may be that, as they claim, these associations are open and above-board in their tedious and mediocre choice; but I may record here, as an instance of the way their names can be taken in vain, thus affording the use of a new weapon to those who should not be entrusted with one, that, when the representative of a most reputable firm of publishers interviewed me for the purpose of procuring my name for his list, he stated how, if I were willing to write a book which he had suggested to me, and would allow his firm to publish it, he could arrange—"wangle" was, I think, the term he used—for it to be chosen as the Book of the Month. Thus, in fact, he offered me, if what he said were true, a bribe amounting to several hundreds of pounds, to come to a firm of publishers which "had a pull". And if, on the other hand, his promise was not capable of fulfilment, at any rate the existence of these organizations had enabled him to say it, and me to wonder how much truth supported his boast.

THE ARTS
OF READING
AND WRITING:
THEIR FUTURE

THE SPRING MONTHS of the year, until the end of June, I spent in Greece and Italy, waiting for the early hot weather which is so pleasant; but the seasons were awry. A bitter wind raced round the corners of the Athenian streets and bellowed under the ruined pediments of the Parthenon. At Olympia sounded a perpetual deluge, which woke all the snakes that usually sleep under the fallen columns, and in the month of June the new Rome, with its wide corridors driven through the heart of the city, lay heavily under the clouds, as though the tremendous alterations which had taken place there had offended its ancient gods.

All this, it may be, was conducive to reading; but where were the books? I tried to buy a copy of the *Città Morta* by d'Annunzio, but found that it had died out of fashion and was not stocked by any shop. English and French books were few. In Athens there was a copious supply of Mr Edward Hutton's works, and a few old copies of *Vogue* and *Harper's Bazaar* lay about on the counters; and for these a queue of Greek ladies ever waited, turning over the pages and looking at the latest fashions without any intention of buying the magazine.

Here in London, on the other hand, I have found the fullest summer, an endless stream of books and but little inclination to read them. To-day, when a golden haze lies upon the city, which, even though it is the least fitted of all European capitals for such weather, seems to blossom like the fullest blown of roses, while the rolling of the passing omnibuses supplies a never failing synthetic thunder as accompaniment, and every landscape, usually so fresh and heavy, trembles under the heat; while the cicadas sing at night among the grass, and the branches of the trees are light as feathers in the faintest wind; it is easier, perhaps, to think about reading and writing than to achieve either. Scattered over London, as I write, people are sitting in the parks with books open before them, finding it hard to read. Eyes wander up from books, any distraction will serve; a dog galloping round, or curled asleep, a child tottering along a path, or an old man talking to himself. And how odd are the people whom the heat draws out, the scarecrows and ghosts of the greatest city in the world! Heat seems to cause them to emerge, just as it produces those obscure and exotic insects, of whose bites die every year a few members of the community. . . . So thoughts wander; but very seldom does the play of these minds concern the art with which the books flapped open on their knees are connected. And here we may pause to remember that, for every one of those we picture with books on their knees, there are dozens crackling their newspapers and actually reading them.

In the past hundred years almost all English men and women, including even the blind, have been taught—but never have they been taught *what*—to read and write. Reading has been offered to them as a drug to soothe their nerves and fill their brief leisure, the equivalent of "soma" in Mr Aldous Huxley's *Brave New World*, and has also been presented to them as something easy, like eating, swimming or "kicking a ball about". Seldom has it been revealed to them as an art, though in truth the reader should be as carefully and patiently trained as the writer. Alas, just as the writing of English—apart from Business Men's English—is seldom taught in schools, so is the reading of it.

Far be it from me to advocate that every leisure hour should be spent in reading Shakespeare. There is a lot to be said for sheer idleness; it may be, even, that the power to muse in hot weather, extending over many generations, has been responsible for the work of Shakespeare himself. Certainly of no hereditary tendency to read the classics will great poetry ever be born, for the perfect use of leisure is to prefer your own thoughts when surrounded by every possible amusement. And so the great mass of people who sit at this moment with books or papers before them, refusing to read, have right on their side. But I fear that for the most part the reason which prompts this attitude is merely that the sensationalism of their pages, which makes its victims ever demand stronger doses, is not powerful enough. . . . Nor am I against sensationalism; but it must be of that kind which, exploding like a bomb, opens the mind, blasting holes and passages and tunnels through conventional thought.

In this kind I have read two books lately, one American and one English, of which the writers seem to me to hold more promise than any of their fellow-writers of to-day. I refer to *Light in August* by William Faulkner, and *Tom's A-cold* by John Collier. The sensationalism of Faulkner's book is concerned with the cruel and morbid struggle between blacks and whites in America; that of Mr Collier, more subtle and more intimidating, with the future of the English race. . . . Sometimes the genius of an author is made plain even by the use of a quotation, and at the beginning of *Tom's A-cold,* in which Mr Collier describes the people who live among the ruins of present-day towns, he places that terrifying passage from *King Lear* in which the old king, seeing Edgar is cold, by chance and through lack of clothes, decides to divest himself of his own. "'Thou art the thing itself; unaccommodated man is no more but such a poor, bare, forked animal as thou art. Off, off, you lendings! Come; unbutton here.' (*Tearing off his clothes.*)"

Wherein the analogy of this passage seems so woefully just is because Lear *purposely* divests himself of his habiliments; precisely in the same way as the modern world, though it plainly sees the dangers facing it, marches quite boldly on towards annihilation. The idea of progress has perished; and though this Victorian faith may have been in itself an illusion, a belief in it is absolutely necessary, even if the world itself only wishes to mark time and not at all to advance. And of the civilization of which men are seemingly so anxious to divest themselves, reading and writing are part.

The old nineteenth-century humanists looked forward to a world in which everyone could read and write, but, on the other hand, I think the time will come when the majority of Europeans and Americans will not use this power, even should they be in a position to acquire it. Already the masses prefer a cinema to an illustrated paper, and an illustrated paper to a printed one; and when, in the near future, the world of amusement provides a greater variety—in days when every house will possess its own theatre: a little box, or screen full of figures, which have volume as well as flatness and can sing and talk and act—there will be no more reading in the average home.

Nor, perhaps, need one contemplate this prospect with apprehension, for by it literature will be liberated once more. That which the camera has achieved for painting, by freeing it from the necessity to record with photographic accuracy, these inventions will accomplish for writing. The reading public will then be as loyal and enlightened as at the present moment are the lovers of poetry. Foreigners have often wondered that the English people, who all through their history have produced poets in profusion, and of a quality unsurpassed by any other nation, should for the most part themselves be insensible to poetry; but it must be remembered that the public for poetry in England is the most loyal in the world. To this kind of public, but on a much larger scale, the writer of the future will appeal. He may be conscious that only a few hundred thousand people, where to-day there is a possibility of millions, will read his books; but he will know that this public will follow with appreciative discernment every word from his pen.

327

ON THE
BURNING OF BOOKS
AS
PRIVATE PASTIME
AND
NATIONAL RECREATION

COMPARATIVELY FEW PERSONS, we have just prophesied, will read printed matter in the future; but I doubt
whether this need inevitably affect the production of books.
Because reading it is not the only thing you can do with
a book—you can also burn it. Newspapers are already used
in the majority of houses to light fires, and the book of the
future may serve a similar but more general purpose.

In a sense, the burning of one's books is a gesture similar
to that of burning one's boats. It marks a definite step. Moreover it affords relief, both to the private individual and to
the general public. The unliterary mind, it may be, finds
more pleasure in the smashing of a plate; but, to those who
know and hate literature, there is no satisfaction comparable
to that of poking some special volume's glowing ashes.

We have been treated to a good deal of the sport in the

past few decades. My first experience of it was when I saw those responsible for the education of my sister warming their hands at the embers of Swinburne's *Poems and Ballads.* Thirty or forty years earlier, no doubt, it would have been Shelley rather than Swinburne. But, though up to the close of King Edward's lifetime books were still burnt as part of the normal upbringing of any intelligent child, it was not until the war years that the setting alight of printed matter became a national recreation. . . . Who can ever forget those enjoyable bouts of newspaper-burning? The circulation of the condemned journals must have risen by thousands; for in order to burn a newspaper one has first to buy it. And any paper which did not suggest that the war was the best possible war, that the lads loved it, and that it would swiftly be brought to a glorious conclusion, was publicly burnt as a matter of course.

Nevertheless, newspapers are, by their very nature, ephemeral, and therefore their destruction does not offer to a cultured person the feeling of release afforded him by the burning of a *book.* Alas! only latterly has book-burning attained to national proportions. At one time it was un-organized and sporadic; and thus unsuitable to an era of organization and efficiency. But the matter has now been remedied. With the rise to power of the Nazi Government, book-burning, in Germany at least, has once for all assumed its proper place. All books that were un-German have been consigned to the stake, and in so doing, who knows but that the Nazis may have lighted such a candle as shall never be put out? Moreover, should a similar situation arise here, where literature is taken less heavily than on the Continent, would it not be the authors, rather than their works, who would be sacrificed?

The reasons for the widespread hatred of literature are to be sought in many morbid complexes. There is the gnawing and continual fear, which the most uninteresting people perpetually entertain, that they may be "put into a book"; a fear which fortunately in some cases makes them nervous of meeting authors, though in others it leads to an irritating amount of rudeness. (Many, it is true, are too shy to be rude individually and alone. These unfortunates are compelled to form themselves into lecture-associations, luncheon-clubs and the like; to which they invite the author to come without payment, and then, having got him there, proceed in mass to insult him.) For any author, more especially a novelist, is regarded by these persons as a collector of specimens, who stalks through life catching the poor creatures unaware and imprisoning them in those curious cubes which he manufactures. . . . (If only a character could know the degree of touching up and of toning down which he requires if he is to appear even as the most humble auxiliary!) . . . Then, too, there is the fact that, since an author is often endowed with the gift of words, he can, when challenged, crush his specimen with ease. . . . It is singular, therefore, that fears thus engendered should incline the character to be rude to the author from the beginning. Surely it would be better to propitiate him?

Again, there is much chagrin at the miserliness which authors display in the giving of their time for advice. They exist to be consulted on every subject, and it is well known that they have at their disposal hours unlimited; but are they willing to bestow it on every worthy cause? No! This is responsible for much annoyance, and I well remember an old lady, unknown to my sister, who wrote to her inquiring if she could explain the secret of how to keep a hot-water bottle *really* hot during the night? Apparently, however boiling the water might be when put into the bottle, it would never remain at the right temperature for more than five or six hours. This occurred during the lifetime of Mr Arnold Bennett, and my sister replied that she happened to be rather busy at the moment, and therefore regretfully found herself unable to devote as much time as she would have liked to the solution of the problem, but that, since both Mr H. G. Wells and Mr Arnold Bennett were proverbially idle, she advised the old lady to write to them instead. They, she was sure, would be delighted to give their advice on a subject of such concern to humanity.

Upon another occasion a rather stout lady, wearing a sombrero hat, and clad in a sensible coat and skirt, appeared at my house and, when I opened the door, quickly threw her foot into the gap, and asked me to take down in coloured silks the embroideries which she would sing to me. She indicated that she had taught this remarkable accomplishment to an Indian student, whom she had specially trained for the purpose. She used to sing: and from her singing he would seize the appropriate design and colour. Unfortunately he had died, and she had concluded, from my writings, that I would serve instead. I assured her that this was not the case, and supplied her with the addresses of various friends whom I thought more suitable for her purpose. . . .

Whether the root of such incidents is in a conscious desire

to waste the time of authors and thus prevent their working, or whether it is merely a matter of instinct, will, I suppose, never be scientifically decided: but book-burnings are their outcome. Speaking for my own part, as long as the book is bought, I do not mind its being burnt; but the end which I fear is that the book will be borrowed, and then burnt: for just as it is known that authors have this infinite time upon their hands, so the public believes them to have an unlimited supply of books; to be, in fact, a sort of lending library of their own works. More than this, nobody who is proposing to organize a bazaar ever thinks twice before asking an author to give his works, and, in addition, to sign them. . . .

It may be worth while now to conjecture which English books would meet the same fate in England as that of the un-German books in Germany, should the government of the day be in the happy position of being able to enforce these decrees? Some authors would be spared because they are not read, and others would be burnt for the same reason. Shakespeare would be spared, one presumes, because he is so little read: though were he a German writer, and had he written of Germans in the same way that he wrote of Bottom, Snout and Starveling, he would most certainly have been burnt. . . . I suppose no writer earlier than the nineteenth century would be consigned to the flames? Shelley is presumably safe: but nearly all modern poets would be burnt, and the works of all such philosophers as Bertrand Russell. D. H. Lawrence would similarly be a favourite for fiery treatment, because perhaps full enjoyment of an *auto-da-fé* is only to be obtained when there is also the support of a fanatical minority.

Which books should be chosen would, I imagine, be

decided by the readers of the newspapers; and I venture to suggest that Mr James Douglas, of the *Sunday Express*, would make a suitable executioner; for in him the moral sense seems to be developed to its finest form and most acute degree.

TA-RA-RA-
BOOM-DE-AY!

The Muse of Alfred Noyes

"When Marjorie walked in the wood
    There was nothing to frighten her there.
She was beautiful, bold and good;
    But the little leaves whispered beware;
For she walked,
    Alone in the
    Wood,
    Like a daughter of Berkeley Square."

"Throned among primrose cushions, in a window of Berkeley Square
Lady Jane and the Pekinese are goggling up in the air,
Where dark against the dazzling sky a British workman stands.
Toiling—Nah! He's lighting his pipe in the pit of his horny hands."

THESE LITTLE QUOTATIONS I have chosen as being the
most typical, the most perfect, examples of Mr Noyes's
bellicose yet tender Muse. Some, reading them, may say that

their author is a subject more for psycho-analysis than for criticism; it is true, for example, that the words "Berkeley Square" occur with a rather suspicious regularity; but this may be due as much to the fortunate rhyming of "Square" with "air", "there", and "beware", as to any more suppressed cause of complex and inhibition. Indeed, there appears at first sight to be precious little inhibition about Mr Noyes's poems.

Both these verses possess that particular quality described as a "true note of singing"; both have in them the sobbing, hiccoughs and castanets of the old music hall and its songs.

A very active man is Mr Noyes. A dozen or so books of verse stand to his credit; it would not, therefore, be fair (Berkeley Square) to expect every poem in every book to be a good one.

But these verses are tiring to read, and must have been more so, surely, to write? No posture is so fatiguing as that of defence, when no enemy is attacking; no attitude more undignified than that of assault, when there is no enemy to attack. Mr Noyes believes in vigorous hitting; but the wooden antagonists which he himself has constructed fall down directly he hits them, and in falling, invariably injure their maker. Two things, it is evident, Mr Noyes cannot abide—the progressive in politics, the Bolshevik in poetry.

As we know, a properly brought-up bull, sharing Mr Noyes's antipathy to Bolshevism, will charge anyone or anything, however faintly tinged with red. But even a bull, an animal perhaps with greater reputation for courage than for intelligence, chooses his colour carefully, whereas Mr Noyes goes further: he sees red first, and then charges! If he charges, the object of his assault must be red.

In the intervals of his many books, between an epic on science, a whirlwind tour of the American universities or a masterly raid on the tomb of Drake, our active hero spends much time in defending Tennyson and other Victorian idols, clearing their characters for ever of crimes of which they have never been accused. But, though privileged to hear Mr Noyes's opinion of the late Lord Tennyson, never—except in our own hearts—shall we be privileged to know Alfred Lord Tennyson's view of Mr Alfred Noyes. It is, however, our own conviction that there would have been trouble between the two Alfreds had they been contemporary; that His Lordship might even have risen from his seat as hereditary legislator to demand the impeachment of the younger Alf.

Mr Noyes's verse, we take it, is intended to follow up and justify his defence of the great who have preceded him. The quality, we are given to understand, shared by Swinburne, Tennyson, Keats and Noyes is that of "singing". . . . But to sing is not really sufficient. No one has ever accused Mr Noyes of not "singing". "Come down to Kew in lilac time" should have been—and perhaps was—whistled by every errand boy in town. "Pagan Marjorie" and "Fey Joan" in the volume before me manifest the same quality. Alas! the effect of all this "singing" is but to make us prefer quiet. If Mr Noyes *must* "sing", it would be easier to bear if he would even sing flat occasionally, or do something unexpected.

But the process of his ratiocination, even more than his singing, is at fault. Mr Noyes argues, in effect, but with much force: "Tennyson was a great poet. He was also,

336

occasionally a great bore. I am sometimes a bore. . . . Therefore I am a great poet."

These same little lapses in logic occur in his verse. In the second poem quoted at the beginning of this essay occurs, in a later stanza, the exquisite line:

But Bill don't read 'em, of course he don't, for Bill has his pipe to smoke.

Now Mr Kipling, who has no greater admirer than Mr Noyes, would, in the frenzy of his democratic patriotism, and in his fidelity to those types which, however unfortunately, he does undoubtedly create, have discarded all his remaining "aitches"—had there been any—and thrown them to the winds. Not so Mr Noyes, for the innate refinement of the latter gent only permits him an occasional deviation from the speech of a Public School and 'Varsity man. The line quoted should surely have been rendered either with realism as (1), "But Bill don't read 'em—o' course 'e don't, for Bill 'as 'is pipe to smoke"; or, more prettily, but with less fidelity as (2), "But Bill dœrs nert read therm —erv kerse he dœrs nert, fœr Bill has his paipe to smœke."

Yet Mr Noyes redeems himself in the last line of the whole poem, where, master of imagery that he is, he sums up the whole magnificent conception in one forcible phrase:

But Bill has lighted his blasted pipe, and he spits into Berkeley Square.

What, then, is the exact position of Mr Noyes among the great, the great who are no more? For it is hard to match him in contemporary poetry. His place, undoubtedly, is among those who have gone before. It is a difficult but fascinating speculation. . . . Nevertheless, if we may be allowed to Kipple for an instant, this much seems certain, that Mr Alfred Noyes and the late Mrs Ella Wheeler Wilcox "are sisters under the skin". The former is less graceful, more strong; the latter more whimsical, more subtle, more feminine, even. As befits her sex and race, her work shows less interest in politics; she was no empire-builder; while Mr Noyes stands in the direct descent, apparently, from Drake and Raleigh, as well as from Shakespeare and Tennyson. He is still a Viking at heart.

Yet Mr Noyes, for all his singing, is very modern, of that there can be no doubt—and sometimes a little obscure? What, for instance, does he mean by that darkling phrase: "the smack of his noon-day cheese"; a phrase that, in its gusto, recalls the old pantomime business, between the clowns, preceded always by the query, "Do you like custard?"?

PROPHECY

ON
PROPHETS
AND
PROPHECY

THE MAJORITY OF mankind is numbered among the prophets; all of us, that is to say, who give ourselves time occasionally to think—and, still more, those who possess the leisure in which to allow their brains to lie fallow. The rarest gift of prophecy is, perhaps, that which applies itself with accuracy to small things: and of this gift I can boast, for am I not able often to foretell—and that without attempting to read it, but merely by the look of the names of the author and publisher—which book will be selected as the Book of the Month? And, further, on one occasion was I not able to announce publicly, through the columns of the press, the name of a winner of the Hawthornden Prize, ten days (so a member of the Committee subsequently announced at the particularly enjoyable prize-giving which ensued) before the Committee itself had been able to make up its mind? But such a gift, though uncommon, is perhaps not altogether unconnected with the possession of common sense, and I am far more interested in the true and ancient scope of prophecy —the rise and fall of nations and even of the world itself. Yet prophecy needs renewing, has grown old and soft.

In the first place, let us demand greater imagination from the prophets, and, at the same time, a greater ambiguity of expression; a return to classicism, as it were. Events must again be allowed a larger opportunity of living up to prophecies; for those who professionally make them have lately become too prone to detail, too niggling-minded; altogether too limited and literal in their output. Why, even those imaginative persons who devote their lives to unravelling the secrets of the Great Pyramid, and revealing them to the English-speaking world through the medium of full-page advertisements in the more dignified morning papers, allow themselves to be too explicit in prognostication. Mother Shipton knew better.

Not, of course, that a prophet ever seems to have been injured in reputation by the failure or collapse of his predictions. Did, for example, the opening of Joanna Southcott's box discourage her adherents? . . . Not in the least! . . . Thoroughly exposed in her lifetime as a mad old humbug, her adherents maintained their clamour for over a century. Like all evil things, her cult throve particularly during the "Great War", and later, in 1924, her followers presented a monster petition to the Archbishop of Canterbury, who completely ignored it. In July 1927, however, the magic casket, which, it had been stated, would reveal so many secrets, was opened by the Bishop of Grantham: to disclose a miscellaneous collection of objects more usually connected with the laying of foundation-stones—cards, coins, ornaments, and a distinctly curious volume entitled *The Surprises of Love: or An Adventure in Greenwich Park.* . . . In no way dismayed by the discovery of these articles, her followers asserted that they had always expected it. The box had been opened in the wrong way, and too few bishops were present at the ceremony. Another box, if opened in the presence of *twenty-four* bishops, would surely reveal the treasures of wisdom destined to save our country. . . . So, too, during the war, the tactical prophets, though hardly ever accurate in a single prediction, flourished like trench-rats and, at the end of years of failure, the chief of them had the audacity to write a book on the failure of prophecy!

What, then, can be done to restore prophecy to the ancient esteem in which it was held? . . . Largely, I think, this restoration is a technical matter. Consider the prophecies of the Apparitions in *Macbeth*, such as:

> Macbeth shall never vanquished be until
> Great Birnam Wood to high Dunsinane Hill
> Shall come against him.

That is the perfection of prophecy; to which rhyme is essential, for the mere arrangement of words in artificial positions which its use entails, must lend a certain essential ambiguity to the content. . . . But the poetry, to be effective, need not be so good. Shiptonesque couplets are more awe-inspiring than predictions couched in prose, and the worst doggerel can carry a great weight of significance. . . . Surely Sir John Squire could arrange for some of his team of Georgian poets, now so largely unemployed, to stop playing

343

cricket and, instead, to develop this new line of business in good, old, country-bumpkin verse, full of burrs, such as:

> When yonderr towerr shall lose its thatch
> England shall win a cricket match?

(And, by the way, how long ago was it that I prophesied, in *Triple Fugue*, Sir John Squire's knighthood, together with that earldom which the future still holds for him?) Or, again, if you wish for more nebulous and sophisticated prophecy, certainly the Lads of the Left, Mr Grigson's and Dr Leavis's laurelled lambs, would be able to supply it.

As for the matters with which the reformed art should deal, we are all a little tired of Jules Verne and his descendants. . . . Their prophecies have for too long been realized, overtaken by fact. Nobody in this century wishes to read a forecast of Edisonian, nineteenth-century machinery. Throughout the ages the two most absorbing subjects have been the conquest of the air and the end of the world; and so they remain to the soothsayers, though one has long been achieved and the other seems well on its way to achievement. . . . The only prophet who, in the second instance, has shown originality is the able author, Mr Geoffrey Dennis, who has devoted a whole book to that unwieldy topic, the end of the world, and, in prose almost too vivid, has discussed every variant of destruction which could overtake us. . . . With this final anthology the matter should be closed.

Chief of the new prophets who foretell new things with originality, and are able to impart to a reader of them a conviction of their truth, is Mrs Charlotte Haldane, whose novel *Man's World* is a remarkable achievement. Then, too, there is Mr Aldous Huxley; but how smoothly, as we watch it from the depths of the slump-years, his *Brave New World* seems to run. . . . And, of course, Mr H. G. Wells, leader among the prophets for the last thirty years: a great prophet, but one, indeed, whose estimates of the future, as I read them, always seem to me fairer and more convincing than his estimates of the past.

No one, of course, would presume to offer advice to these: but to prophets less gifted I would counsel, in addition to adopting rhyme, that they should pay a far greater amount of attention to death-rays and plagues, scientifically provoked, and also, perhaps, to Dr Picard's adventures with—or in— the stratosphere. They should also, before graduation, devote themselves to a prolonged study of biblical language and rhythms; which are able to invest even the slightest threat with a most ominous and sinister burden of meaning. . . . Certainly Isaiah and Jeremiah understood their business to perfection: like Mr Wells, they prophesied continually (which in any prophet is a great asset); and, unlike him, they prophesied only evil. And that is what we enjoy. . . . Every prophecy, to be really popular, must be flavoured with menace; since man likes to imagine himself, poised on the flying second, heir of the ages, a proud and prosperous figure outlined against a barbaric past and a decadent future. His own future happiness, his own continued future, is assured by the means of some such conception as heaven; but oh, as he grows old, the future of the race is black, black, black . . . and ever has been!

ON
CENTENARIES

EVERY DAY IS somebody's centenary—of a real somebody as well as of countless mute inglorious Miltons. (Just
recently we celebrated Rossetti's centenary—false one,
though, for it was reckoned from his birth instead of from
his death.) And there are also tercentenaries, growing in
popularity.

Since it is necessary for great nations to have great men,
we are obliged, I suppose, to celebrate their centenaries;
otherwise the public would not hear of them. The mere
startling newness, to most people, of the information imparted to them during a centenary makes it palatable. The
most remarkable change—we are told by the librarians in
congratulatory speeches—manifested in the reading of the
public is the growing demand for biography as opposed to
fiction. But the reason for this change is identical with the

reason for the popularity of centenaries: the public is intensely surprised at the facts and incidents with which these books present them.

Thus, the great sale of Ludwig's *Life of Napoleon* was largely due to the majority of its readers never having been aware of the existence of the Emperor. Every fresh fact, toned down and made easily digestible, afforded a little thrill of surprise and wonder. "And so near our own taime! Well ai am serr-praised" was the most usual comment the book evoked.

And when literary men or artists of any kind are the objects of centenaries, the celebration offers to the great British public an opportunity to cover its tracks. If only it can show sufficient slobbery and snobbery at last, a hundred years after the artist's death, the rudeness and neglect to which he was subjected in his lifetime (and to which his successors are subjected to-day) will be smoothed over and forgotten.

Even now, though, it is not too late to be rude to Rossetti, for the British public requires a full century to accomplish its entire swing from obloquy to cringing, and he has only been dead sixty years. Thus, a charming journalist from an enterprising North of England newspaper called on me the other day to try and induce me to be rude about him.

In a sense it was tempting. It is hardly fair to expect a poet of to-day to be entirely taken up with the work of his grandmother, so to speak—though, in this country, there are many still concerned with such. Personally my preference is for the work of to-day, or for the work of several centuries ago. Yet much as I value the work of the generation of Keats, Shelley and Byron, or of Tennyson and Rossetti, I can hardly feel the thrill of discovery that goes through the British public

347

at the mention of any of their works. "From my youth up I have been acquainted with the works of the best authors, but it was not until later that the work of Keats crept on to my shelves," wrote an old lady in protest to me on one occasion.

Yet, has the centenary business a future? . . . I wonder. . . . Monkey glands constitute a serious threat to it: for we must face facts. Science has triumphed in its noble attempt to prolong the life of the ordinary rat to three times its natural span, and we shall surely follow in the wake of the rat, so that soon the author himself may be forcibly kept alive to celebrate his own centenary; that is to say, the celebration will be held in honour of the hundred years which have elapsed since his spiritual and mental, rather than his physical, decay. If the poet were to die young, all would be well: the occasion could be extolled in the good, old-fashioned way— and we usually encourage our poets to die young. But, should he by some strange chance survive the persecution which will be his lot, and live to the age of eighty or ninety, he would then have become a Grand Old Man and would not be allowed to shuffle off this mortal coil. Forcible monkey-glands may well succeed to forcible feeding. An operation of this sort, if voted by the people, might be substituted for burial in the Abbey. . . .

On the other hand, granted that the British public have a liking for Grand Old Men, how would it be possible to take an interest in a man of only eighty or ninety when, still living amongst us, completely animalized and idiotic, there were others who had attained two or three hundred years?

Meanwhile, since we can settle nothing, let us get on with the game.

MORE
ABOUT
MONKEY
GLANDS

LET US NOW consider—apart from the effect on literature that would follow the more general adoption of the
monkey-gland operation—some of the political changes that
would result from extra longevity.

The first direct consequence would undoubtedly be a
renewed access of autocratic power, for there is never a
revolution against a king, however good his rule, if he has
reigned for over forty years. The Emperor Francis Joseph is
a case in point. In England especially is there the cult of the
Grand Old Man. Hated, for instance, as are artists here, even
Titian has gained a certain false popularity owing to the
enormous age to which he lived. But politics, though sunk
in esteem, are more popular than the arts, and were Mr
Gladstone still alive, however unpleasant his policy, he
would be beloved of all parties. What a roar of applause,

349

then, would greet any politician of over *two* hundred years! It is possible, though, that the Conservative Party would have an unfair pull—for a Socialist Prime Minister might not have sufficient private means to avail himself of the rejuvenating operation, and would so be deprived of the fruits of office. On his behalf, for the sake of fairness, there would have to be a levy on the Trade Union Funds. Yet would this be strictly in accordance with Socialist principles?

But so long as it stops at monkey-glands I, for one, shall not complain. Unfortunately, however, since the human body is apt to reject any alien substance, the gland of a young man is considered safer than that of a monkey for prolonging the life of an old man. Even now, it is said, there are American cities, inhabited by the super-rich, in which the glands of no young poor men are safe. Men tell, for example, how a navvy was walking through a street in Chicago the other day, when something happened, and the next thing he knew, ten days later, was that he lay, a glandless, ductless, and semi-conscious cretin in a hospital ward, while in a neighbouring palace—no doubt, a palace composed of Tudor rooms torn from their setting, and Louis XV *salons* clawed out of French *châteaux*—a multi-millionaire ran, skipping and rejuvenated, round his room.

But opportunities such as this must necessarily be rare in peace-time. Imagine, then, the renewed popularity of war! Young men, as they lay dying on a battlefield, would be rushed off to stations fitted with every modern surgical appliance, where well-trained operators would remove their glands and place them in cold storage for the use of the old generals, still safely behind the lines—or, better still, for rejuvenating those elderly statesmen who had so cleverly provoked the war. Moreover, with a lifetime of over two hundred years, even our generals might master military strategy, while with better generals on each side, wars might be indefinitely prolonged: a comfort and blessing for all of us.

IN
THE
REALM
OF
ART

THE
BALLET

THE ART OF the ballet, of executant arts the richest and most sumptuous, usually flowers, like certain rare plants, but once in a hundred years. In the short period of blossoming, it attracts the widest and most attentive interest, but, fot the remainder of the century hides itself away, despised and fugitive; a convention, an amusement that amuses no one, but has become, through long custom, a ritual part of some ceremony or diversion.

It may be asked why the flowering of this art form is of so rare occurrence? The answer is, it needs so unusual a combination of talents: a great producer, dancers of genius and a new fusion of the scenic arts with music. Moreover, in order that the supreme dancers, who appear only once in a century, should be able to attain to the utmost heights and depths of expression and technique, four whole previous generations of dancers must be schooled in abnegation. Countless crushed inglorious Pavlovas and Karsavinas go to the making of those exquisite and unforgettable artists.

To understand that which the Russian Ballet accomplished, it is necessary to look back a quarter of a century. Twenty-five years ago, ballet in England was a thing obsolete but still slightly exotic, which could occasionally be seen at a music-hall, while diamond blazing shafts of light, composed in equal parts of heavy tobacco smoke and limelight, played down upon it; a decadent art of Italy (all dancers then sported Italian names, as now they sport Russian) which no one, least of all the art-lover, took seriously. Most dancers of any celebrity seemed old: age lay over them like a frost, stiffening their limbs and powdering their hair. Groups of tiptoeing women in inappropriate wide skirts of white gauze, leered and pirouetted archly for the coy appreciation of so many corseted and posturing old gentlemen. The entertainment, in consequence, had become so essentially arch, in gesture and expression, that for men to dance in this fashion was generally regarded as absurd. It *was* absurd. . . . But then, no one paid much attention to the performance—everyone talked and laughed throughout the ballet of those days.

Since its life was confined to certain moments in the programme of a few music-halls, and since the music-halls of those days possessed a broad appeal—broader than at present— it may be that ballet as a diversion was more familiar to the great public than it is to-day: but it must not be thought that, because still surviving, it was popular in the music-halls. It was *not*. A vestigial ornament of the programme, it existed only as the unworthy and neglected descendant of something that had formerly been of use to the management as an attraction. Now it bored the patrons profoundly; but the English are patient, and further, it had become associated in their minds with the last item in the programme or before the *entr'acte*. It retained therefore a certain ritual significance, like soup at dinner, still consumed automatically by many who neither need nor care for it. But it lingered there, obviously a dying thing; and the chatter from the promenades (where walked the strangest and most disquieting phantoms, odorous with the fashionable perfumes of half a century before, clad in voluminous, muffling dresses, crowned with huge hats, and displaying to the appreciative males there gathered together busts and hips of a now forgotten rotundity) quickly engulfed it.

So it remained, in a long process of death, until 1910; and then, suddenly, entered surprise. Within a year or two Serge Diaghileff's Russian Ballet had appeared in Paris and London and had taken both the fashionable and artistic worlds there captive. An art, undreamt of hitherto in its freedom as much as in its discipline, had been reborn, and had become the chosen interpreter of music and of the modern visual arts. The all-pervading coyness had been banished, and every variation of tragedy and true comedy had been substituted for it. Each new ballet revealed a fresh world, and great as was the corybantic virtue of its stars, the *corps-de-ballet* seemed hardly less faultless. The most imaginative scenic artists—as later, the most eminent painters—were eager to aid this triumph, and in the young Stravinsky was found a Russian composer of the first rank. The theatres in which the ballets took place were crowded and the rapturous applause, it seemed, would never die down. And Diaghileff, a genius, was one who fortunately preferred success to failure. For in spite of his innumerable experiments—some of which were later to be financial, though none artistic, failures—he had no wish, like so many Russians of every profession and like various English producers, to be misunderstood.

The ballet which he created, and continued to create until his death, was the lion of the moment, and of every world; and Diaghileff revelled in its renown. To have written a libretto, or designed the scenery, or composed the music of a ballet for this extraordinary man, always carried with it, among artists of any kind, a certain evidence of authenticity; though, on the other hand, it was responsible for much jealousy among those writers and musicians and painters who were convinced that they ought to be commissioned by the great man, and who were, as a result, furious when he failed to notice their merits. Signs of this jealousy are to be observed even to this day, and I well remember the rage of an artist, who at the time was considered interesting and progressive, when, after he had pestered me to arrange a meeting with Diaghileff, the Russian producer looked at one painting and then asked to see no more. Fortunately the former artist has now become a writer, and in this direction can pursue old feuds, even though their objects are dead.

The Diaghileff Ballet enjoyed three periods; of which, contrary to the opinion of many, I hold the third to have been the best and most interesting, if not the most prosperous. The pre-war period consisted chiefly of ballets built upon Russian themes and executed by Russian artists. It was predominantly national. The most significant, the most typical ballets were, *Scheherazade*, *Thamar*, *Petrouchka*, *Le Sacre-du-Printemps* and *L'Après-midi d'un Faune*. This last was an exception, a ballet to the music of the then living Debussy (that genius whom I once saw plain, and spoke to; though to my shame I can recall little of him, neither appearance nor talk). *Carnaval*, *Spectre de la Rose* (which for the art of pure dancing surpassed all else) and *les Sylphides* were, too, not national in origin, but they were thoroughly Russian in interpretation. *Sacre-du-Printemps* was an unforgettable event, astonishing in its magic, and so moving that audiences frequently fought over its merits. (It was on the occasion of its first performance, as Jean Cocteau relates, that the aged Duchesse de X. waved her arms in the air, shook her fist at the stage, and remarked, "And it's done to make mock of *me!*")

But to the other ballets, as yet not even the most conservative critics could object. The scenes evolved were solid enough or wistful enough for all to understand: of barbaric splendour on one hand, or of an elegiac and poetic nostalgia on the other, they were yet to my mind less stimulating (although they, too, then possessed all the fascination of novelty) than the ballets which were to be born after the war. Though it cannot, I think, be disputed that in Karsavina and Nijinsky were presented the two most perfect dancers of their, or any other, century. Their technique and interpretation could never be excelled. Nevertheless if, in after years, one heard people remark that "The dancing isn't as good as it was. I saw them before the war," it had to be remembered that in England there is a particular and pernicious type of bore that loves to dwell on a past into which Time has forbidden the younger generation to enter; for the past, thus flourished in your faces, is an assertion of importance, becomes an attribute of virtue rather than age. It must also never be forgotten that, when first seen, the Russian Ballet was the more astounding because so undreamt of, so unstaled by custom; and that the people who saw it were more intelligent, because younger, than they are now. (Nothing, I am convinced, in my own despite, destroys intelligence so much as the passing years.) Indeed, it can be imagined that to a generation fed exclusively on the plump Wardour-Street perspectives of Wagner, and Verdi as performed in Covent Garden, or on the siren smiles among the perpetual almond and peach blossom of Daly's and the Gaiety, the first performances of the Russian Ballet revealed paths of an unequalled magic, whereon pirouetted the very nymphs of music and poetry; and that this sudden encountering of beauty was of necessity an experience denied to the next generation, at once more cultivated and more sophisticated.

The second period of the ballet, which opened for the English in the last winter of the war, centred round the next two great stars, Lopokova and Massine, and, beginning with the delightful eighteenth-century fantasia *The Good-Humoured Ladies*, found its culmination in the grotesque beauty of the Derain-Rossini *La Boutique Fantasque* and the Picasso-de-Falla *Tricorne*. With these last two ballets the art had finally divested itself of period-culture—and so, perhaps, of an appeal for "millionare art-lovers"—and of exoticism, and came forth boldly as the champion and inter-

preter of modern art, as much as of music. And in its two
chief exponents, it possessed two artists who presented it
with a never-failing verve, a sense, hitherto unrivalled, of
fantasy. The poetry of it had become essentially modern, and
the surprising beauty of *Alice in Wonderland* was now nearer
to its spirit than the smooth, accustomed beauty of Keats.

As for the third period, of which Lifar and Danilova were
the protagonists, it was seething with life. Each year the chief
dancers showed their gifts to more perfection and the thing
which they so ably strove to express became more interesting.
But the sudden death of Diaghileff in Venice during the
summer of 1929 showed all at once how much in reality
had depended on him. He had been a kind of Tsar, a court-
of-appeal, and no detail had stood outside his range. The
audience, which with so much care he had built up, was left
seeking for something to replace his productions. The ballet
itself was split up and some of its roots have flowered again,
though less exuberantly.[1] Diaghileff had lifted the ballet
out of the public-house atmosphere in which, in England,
we first discovered it and had established it once more in the
court-theatres of the world as one of the art forms. Now the
danger is that here it may relapse, not into the public-house,
but, far lower, into the artistic tea-shop. Peasant pottery and
homespun must be eschewed.

[1] This was written before the formation of Colonel de Basil's very
remarkable company.

ON
INTERIOR
DECORATORS
AND
DECORATION

THE LAST DECADE or two has given birth to every kind of decoration; period rooms (preserved lavender and masses of brass work, or, equally, Park-Lane-and-Fifth-Avenue Louis Quinze, with furniture like gilded spiders), Venetian rooms, peasant rooms (matting and greasy pewter), beige rooms (when it is as though every wall and curtain and ceiling had turned to dust and ashes, the stripped furniture to bones), black rooms (oh, those pre-war black rooms, with their massed ballet-russe cushions and oriental lampshades!) white rooms (half hospital and half snowdrift), Victorian rooms, Edwardian rooms and rooms of the Stern School of To-morrow. Simplicity and complexity win by turns, it will be seen, like the old-fashioned political parties in nineteenth-century general elections.

Whole armies, whole rival schools, are engaged in this

work, which they deem so easy. Any ruined woman of fashion can at once sell her own house and begin "doing up" other people's, and nearly all the unemployables of the richer classes tend to become, according to their temperament, either interior decorators or car-touts, just as in the 'eighties they used to work for wine-merchants. To-day, every nice girl loves an interior-decorator and can prattle to him of the "sweetest little Victorian objects". Whole cohorts of followers, as much as the protagonists themselves, see the world in terms of interior decoration; and, indeed, in example of this, last year on the Acropolis I was fortunate enough to observe a lady decorator, almost as ancient and famous as the Parthenon itself, first survey that temple with an appreciation of which I had not hitherto suspected her capable, and then sum her impression with the cry, "It's just me. It's beige!"

At the moment, Stern-School-of-To-morrow rooms are in vogue: a style which, it must be admitted, is at least practical, and suited to flats—into which in time we shall all be driven—rather than to houses. The typical room of this kind is low-ceilinged, shaped like a lightly built cigar box painted white inside, has windows that sail right round it and is full of angular, aluminium furniture and of plugs and wires. No wood enters into the scheme; and with this omission, at any rate, I find myself in agreement, having always held that wood constitutes, both for furniture and fittings, an ugly and unsuitable material, and one which, much less beautiful and appropriate than marble, steel, glass or numberless composite substances, only becomes tolerable when painted or gilded.

The implied theory which underlies the creation of such apartments, however, seems illogical: that because we live in an age which has created the airplane we ought to inhabit rooms forced as much as possible to resemble that machine. . . . Now, that the prevailing method of locomotion of any epoch affects its art indirectly I am willing to concede; that, for example, both Degas and Seurat introduced into their paintings something of the bicyclist age in which they lived; that Gainsborough's work is often akin in feeling to the coaches which, in his day, rumbled and rocked down the leafy lanes of his native Suffolk; and that the work of all Victorian Academicians—except that they so seldom, as it were, got up steam—has much in common with the snorting, gritty railway trains in which they travelled. . . . But why, because we risk our lives in airplanes, should we be, after this fashion, compelled to inhabit houses that resemble them; *why*, any more than the bicyclist-man should have been obliged to live in rooms that, full of spokes and spiders and rubber tyres, resembled bicycles, or the man-of-the-car in a Rolls mansion or a Ford maisonette? On the contrary, if you have really travelled much in an airplane, the probability is that, in your more leisured and static moments, you would crave surroundings of a very different nature—lofty rooms, richly upholstered and full of heavy objects as opposed to these bare and lightweight aluminium constructions. . . . Otherwise, why not live in the airplane itself, after the manner of those who dwell in discarded railway carriages; though they, I fancy, do so less from choice than owing to a local housing shortage?

Nevertheless, metal furniture of the Stern-School-of-To-morrow sort possesses, it must be admitted, the merit of a certain permanence. It is, obviously, of an enduring nature:

whereas one of the chief faults of most modern decoration consists precisely in a lack of any sense of permanence; this being perhaps due to the political circumstances of our age. Indeed it may be argued, further, that as a rule the decoration and furniture of rooms to-day seem calculated to last either too long, or too short a time; because they are either so plainly temporary that it is as though you were living in a tent, or else they induce the uncomfortable feeling that they will survive every century and every catastrophe.

Alas! the interior-decorator has degraded his art from a species of architecture down to the level of that of a fashionable dressmaker or beauty expert. His aim *should* be to make a house interesting and beautiful *in spite* of its owner; but he can now only coax his clients into giving him an order by assuring them that "it will set off your personality so well" or, when they are middle-aged women, that "the colour shows off your beautiful white hair . . . so lovely, with a young face". . . . In this way the impression is produced, in every man and every woman who has enough money to spend, that they have a definite personality, whether strong or restful; whereas in all probability they have none at all. Few people possess one in any age, but never so few as to-day. . . . On the other hand, there are more fake personalities in circulation than ever before, and just as nothing is so tedious as one of these loud, assertive shams, always telling you of their doings, circumstances and ambitions, thus, too, nothing is so disagreeable in decoration as a house with a false, a concocted individuality.

And yet, any house which is painted and arranged under the superintendence and for the pleasure of its owner, however dull, is always more interesting, and usually more beautiful, than one created by a decorator, however talented. (To that extent, at any rate, personality counts; in contradiction, it may be, of what I have written. . . .) Nevertheless, if you are responsible for the decoration of a house, never deliberately consider the individuality of the owner, which, if it exists, will always make itself felt; pay attention only to the house itself, its shape, style and history. And above all, I would counsel you, avoid the point of view which insists that such an object will not mix—or "go", as the cant is— with another of a different kind in the same room. Anything mixes with anything else, but only on the condition that the owner really likes it, really wants it in that particular place; does not put it there out of, let us say, a desire for display or a feeling that he must put it somewhere. Do not, again, be afraid of collecting too many things in a room. A crowded room has its beauties, as much as a fashionably empty one. In fact, allow the rooms, and the objects in them, to speak to the visitor with their own voices.

ON
EXHIBITIONS

EXHIBITIONS OF THE smaller kind, whether to illus-
trate a special tendency in some branch of dead painting, or
whether to show us the living work of painters, are always
justifiable and often praiseworthy. The modern painter—
even if the public does not often see the necessity—must
live; must advertise his work and show it, if only in order to
obtain critical comment, however inept. For the painter,
writer and musician, even though, as so often, their natures
tend to melancholy, remain always sanguine in this respect:
that on the next occasion the critics will not merely notice
their work, but that their notices will surely be of use, indicating real virtues and pointing out real faults. Thus their
hopes are doomed ever to be disappointed.

So much for the smaller exhibitions; but these great
exhibitions at Burlington House—the Italian and French,

Spanish and English—of what use are they? They merely represent some process in the nature of a winding-up of European art; a consideration of the stock in universal bankruptcy. We have already finished, docketed and explained away in this manner the gracious arts of France and Italy, and the robust ones of Holland and Belgium. . . . What risks, too, were dared in the course of this woeful stocktaking! Think of that stormy day in December on which no news was received of the art-ship—the *Leonardo da Vinci* (was it called?)—on which were stored the greatest treasures of ancient Italy. . . . And yet, if a marvellous tradition *had* to perish, what a beautiful death it would have been! Imagine for a moment that the treasure-ship had never arrived, and that all this nourishment for ancient, academic art-lovers had sunk beneath the curling blue waves of the Mediterranean; what an end for it! Perhaps in the "Birth of Venus", rising from her shell, so lightly borne upon green ripples, Botticelli symbolized the birth of a new Italian tradition, and it may be that it would have been fitting for this pale, golden-haired goddess to return to her native depths, accompanied by all her train of tortured saints and triumphant satyrs. What a legend of the old world, equivalent to the myth of Atlantis, would have lingered for men to tell in the days to come; those encumbered, yet empty, days of our grandchildren, squatting among the battered and falling skyscrapers and the wrecked machines.

Some primitive sculptor, roughly shaping a human bone into the vague likeness of an animal, would have been able to relate to his progeny how the old world was once full of things called pictures, and of sophisticated forms of an exquisite poise and balance, and of how men grew to hate them, and first of all gathered them together and crammed them into a room in London, and then packed them, every one, on a ship and drove them out into the depths of the ocean. "And", he might continue—for, in time, these stories would, no doubt, vary from the truth— "somewhere the *Flying Italian* still sails" (they would have forgotten the age of steam), "floating palely among the Polar wastes or making a fleeting appearance in the Sargasso Sea or in the coral channels of the South Sea islands, and many men have set out in their rowing-boats to try and find this treasure": for in the years to come, as in the past, treasure will draw men; and in that future day there will already be chiefs living in their kraals, pitched among the ruins, eager to give as much as two or three glass beads and a bottle of spirit, distilled from the berries that will yet grow on Salisbury Plain, for a broken marble head. . . .

At any rate, Venus would have been spared the indignity of those curious mauve stains, akin to the blotches caused by indelible ink, which now mar the perfection of her canvas. What are they, one wonders, and why were they not there in the days before the exhibition at Burlington House?

However that may be, the Italian exhibition constituted a real feast for the art-parasites; they could visit it, and there devour all that exists in the way of beauty, with no trouble to themselves and no benefit to posterity. Nevertheless, did they appreciate it? For the art-lover, to enjoy properly his idle treat, should be given as much trouble as possible: he ought to be forced to ask special permission to see his favourite picture, to be turned away time and time again, and, when finally admitted, to be obliged to climb a ladder in order to examine it properly. Then he would appreciate it to his full, never forget the occasion, relate, to anyone who would listen to it, this tale of his extraordinary adventures. Similarly, pictures in galleries should not be too luxuriously, too easily, disposed upon the walls. The art-lover should be made to hunt for his favourite picture as though it were a needle in a haystack, to search crowded walls over and over, and finally to identify it high up in a hideous scramble of lesser work. Such is the ideal.

Did Botticelli and Signorelli, Giotto and Tiepolo, Donatello and Bernini, Vermeer and van der Weyden, van Eyck and Rubens, Hogarth and Gainsborough labour for the good opinion of this musty crowd: so you may question your familiar spirit as you see the throngs, in their skirts and feather boas, pressing into the rooms of Burlington House, with all art spread out before them for their rheumy and wheezing comment.

How ancient they are, these bent backs and parchment faces, how smothered in obsolete clothing! Yet their contemporaries, I apprehend, loved art more than do mine. They belong, at any rate, to a generation to whom the term *pictures* signified oil paintings, and not the flickering, fleering goings-on at a cinema. On the other hand, the word *modern* suggests many a past page of beauty to them; Burne-Jones and his palely aching angels, Rossetti in his lovely trance of full-throated maidens, William Morris at work translating the lines of Gothic cabbages on to the walls of the industrial England which he so abhorred, and Ruskin trumpeting forth so expressively his crazed criticism. . . . Sometimes, of course, the ideal world of these wrinkled gazers on the past is not so lofty a one. They may, for all we know, only have been the humble admirers of Poynter and his academic associates. . . .

THE END

Date Due